Wakefield Press

THE DIGGERS' DOCTOR

Ashley Mallett is a born storyteller and former Test cricketer. His ambition was to take 100 Test wickets, a feat he achieved in his 23rd match, along with Shane Warne, Glenn McGrath and Graham McKenzie. Ashley continues to write cricket for the *Age*, *Sydney Morning Herald* and *Cricinfo*, and to coach Australia's best and emerging spin bowlers, either as head of *Spin Australia*, an international spin bowling coaching program, or with Cricket Australia's Centre of Excellence in Brisbane. Ashley has worked with a number of recent Australian, English and Sri Lankan spinners including Graeme Swann, Rangana Hereath and Nathan Lyon. Away from the cricket scene, Ashley teaches Write Biography in Adelaide. *The Diggers' Doctor* is Ashley's 32nd book.

By the same author

Autobiography
Rowdy
Spin Out

Biography
Clarrie Grimmett: The Bradman of Spin
Trumper: The Illustrated Biography
Chappelli Speaks Out
One of a Kind: The Doug Walters Story
Thommo Speaks Out
Nugget: Man of the Century
Scarlet: Clarrie Grimmett – Test cricketer
No Beating About the Bush

History
The Black Lords of Summer
The 1868 Aboriginal Tour of England and Beyond
The Catch that Broke a Bank

General non-fiction
Bradman's Band
100 Cricket Tips
Eleven: The Greatest Eleven of the 20th Century

For Children
Master Sportsman Series – Hutchinson of Australia

United Kingdom editions
Lords' Dreaming: The Story of the 1868 Aboriginal Tour of England and Beyond
Hitting Out: The Ian Chappell Story

The Diggers' Doctor

The Fortunate Life of
Col. Donald Beard, AM, RFD, ED (Retd)

ASHLEY MALLETT

Wakefield
Press

Wakefield Press
16 Rose Street
Mile End
South Australia 5031
www.wakefieldpress.com.au

First published 2014
Reprinted 2014 (twice), 2016

Copyright © Ashley Mallett 2014

All rights reserved. This book is copyright. Apart from any fair dealing for the purposes of private study, research, criticism or review, as permitted under the Copyright Act, no part may be reproduced without written permission. Enquiries should be addressed to the publisher.

Cover designed by Stacey Zass, page 12
Edited by Julia Beaven, Wakefield Press
Typeset by Wakefield Press

National Library of Australia Cataloguing-in-Publication entry

Author:	Mallett, Ashley, 1945– , author.
Title:	The diggers' doctor: the fortunate life of Col. Donald Beard, AM, RFD, ED (Retd) / Ashley Mallett.
ISBN:	978 1 74305 306 5 (paperback).
Notes:	Includes bibliographical references and index.
Subjects:	Beard, Donald, 1925– .
	Australia. Army – Surgeons – Biography.
	Surgeons – South Australia – Biography.
	Korean War, 1950–1953 – Personal narratives, Australian.
	Vietnam War, 1961–1975 – Personal narratives, Australian.
Dewey Number:	617.092

Contents

Foreword		vi
Preface		vii
Chapter One	Miracle at the Battle of Kapyong	1
Chapter Two	Early Days	24
Chapter Three	Fail and You're in the Army	37
Chapter Four	The Road to War	51
Chapter Five	Home from the Front	56
Chapter Six	1953: Marching with the Queen	62
Chapter Seven	England	73
Chapter Eight	Margaret – 'The love of my life'	84
Chapter Nine	Vietnam: The Diggers' Doctor	97
Chapter Ten	War's Daily Battle	120
Chapter Eleven	'The Don Bradman I knew'	126
Chapter Twelve	Gems and Rough Diamonds	144
Chapter Thirteen	Power of the Human Spirit	156
Chapter Fourteen	Hawkeye's Guardian Angel and Other Miracles	172
Chapter Fifteen	'My fortunate life'	182
Bibliography		200
Acknowledgements		201
Index		203

Foreword

Here is a wonderful story of a great Australian, Colonel Donald Beard; a story of his life endeavours, duty and leadership. It is a story of serious service as a fine surgeon in both peace in Adelaide and as a war surgeon in the Korean and Vietnam wars. He also served as the regimental medical officer in the famous 3rd Battalion (Old Faithful) in the Battle of Kapyong, then through the fearful winter of Korea where our soldiers, wearing service clothing, footwear and headwear all designed for temperate climates, suffered terrible illnesses caused by the fierce cold.

This book describes, with many anecdotes, his adventures in various other employments including being chosen to be a member of the Australian contingent to attend and serve in the coronation service of our Queen in London in 1953; his cricket career in the latter days of Bradman in Adelaide; and service in the Royal Australian Army Medical Service, where he rose to the rank of colonel to be the senior army medical officer in South Australia. Other stories involve acting, tours of the Western Front, and being once a patient in the famous US MASH in the Korean War. This book also presents a great deal of humour and excellent accounts of his very many friends, colleagues and mates, and it details his family life as a child, and later his marriage to Margaret – 'the love of my life'.

This is a valuable book for it covers the life of a great Australian and the lives of people from the 1920s to today.

Major-General W.B. Digger James AC, AO (Mil.) MBE, MC, MBBS (Syd.), FRACS
Auchenflower, Queensland

Preface

In a good surgeon; a hawk's eye, a lion's heart and a lady's hand.
  Leonard Wright, London, 1589

Sir Donald Bradman introduced me to the South Australian Cricket Association medical officer, Dr Don Beard, in October 1967. I had just arrived in Adelaide from Western Australia to try my hand in getting a game for the South Australian cricket team. My spin bowling opportunities were restricted on the flint-hard WACA pitch. WA relied on a barrage of pace from one end led by Graham McKenzie (soon to be joined by a young firebrand named Dennis Lillee); at the other end was the great England left-hand spinner, Tony Lock. During my first State training at Adelaide Oval I dislocated my finger and Sir Donald drove me in his silver four-cylinder car to have my finger treated at Doctor Beard's Marryatville private residence.

I did not recognise the significance of this day, but I soon learnt that this surely was the luckiest break of my life, for I got to talk one on one with Sir Donald Bradman and I came to know Doc Beard. The doctor was a tall and slender man with a bushy grey moustache and kind, smiling eyes. His manner was confident, yet surprisingly gentle. He took hold of my right hand and eased the joint of my third finger back into place. It hurt like hell but I wasn't going to make a sound. So began my long association with both Sir Donald Bradman and Dr Donald Beard.

A regular to Sheffield Shield matches staged at Adelaide Oval, Dr Beard always visited our dressing-room during a game to check our injuries and any other health problems. Then early in 1968, the Doc seemed to go missing. We soon learnt the reason for his absence. The Doc, also a colonel in the Australian Army, had gone back to war. In 1951 he had served in Korea, running a Regimental Aid Post on the battlefield. Now he was to head a surgical team at the 1st Australian Field Hospital at Vung Tau, South Vietnam.

Over the years I began to learn more about Dr Beard's remarkable experiences in war and peace. A man of substance, who has led an extraordinary life as a surgeon, he is a leader and man of great compassion, humility and charm. His life has been enriched by his giving to people from all walks of life. He embraces people, their work ethic, their humour and their passion. Surgery, cricket, music, theatre, reading and his love for Margaret, the greatest love of his life, has warmed Don Beard to thousands. Some are eminent, well-known figures, others are less distinguished but all of them are equally important to him. He got to know myriad cricketers, including Sir Vivian Richards, Wes Hall, Geoff Boycott, Ian Chappell and Dennis Lillee, and he was a close friend of Sir Donald Bradman.

Once Sir Donald amazed dinner guests at Don and Margaret Beard's Norwood home by agreeing to bat against the doctor's two teenage boys, Matthew and Alastair, on the green-tinged wicket at the rear of their back garden. Arguably the fastest bowler to draw breath, Jeff Thomson arrived and said, 'If Bradman's batting, I'm bowling,' and picked up a ball. He still speaks of the occasion and 'how good must Don Bradman have been in his prime'.

As a child I was run over by a car crossing the road on my way to school in Sydney and it left my spine out of kilter. Years later I had a hip replacement, then the other hip started playing up, so I consulted Dr Beard at his home. He told me that I needed to see a good physiotherapist. 'The best one I know is Matthew Beard,' he said confidently.

One day during a visit to Matthew's rooms for treatment, we were discussing writing and my latest project. I mentioned that a biography of Donald Beard would be a fabulous project for me.

'Oh,' Matthew said with a grin, 'we've been trying to get Dad to tell his story for years. His life has been incredible and it is a story that I am sure would interest many people.'

A few days later I saw the doctor looking through a stack of books on a table outside Dillon's Bookshop on Norwood Parade. I approached from behind, placed my hands on his shoulders and said quietly: 'It is time I wrote your story.'

He looked straight ahead: 'Yes,' he agreed, 'it is. It's time.'

One

Miracle at the Battle of Kapyong

The noise of the bullets hitting the outside of the tank was incredibly unnerving, however the only real worry was having the tracks blown off by stick grenades.
                                                        Captain Don Beard, 3rd RAR

As the Diggers fixed bayonets and steeled themselves for the coming battle, the cold breath of oblivion swept down the Kapyong Valley. All four companies of the 3rd Royal Australian Regiment (RAR) had dug weapon pits in stony ground on the steep slopes either side of the valley. Having crashed through the defences of an entire Republic of Korea (ROK) Division only a few miles up the valley, the Chinese cleverly merged with the retreating South Korean soldiers and refugees fleeing the war zone and infiltrated the 3rd RAR battleline. Dressed as civilians, the Chinese took advantage of the fact that UN aircraft would not deliberately bomb or strafe the columns of fleeing refugees. Hundreds of Chinese fighters infiltrated the UN defences and, in the dead of the night of 23 April 1951, they attacked.

The Chinese offensive came as a tremendous shock to the Australians, who were preparing to commemorate Anzac Day two days later. An invitation to attend the festivities had already been accepted by the Turkish Brigade, encamped four kilometres away. Stacked supplies of flood and beer were left in the wake of a general call to arms for this was the start of the Battle of Kapyong.

First came the incessant sound of whistles, bugles and trumpets before each Chinese attack. They used mortar and small-arms fire and many times there was fierce hand-to-hand combat. As the battle raged, Captain Donald Beard, the Regimental Medical Officer, tended to the wounded at the Regimental Aid Post (RAP) in a ditch in a paddy field across from the 3rd RAR headquarters. As bullets came across the ditch, RAP Sergeant Noel Tampling cried out, 'Keep your head down, Doc.' He was addressing Captain Beard, who, at a height of 6'4" (193 centimetres), was a likely target, given that the bullets were ripping through the aid post halfway up the walls of the low tent.

'What's going on?' Captain Beard replied, as he calmly continued to dress a soldier's wound. The RAP was in turmoil. Australian soldiers were being carried there at a frightening rate, their injuries often terrible, and the medical assistants and the padre were rushed off their feet.

'It was all very strange with everything going on at once – small arms, shelling, Chinese banging drums, screaming, and shouted orders from both sides. The sensation was a mixture of real and unreal with little time to take much notice because of the job in hand.

'It went on all night with the Chinese firing across the paddy field,' he recalled. 'It was strange with streams of tracer bullets looking like glow-worms. On top of the noise of the firing was the banging of drums, and the sound of whistles and bugles used by the Chinese to fire up their troops and to frighten us.' The Australian companies returned fire with everything they had; the air 'seemed full of missiles but everyone was so flat out there was almost no feeling of fear'.

On the morning of Monday 24 April, the Battalion Headquarters and the RAP (which comprised Captain Beard, his corporal and stretcher-bearers) were instructed to withdraw. The Commanding Officer Lieutenant Colonel Ferguson believed the situation was dire and that a strategic withdrawal in this circumstance would be the better part of valour.

'Just before dawn I decided that the position of my headquarters would not enable it to regain control of the battle and that I should withdraw to a higher ground occupied by the Middlesex Regiment. Hopefully, with better communication there, I could regain control and thus provide the full weight of supporting fire, including aircraft and artillery support, both of which were vital if the forward companies were to receive the relief they so urgently needed,' stated Lt Col. Bruce Ferguson in *The Battle of Kapyong* by Bruce Green.

The Doc said there had been some controversy about the whereabouts of the CO during the night of 23 and 24 April. 'As far as I was concerned he was still with me and he gave the orders to withdraw in the morning to the Middlesex Battalion HQ.'

All medical staff helped patients to safety. Under intense fire from the Chinese, and with heads held low, they ran and stumbled hundreds of yards across the paddy field, carrying casualties to the RAP stretcher jeep and the 60th Indian Parachute Field Ambulance waiting to evacuate all the casualties.

'We survived the trip through the Chinese infiltrators now dug in on the slopes of the valley and reached the safety of the 27th British Commonwealth

Brigade,' he said, 'but I recall little of this period. It is almost as if it never happened. How long did it take?

'My relief was short-lived. Lieutenant Colonel Ferguson called for me and said that one of the companies was short of ammunition and had many casualties. He intended to go up with ammunition and he asked that I join him to attend to the wounded. Lt Col. Ferguson had enlisted the aid of the US 72nd Heavy Tank Battalion. I thought to myself, Oh, bother that for a joke. I've just got out!'

More than 30 Australian soldiers had been wounded, some critically. They were lying on cold, rocky ground, their bodies covered by coats, on land behind enemy lines. The Chinese had broken through, scattering the ROK soldiers and the Ferguson rescue mission was death defying. Those to be saved were trapped behind a line of thousands of rampaging Chinese soldiers rushing down the Kapyong Valley. Captain Beard found himself riding inside a Sherman tank, stuffed with ammunition and medical supplies. As the tank careered along Kapyong Valley floor, it ran the gauntlet of continuous small-arms fire.

'The noise of the bullets hitting the outside of the tank was incredibly unnerving, however the only real worry was having the tracks blown off by stick grenades. We reached the company positions and the tanks laid down a protective perimeter of 50-calibre fire while we unloaded the ammunition and I attended to the injured men,' he continued. 'Soldiers' wounds had to be dressed and the injured carried to the tanks. Once again there was no real sense of danger.'

Medical assistants on the front line had to make do with meagre resources in their medical bags. With minimal morphine and only a couple of stretchers, many of the injured Diggers had to lie in pain on stony ground. Captain Beard found that only one or two of the wounded men could fit into each of the Sherman tanks. Lt Col. Ferguson asked: 'How are we going to get the rest out?'

Captain Beard had the solution: 'We can't leave them here. They would be either shot on the spot or taken prisoner. And they need immediate medical treatment. We'll have to take a chance, lash them to the sides of the tank and go as fast as we can down the valley and hope they miss us.'

The men, expecting Chinese gunfire from both sides of the road, feared the worst as the Sherman tank sped back down the valley. The poor devils strapped to the outside of the tank needed a miracle. The miracle came in the form of the Chinese soldiers who ceased fire as the tanks, with the wounded strapped to their sides, sped past.

'The Chinese stopped firing. They let us through, for which I'll be ever grateful.' Captain Beard stressed, 'The Chinese were good soldiers and fair soldiers ... except if you were taken prisoner.'

After the first evacuation from the front line, Captain Beard attended to the casualties and supervised their evacuation by the 60th Indian Para Field Ambulance. He again accompanied Lt Col. Ferguson to the front line, their Sherman tank speeding up the treacherous Kapyong Valley road, holding firm against the withering Chinese fire from both sides of the valley slopes, bullets ricocheting off the tank's outer steel skin while those inside once again prayed that no stick grenade would hit the tracks.

'I'm not sure how many times we repeated the run, but the same thing happened. We were attacked continuously on the way up the valley, and then the Chinese stopped firing as we returned with the wounded men strapped to the sides of the tank,' Captain Beard said. 'Even though the 3rd RAR was holding the massive Chinese offensive, it was obvious they would sooner or later completely overrun us, as they did to the British Gloucester Battalion to our flank, and the entire battalion was taken prisoner. At one stage their medical officer was out attending to casualties when the Chinese were advancing. He sent a message over his radio, "I think I'm going to be surrounded." A few minutes later he sent another message, "I am surrounded." And that was the last they heard of him until two years later when he was one among thousands of POWs released when hostilities were called to a halt.

'One of the prisoners was Major Farrar-Hockley, known by Australians as 'Major Horror Fuckley.' Later he escaped from the Chinese POW camp six times, but was recaptured six times and beaten. Each time he survived. He became a major general and was the man in charge of arrangements for the funeral of Princess Diana. He was a very brave man.'

Captain Beard has kept in touch with him since the Battle of Kapyong, as he has with the medical officers of other units, including Captain Douglas Haldane, RMO, of the Argyll and Sutherland Highlanders.

'We became good friends, a good example of close friendship developed during the war.' The Doc recalled, 'My wife and I stayed with the Haldanes in Glasgow and they visited us in Australia.'

While Capt Beard was attending the growing list of casualties, the Diggers were fighting at close quarter, trying to halt the Chinese advance. 'I don't know how they managed to hold their positions and keep fighting against fierce opposition.' A Company CO, Major Ben O'Dowd, tells of that desperate action:

In the moonlight our effective killing range was about 10 metres and our killing time about two to three seconds – the time it took for their heads and shoulders to appear above the edge of the ridge and for them to run to the forward (fighting) pits. As soon as shapes appeared out of the gloom our soldiers would produce as much rapid fire as each individual rifle was capable.

Reluctantly the 3rd RAR withdrew, to reform a stronger, more stable line with the rest of the 27th British Commonwealth Brigade. 'It was a magnificent action,' he recalled. 'The men withdrew slowly, but at the same time they fought off the Chinese, supported and covered each other.

'Back at HQ, news of the fighting reached us. One by one the companies returned and were redeployed. Sadly, as the last company came out it was mistakenly napalmed by American fighter-bombers, which did not realise there were still UN troops so far north. Four men died and many suffered severe burns.'

Private 'Nugget' Dunque, D Company's medical orderly, recalled in the *Battle of Kapyong*:

After the napalm hit I began to go around in my capacity as the medical orderly and pull people out … I then saw the most appalling apparition. A man with no flesh – his hands were dripping flesh – completely naked. As he walked, I saw these huge bloated feet. The sticks and stones came up through his feet. He sat down next to me. I didn't know who he was. He looked at me and said, 'Jesus, Nugget, you're having a bad day.'

But the decisive Battle of Kapyong, the major battle of the Korean War, effectively stopped the Chinese advance as they headed to recapture Seoul. In the wake of that extraordinary fight, Seoul was saved: the Chinese never got further south than the Kapyong Valley. As for the Australian soldiers who battled so bravely throughout the fierce fighting, Capt Beard said: 'I am proud to have played my part in the medical care of these magnificent Australian soldiers. I am proud of the battalion which stopped the Chinese, who must have been tiring after their long advances in the snow.'

For their gallantry in the Battle of Kapyong, 3rd RAR, along with the 2nd Battalion, Princess Patricia's Canadian Light Infantry and Company A, 72nd Heavy Tank Battalion (United States), was awarded the United States Presidential Distinguished Unit Citation. Any withdrawal on the battlefront is a testing time; it tests a man physically and mentally and the morale of the men as a collective. Men of the 3rd RAR had been under extreme stress for weeks and while it is instinctive for a soldier on the retreat to rush from danger as would an animal with survival his only motivation, the 3rd RAR moved at a steady pace. They'd stood in fall-back positions, awaited the enemy and provided covering fire for the rest of the battalion to find fall-back positions further down the valley.

There was no break in discipline and the officers reckoned the withdrawal went smoothly, like a well-planned training exercise. While the Battle of Kapyong was won by the fighting spirit of the Diggers, on the nights of 24 and 25 April 1951, Princess Patricia's Canadian Light Infantry held the line with a stubborn defensive action which froze the Chinese momentum. They managed to bring artillery down on forward weapon pits to hold the Chinese advance. They were heroes, but so too were the men of the medical corps. Not all heroes of war are dropping bombs, firing rifles and rushing in a bayonet charge at a slit trench filled by heavily armed enemy soldiers.

In Major Ben O'Dowd's book, *In Valiant Company*, he writes of Captain Donald Beard:

> Dr Don Beard had been a major during the early days of the Korean War, a surgeon in the general hospital in Kure. The RMO of a battalion is a Captain, so the rank of Major made him secure from the discomfort of active service with us. However, early in 1951 we again found ourselves minus an RMO, and Don busted himself back to Captain to tend to the medical needs of our soldiers. This responsibility fell to him at a period when we were losing more men from frostbite than any other cause, the problem being exacerbated by the mobile state of 3 RAR's operations in that period. I have no doubt there were times when he regretted this unselfish move, but the Diggers never did.

The Battle of Kapyong involved a 15,000-strong Chinese division attacking the Australian, British and Canadian battalions and the New Zealand 16th Field Regiment in two days and nights of fierce fighting near Seoul. The Australians were grateful to their Kiwi cousins manning the big guns, for it was the New Zealand 16th Field Regiment that kept lobbing their 25-pound shells to help slow the Chinese advance.

'The Kiwis enlisted cooks and transport drivers to help their cause, but they were able to maintain a relentless and accurate barrage throughout the day and night as the Australians made good their retreat,' he said.

'An observation officer called down fire on the advancing Chinese and, at times, just ahead of the Australians. Eventually they were firing directly under open sights and this is an appropriate moment to congratulate them and thank them for helping to deliver us to safety. You would have thought we were enemies when we threw stones and clods of earth at each other, but next minute we were helping each other, even in danger. We loved them. It was Anzac all over again. We will be eternally grateful. Once I had to "run the gauntlet" in my jeep through their lines and was "set upon", even hosed from the fire truck and then at the end of the line I was stopped and they invited me for a cup of tea. It is difficult to describe the relationship between the Aussie and the Kiwi but we are fortunate in that relationship.'

The four companies of the 3rd RAR totalled 600 men. Fighting against some 4000 fanatical Chinese fighters their sacrifice will never be forgotten.

Jeffrey Grey in *The Commonwealth Armies and the Korean War: An Alliance Study*:

> The main brunt of the assault fell upon 3rd RAR (3rd Battalion, the Royal Australian regiment) and 2 PPCLI (2nd Battalion, The Princess Patricia's Canadian Light Infantry), the former suffering 32 dead and 59 wounded, the latter 10 dead and 23 wounded. Between them, and with the aid of the New Zealand gunners (16th Field Regiment, Royal New Zealand Artillery) and an American tank company (Company A, 72nd Tank Battalion), they fought an entire enemy division to a standstill.

Captain Reg Saunders, the commander of C Company, Aborigine, and later to become a life-long friend of Don Beard, said immediately after the battle: 'At last I felt like an Anzac and I imagine there were 600 others like me.'

Donald Beard was a reluctant volunteer for the war in Korea. Having studied medicine at the University of Adelaide during World War II, he graduated in 1947.

'We felt guilty about not contributing to the war and many joined the Citizen Military Forces,' he confessed. 'Medicine was one of the protected industries. But if you failed any exam you'd be in the Army next day. Yet we felt guilty staying at home, studying in safety while our relatives and friends were risking their lives on the front line. Four of us, Graham Wilson, Hugh Douglas, Brian Cornish and I volunteered for the Interim Army and in December 1948 we were sent to Japan for a year as medical officers to the British Commonwealth Occupation Force.'

The others returned to Australia in December 1949. Major Beard volunteered to remain for six months while the force was being closed. He was due to return to Australia on 27 June 1950. Four days before the Doc's expected departure from Japan, his friends farewelled him on a small steam launch in the Inland Sea, off Kure. As the steam launch approached an island with natural steam baths, on which, in spite of General MacArthur's non-fraternisation policy, festivities had been arranged, news came over the radio that the North Koreans were massing on the 38th parallel in Korea, the 'line' separating north from south.

'During the afternoon there were news items on the radio reporting an attack by North Korea on South Korea. Next came news that the UN was to intervene on behalf of South Korea. We tried to turn off the radio but the girls felt that we should continue to listen in case we were needed,' Major Beard said. 'Inevitably the announcement came that all UN personnel were to report back to their base units. We were not happy about going. We scarcely knew where Korea was nor whether or not we were involved in the UN and I was due to return to Australia in two days. But return to base we did.' The party was over.

'The girls became slightly less attractive and the beer turned sour. Parades were ordered and the commander said, 'All those who volunteer for Korea, one pace forwards.' Suddenly I realised that I had volunteered. It was not one pace forward but a reluctant shuffle and I found myself volunteering for something I really didn't wish to do. Instead of two days, it was another 18 months before I got home.'

Major Beard did not initially go to Korea. His role in the British Commonwealth General Hospital in Kure, Japan, necessitated his delaying his departure to care for casualties flown by the RAAF from Korea. On the night of 26 July 1950, acting prime minister, Arthur Fadden, told the world that Australia would deploy ground troops to Korea (he offered the 3rd Royal Australian Regiment) as a third battalion to fight alongside two British battalions (1st Middlesex Regiment and 1st The Argyll and Sutherland Highlanders) under the command of US General Douglas MacArthur's UN forces. A day later, PM Robert Menzies addressed a joint sitting of the Senate and Congress in Washington, promising the deployment of the Australian troops 'to be serving within weeks' and suggesting that the Australians, New Zealanders and British troops eventually form a Commonwealth Division.

While a war was not in his career plan, Captain Beard believes that the experience in Korea taught him to 'become a real doctor and a decent human being'. He is a man of peace: a physician dedicated to the care of his fellow human beings; the saver of so many lives. However, there were times during his illustrious career that Donald Douglas Beard was a doctor at war. His full-time army service began in February 1949, when he was appointed a medical officer with the British Occupational Force, Japan, rising to the rank of Major in December 1949. At the end of World War II Korea was arbitrarily divided at the 38th parallel; a Soviet-supported North Korea and a US-backed South Korea came into being. As the US and Soviet Union removed their forces both the North and the South stated they were working towards a united democratic nation, but in reality they envisaged themselves becoming independent republics.

They were ideologically and politically opposed. On 25 June 1950, North Korea forces invaded the South, taking control of Seoul and forcing the South Korean fighters all the way to Pusan at the southern tip of the peninsula. The United Nations, perhaps fearing the outbreak of another global conflict, acted swiftly, demanding a North Korean withdrawal. But the North ignored the UN demand and the US moved to support the state of South Korea. As Commander-in-Chief of UN forces, the legendary General Douglas MacArthur immediately initiated a bold amphibious landing at Inchon, on the west coast, and another landing on the east coast. This trapped thousands of North Koreans. It was a brilliantly conceived and executed pincer movement, and proved decisive.

By October the North Koreans had been forced back to the 38th parallel. General MacArthur, who had made the bold prediction 'We'll be home for Christmas', then overstepped the mark, storming over the 38th parallel and driving the enemy forces almost back to the Manchurian border. MacArthur's provocation brought China into the conflict.

'At the front almost half a million Chinese soldiers suddenly appeared out of the snow,' Dr Beard recalled. 'They emerged from their snow-bound holes where they had hidden during the day to advance south during the night.'

The Chinese fighters ruined MacArthur's plans to claim victory by Christmas. MacArthur's action infuriated US President Harry Truman. He sacked his decorated General less than two weeks before the Battle of Kapyong because he was making too many political decisions and press statements, inflaming those in the Pentagon.

With China now involved in the conflict, the Korean War took a new and more dangerous turn. Now the war polarised itself along East–West lines, with the two great ideologies of the Cold War – communism and democracy – facing each other. China brought to the North arms and a seeming never-ending supply of soldiers and the Soviets offered hundreds of 'advisors'. The United Nations brought an opposing force in the south. Led by the US, the UN also comprised forces from the UK, Australia, New Zealand, Canada, the Philippines, Norway, Greece, Colombia, Belgium, Luxembourg, Italy, South Africa, Ethiopia, Thailand, The Netherlands, France, Denmark, Sweden, Turkey and India.

When war broke out the 3rd Battalion Royal Australian Regiment (comprising many veterans who fought in World War II and had been on occupational duties in Japan), together with the New Zealand 16th Field Artillery Regiment, were the first units to offer help to the United Nations force in Korea. Almost immediately the 77 Squadron RAAF began flying air strikes for the UN. General Douglas MacArthur was enthusiastic about Australia's 77 Squadron being involved in the Korean conflict:

> I'd like to get those Australian fighters too ... the squadron pilots are first-class and especially Flight Lieutenant Bay Adams, who always won the gunnery battles each year in competition with US pilots. We particularly need over Korea long-range fighters like the Mustangs ... I am going to take out those North Korean airfields. I am not going to have their planes killing my airmen without hitting them where they should be hit.

Within three months the Allies desperately needed men, arms, medical supplies and doctors at the front line in Korea. As with Don Beard, some of the young men who didn't fight in WW II because of their medical studies felt guilty about not having served while others their own age fought and died.

Indeed this guilt was the major motivating factor for them to serve in Japan and ultimately what prompted the Doc's 'reluctant shuffle' to volunteer for Korea.

'I received a call from the Assistant Director Medical Services (ADMS), Colonel C.W. Nye.

'"Now you've volunteered for Korea and we want you to replace our Regimental Medical Officer, Captain Bryan Gandevia. Would you relinquish your majority?"

'"Yessir!"'

The position of Regimental Medical Officer in Korea was available for a doctor with the rank of captain. Captain Gandevia had fallen sick and the battalion required a new RMO straight away.

'Now a crown on the shoulder was something to be proud of. I think the two best promotions you can get in the Army are corporal's stripes and the crown on your shoulder.' A few minutes later Major Beard's crowns were on the ADMS's desk and replaced by a captain's 'pips'.

While Dr Beard was just getting used to the shiny crown of rank sewn on both shoulders, he was asked, 'When can you leave?'

'Tomorrow,' he said jokingly.

'Right,' said the ADMS, 'the RAAF can fly you out at first light. And finally, I cannot tell you the position of the battalion, it is retreating with the rest of the United Nations forces.'

'Yessir!'

Captain Beard, along with every other volunteer, had to undergo extensive medical examinations and became a veritable pincushion with inoculations against smallpox, typhoid, typhus fever and encephalitis. A resistant strain of malaria had also developed and the Army had commenced giving its troops Paludrine. The ADMS briefed the young doctor. An RAAF plane would take him to Taeju, but because the battalion was withdrawing there was no map reference and he was expected to 'move north to find the 3rd RAR'.

The world moved rapidly. Frantic hours of preparation flew by, including a farewell and several parties, before a Japanese driver knocked on the doctor's door at 0430 hours to drive him 50 kilometres to the RAAF base at Iwakuni.

'My gear was all over the place,' Captain Beard continued. 'I stuffed it all in a sausage bag. We reached 77 Squadron and I clambered aboard. We flew out in a snowstorm. I was tired, cold, anxious – and I had a king-sized hangover from the farewell. What was I letting myself in for?'

At Taeju, the Dakota turned, taxied back down the runway and left the doctor on the tarmac, a forlorn figure standing in the light snow under sullen clouds. Cold, disorientated and apprehensive, Captain Beard ventured into the US Air Force orderly room and asked the whereabouts of the 3rd RAR. He was told they had not known of any Australians being in Korea. An American sergeant told him that the Australians must be somewhere north, but everyone was withdrawing.

'"It's the big Bug-Out," the airman blurted. "You won't be home for Christmas as General MacArthur promised. And you can't set off in that light clothing," he said. "Take this," and he handed me a fur-lined flying jacket. I was lost and bewildered and walked off with the sausage bag over my shoulder, surrounded by the troops of the 21 nations heading south.'

After trudging along the road packed with retreating soldiers for several hours, the young doctor spotted a slouch hat on a man sitting in an Army jeep. Captain Beard had set eyes on an Australian Army records officer also seeking the battalion to ascertain casualty numbers. They joined forces and headed north against a tide of UN forces and civilians. At nightfall he and his newfound Australian friends, the records officer and his driver, stopped at a Korean hut, hid the jeep and took turns in keeping watch.

'We were cold and hungry, but I did have a loaf of bread, in which was stuffed a bottle of whisky and I did not think that my friend in the battalion, for whom the whisky was an intended gift, would mind if we had a crust of bread and a sip or two.'

During the night there was a commotion and the young doctor, the army records officer and his driver peeped out from their hut to catch sight of a large body of men in white smocks moving down the road. There was no way they could tell whether the men in white were friend or enemy, army or civilian, but they remained in case the men in white were friendly. They did consider sneaking out the back of the hut and wriggling along the ditches to the south but feared being branded cowards. They each had another nip of whisky and settled down where they were for the night. At first light the three men again headed north against the flood of retreating civilians and multi-national forces. They were concerned about the direction they were taking. Could they be heading straight into Chinese hands? Finally, after three days, they just happened across the 3rd RAR.

'I reported to the CO (Lieutenant Colonel Ferguson) who said, "I'm glad to see you ... we've got casualties," and pointed to a ditch in the rice field. Next he informed me that General Walker, Commander of the 8th Army, had been killed and General Ridgway, who had taken command, issued the order: "The retreat has finished, we must stand and fight!"

It all seemed unreal to Captain Beard. He thought, Beard, how did you get yourself into this? But he straightened himself to his full height and walked dutifully to the ditch and set to work, with the help of RAP Sergeant Tampling and Corporal Martin, 'to dress the wounds, apply splints, administer morphia and get them ready for evacuation by the 60th Indian Field Ambulance'.

It was cold and snow feathered the ground on 9 January 1951, the day Captain Donald Beard, the Adelaide graduate who had served in Japan for a unit of the British Commonwealth Occupation Force, was welcomed as the 3rd RAR's new medical officer in Korea. Initially he questioned his decision to volunteer for Korea, 'Yet I very quickly realised that I was no longer on my own, but I was in a strong, solid unit, where I felt safe. It was reassuring. Those brave soldiers made me very humble and they turned me into a doctor.' His arrival coincided with the heaviest snowfall the battalion had experienced and the coldest winter in history and upon reaching the unit he was not even aware of its location.

Within a few days of his arrival Dr Beard found the extreme cold in Korea having a detrimental effect on the physical wellbeing of the soldiers. He recorded in his monthly report at the end of his first month on the front line:

> The problem of tender, blue, painful feet and sickness due to the extreme cold has increased. The average daily evacuation is 12. As much as is humanly and tactically possible is being done to keep feet dry and warm. With the present fall of snow a further problem of snow glare arises. This has been alleviated by rubbing charcoal below the eyes and by warning troops not to look at the snow, but rather glance at objects in the distance.

'The charcoal helps lessen the impact of the reflection of the upper face into the eyes,' Capt Beard explained. Interestingly, today we see footballers and cricketers with dark lines on their faces when they are playing at night under the glare of stands of giant spotlights. In that harsh, cold and dry Korean winter of 1950–51, the average daily temperature dropped to 30 degrees below freezing. The dreaded frostbite was ever present. Soldiers' feet were badly affected. Just prior to Dr Beard arriving in Korea, the Australian soldiers stopped using leather US-made waterproof boots, called a 'snow-pack', because at night the men were immobilised in their trenches and the sweat which built up in their socks began to freeze. By the time Captain Beard reported for duty the following month the Diggers were wearing either the leather-lined American combat boots with rubber soles, or the Australian Army leather boots.

Prevention was the key, but it was a constant problem because of the inability of soldiers in that environment to keep their feet dry. Captain Beard ordered the men to put on dry socks before they slept. Wet socks were taken off and placed under the Diggers' shirts, where they dried overnight. Wet socks didn't add to the aroma of that body of soldiers but it did help lessen the incidence of frostbite. Sick parades in Korea were often lengthy affairs. He had to decide whether his simple treatment and reassurance was sufficient for a soldier to return to his weapon pit, or whether he needed to be evacuated. Such a decision often weighed heavily on his mind, for he knew that the battalion was short on manpower and a man who was evacuated often took a long time to be cleared fit to return to his unit.

'I gradually learnt diagnosis without investigation, including X-ray and pathology. It stood me in good stead throughout my medical lifetime.'

Despite the strategies to keep socks dry and the change to better quality boots to ward off the cold, 60 troops from the 3rd RAR suffered so badly from frostbitten feet that they had to be evacuated to Japan for specialist care away from the front line. Some of the men were in such bad condition that the surgeon, Lieutenant Colonel E.S.R. Hughes, had to amputate part of their feet. Because of the military situation, sometimes soldiers in the 3rd RAR needed a temporary treatment before their evacuation. Massage of the feet with oily brushless shaving cream was extolled by the doctor because the cream remained semi fluid at low temperatures and it was useless for shaving. After some weeks the men twigged and the young doctor was, for a time, known as 'Barbasol Beard'.

'The CO was desperate to do something about the mounting number of frostbite casualties. It was of grave concern given we weren't at that time receiving reinforcements. I don't recall exactly how I got my brainstorm, but I decided to distribute as many tubes of American shaving cream – Barbasol, I think – because it contained lanolin. Australians didn't use brushless shaving cream in those days, but I tore the labels off anyway and announced that it was a special frostbite prevention and treatment lotion.

'I'm unsure whether the lanolin really worked, but all that rubbing and flexing of hands and feet certainly helped. Everyone felt better, and the CO thought I was a pretty good RMO.' Major Ben O'Dowd wrote of Captain Donald Beard:

> Any Digger who felt inclined to go to sick call knew that he would simply get more strange ointment in a tube and be told to rub it into his feet when he changed socks, a daily requirement. Peeling off wet socks in the dead of winter was no picnic, but the hard-working hands and numb feet all profited from the exercise. O'Dowd and his men also discovered that the magical foam slowed the effects of frostbite and reduced the chance of having bare hands freeze to the metal of their weapons, which often required maintenance work that could not be done with gloved hands.

When the Barbasol ran out, they used lard. Drugs and dressings were inadequate and in short supply.

Captain Beard had to improvise as he did in treating sore throats with a mix of jam and aspirin, and indigestion with carb soda he found in the unit kitchen. He called aspirin the 'miracle' drug. The icy winter of 1950–51 was the 3rd RAR's greatest enemy.

'It wasn't just snow, it was ice,' he said. 'You slept in it, dug a pit at night and slept in the hole in the ice. All my medical equipment, all the drugs and solutions which were required to inject patients I placed inside my chest pocket and the warmth of my body kept the medicines from freezing.'

Included in the monthly ration was a bottle of beer and Captain Beard discovered that by the time it arrived in the afternoon it began to freeze. The solution was to stuff the bottle of beer in a sock and sleep with it all night, then drink it at first light before it froze. 'It was great!'

He also found that psychological problems had developed among a group of the men who felt that they had been forgotten by Australia. 'I decided to go out into the trenches to help the company officers to boost morale,' he continued. 'Spirits were falling for a number of reasons: the weather, inactivity, concern about the next attack, and the fact that the newspapers in Australia were making little mention of the war.' He found that his counselling among the troops had become more important than his RMO role as a 'dresser of wounds'. Hippocrates had said in 300 BC: 'Who would become a surgeon must first go to war.'

Improvisation in the face of extraordinary odds was the key to Captain Beard's management of the RAP. The regiment had just one medical orderly per company. In comparison the Americans had four or five, so the Doc asked the Catholic and Anglican padres and the Salvation Army representative to help and 'they did a great job'.

During the Korean War a man of the cloth became a hero among the troops. He was Father Joe Phillips, the Catholic padre attached to the 3rd RAR, and his men loved him. As a military chaplain, Fr Phillips served in North Africa, Palestine, Syria and New Guinea during World War II, with the British Occupational Force in Japan and then for the entire duration of the Korean War. In 1952 he was awarded the MBE for his services in Korea. The citation read (in part): 'Irrespective of danger he has carried out his duties … He is completely fearless and tireless … and has won the respect and admiration of all ranks.' As the Battle of Kapyong raged, Fr Phillips was among the stretcher-bearers. And when there was a lull in fighting on the battlefield, Father Joe was the battalion's SP bookie. By the time the men placed a bet, the race was already over back home in Australia, however, because of the secrecy between the front line and army officials at home, there was rarely a sudden surge on an 'outsider'. If there happened to be a flood of bets on a particular horse, Father Joe was always on the case. He would simply declare, 'Sorry, fellas, all bets are off!'

'The Americans didn't have a clue about Australian racing,' the Doc laughed. 'All the men tried to find out the winner of races, but try as they might no one won an unfair advantage.'

In November 2002, Father Joe Phillips died. He was aged 99 and the Catholic Church invited Donald Beard to deliver the good Father's eulogy.

'I considered the invitation an honour, as I was Church of England,' the Doc said. 'The Bishop said they were giving Father Joe a funeral in the Cathedral. I accepted because I thought it was St Francis Xavier Cathedral in Adelaide, but in fact it happened to be the Cathedral in Port Pirie, 150 miles away. I had to change plans, get leave from work and drive to Port Pirie. It was a wonderful service for a man who had done so much. Afterwards there was a procession led by the Bishop and me around Port Pirie; then came the hearse, then 21 Carmelite priests from throughout Australia. After the procession we returned to the Cathedral for a sumptuous lunch, prepared by the ladies of the parish.

During the Korean War Captain Beard took an interest in a young Korean 'stray', Kim Yung-choi, making the 14-year-old an orderly in the regiment. Later he sponsored the boy, who he found to have been 'both industrious and loyal to a fault' and had no immediate family in his war-ravaged homeland, to come to live in Australia. 'Initially he cleaned up round the aid post, but I taught Kim to dress wounds and set splints and he became a very important part of the medical team.'

Captain Beard considered the Indian Army's 60th Parachute Field Ambulance as 'our real saviours'.

'Not only did the Indians evacuate our wounded swiftly to a mobile US Army Surgical Hospital (MASH), but the CO Lieutenant Colonel A.G. Rangaraj would suddenly appear at my side to help stabilise the most serious cases.' The two doctors became the greatest of friends. Later Doctor Beard visited his friend in India and admired Doctor Rangaraj's sage advice and thirst for life. At the age of 80, Dr Rangaraj made a final parachute jump. He lived to the age of 95.

'The Indian 60th Parachute Field Ambulance physician was Major Rangaswami, with whom I also became friends,' he said. 'As there was no renal transplant unit in India at that time, years later I arranged for his son to come out from India with his grandmother as live donor to the Queen Elizabeth Hospital in Adelaide for a kidney transplant, which proved successful. In 2007 Rangaswami was to come to Adelaide and stay with me for the Australia–India cricket Test. Unfortunately, a few days before he was due to arrive he had a heart attack and died. I was greatly saddened.'

'I fell ill with fever and sore throat, coughing blood into the snow, and was taken to the MASH for treatment for pneumonia. The unit worked very well under great difficulties and dreadful weather. However, at the MASH I didn't like men being brought in and carried over me as I lay on a stretcher. Sometimes blood from the wounded men dripped on to me as I lay there. After a couple of days the CO wanted to evacuate me to Japan. I didn't relish the idea of clean sheets in Kure then a return to the hole in the ground in Korea, so I requested a transfer to the 60th Indian Field Ambulance where I was brilliantly treated by rum and curry and a week later I was back in the battalion in time for Kapyong.'

On 22 April 1951 a united church service was held in the Kapyong paddy fields for the Australian, British, Canadian and New Zealand troops. Unlike the previous months of snow and bitter wind, the men were bathed in God's sunshine. There were plans for the Australian, New Zealand and Turkish soldiers to celebrate Anzac Day in three days' time; an opportunity for the old foes of World War I to remember those killed at Gallipoli and to drink to the future on this foreign battlefield. Extra supplies and beer were stockpiled ready for the celebration.

On the night of 22 April, the New Zealand 16th Field Artillery Regiment treated the Argylls, who were due to leave the warzone the next day, to a farewell party. The Kiwis dished up a Maori-style feast for the British troops, scrounging rare fresh sides of meat and vegetables wrapped in leaves and cooked in rock ovens under the ground. However, just before midnight thousands of Chinese from the 3rd Army attacked the hapless South Korean 6th ROK Division, cutting a swathe through their ranks, and began the surge down the Kapyong Valley heading for Seoul.

Early on 23 April, the 3rd RAR, British, Canadian troops and the NZ 16th Field Artillery Regiment were ordered forward to occupy a blocking position in the Kapyong Valley, near the hamlet of Cucktin-ni.

'We never did learn what happened to out stockpile of beer.'

Instead of flying home the British would fight another battle and the Anzac celebrations for the 3rd RAR, the New Zealanders and the Turks would be put on hold. Against overwhelming odds, throughout the days and nights of 23 and 24 April 1951, the Australian soldiers and the medical team of the 3rd RAR showed true valour in the spirit of Anzac. The men had heard rumours and 'furphies' of an imminent attack and it came with frightening realism.

The 3rd RAR moved up the valley and the companies spread out on the hills either side of the road. They found the frozen, stony ground tough work as they dug in, preparing for the firefight.

Dr Beard reflects on the Battle of Kapyong, which takes a place of pride in the annals of Australian Army history. 'When the battle was over there was a strange feeling. We had survived but we were distressed at the loss of 32 great colleagues and 59 severely wounded men. We should have felt good about the battle, but we did not. There was still much fighting to do and we did not know when the Chinese would attack again.

'What did it do for me? I realised even more the value of the Australian soldier. The Australian soldiers were strong and brave and were well led. They looked after each other and the other companies. There was no panic; it was a fighting withdrawal and they took with them the wounded. All this was done for the United Nations, which had been asked for help by South Korea, a country about which they knew very little. They did their very best without thought of recognition nor recompense. It was just as well, because there was very little (of either) for many years.'

In the wake of the Battle of Kapyong, the 3rd RAR battalion became known as 'Old Faithful', for the Battalion itself has welded into a great unit and fought in the spirit of Kapyong in many battles including conflicts in Timor, Afghanistan and Iraq. On 24 April each year, Colonel Beard takes part in the Kapyong Parade; originally held at Battalion headquarters Holsworthy, NSW, the ceremony is now held at Lavarack Barrack, Townsville. He proudly mixes with his surviving mates of Kapyong and the current 'fine, fit new soldiers of the 3rd RAR'. For 50 years Colonel Beard has read the Presidential Citation at the annual Kapyong Parade and in 2010 conducted the ceremony of affixing the battle streamer to the regimental flag.

The Battle of Kapyong stopped the Chinese Army's advance in its tracks. After the Battle of Kapyong, the battleline moved northwards, with the Australians up with the leaders in the advance until the old demarcation line near the 38th parallel was reached and Panmonjong was set up. On the way, in October 1951, another famous battle was fought by the Australians at Maryang San. Reflecting on the Battle of Kapyong, Donald Beard looks back with pride, but Korea also holds memories of great hardship for the men.

'In the mountains the men had to contend with terrible terrain, freezing temperatures and deep snow. Casualties were carried on stretchers up the sides of mountains, the bearers knee-deep in snow. There were many mishaps.

The injured were usually in a state of semi-consciousness. When a stretcher-bearer fell, the injured soldier crashed to the ice. These falls, most of which were unavoidable, caused greater misery, further injury to the wound and, in some cases, the solder died. Eventually they would reach me at the aid post. I adjusted their dressings and splints and gave them morphia.

'Further evacuation of the wounded was carried out by Indian stretcher jeeps. They had to negotiate rough tracks to reach the 60th Indian Parachute Field Ambulance and from there the US MASH, where primary excisions of the wounds was carried out and intravenous penicillin administered. Most of the seriously wounded men were evacuated by RAAF Dakota aircraft to Japan. Finally, those injured men were placed on an ambulance train and taken to our military hospital in Kure, which was run jointly by the Australian and British forces.

'There were teething problems at the MASH. It had never before been possible for a hospital to be based so close to the front line. It meant that casualties were brought to medical aid quickly, when on previous occasions, men suffering similar wounds would have died. MASH units were often confronted by a flood of casualties, most of whom were suffering multiple wounds. Nursing staff was, for the first time, close to the front line. This brought its own special problems. Surgeons who had deferred their national service during medical training suddenly were swept up in the Korean War. This happened to the surgeons at a stage in their experience when they thought they would go into private practice in the US.

'These surgeons were dedicated to the care of the soldier, but not so dedicated to regimental discipline, which made it difficult for the Commanding Officer. But out of it developed a wonderful unit, which again showed its value in Vietnam where the similar Australian unit was the 1st Australian Field Hospital. In Korea helicopters did not have anywhere near the impact they had in Vietnam. Because of the isolated position of the mountains where the Australian battalion in Korea was based, it was rarely possible for casualties to be evacuated by helicopter. A helicopter of the 1950s could not lift casualties from a point higher than 1500 feet, nor could they operate at night, nor in bad weather.'

'When a man was hit, initial aid came from his fellow soldiers. Then a medical assistant, of which there was one attached to each company, would come to his aid. I had trained these men to give morphia injections and they dressed the wound. Next stage was the stretcher-bearers. Each company had two stretcher-bearers attached to it. They were either volunteers or members of the battalion band. Along with their band training and blowing of bugles, they trained as stretcher-bearers. Others in our battalion helped, such as the Roman Catholic padre (Father Joe) and Salvation Army representatives. The leader of the band, Sergeant Tom Murray, was awarded a George Medal.'

Capt Beard's Regimental Aid Post (RAP) could be back at HQ in a tent or in the field, perhaps a stool alongside a tree flying a Red Cross flag. There the men would receive new dressings and firm bandages around chest wounds. The bleeding would be stopped, splints put on broken limbs and all the men would be prepared for evacuation. The seriously wounded men were evacuated to the 60th Indian Parachute Field Ambulance for further dressings, thence to the MASH for initial surgery and afterwards flown by RAAF Dakota to Japan.

'After Kapyong, the Chinese did not immediately attack again,' he recalled. 'They were exhausted and short of supplies. We sent out probing patrols and frequently the Chinese folded and disappeared. We expected a trap, which may or may not eventuate, and so once again we fought northwards towards the 38th parallel.' In June Captain Beard learnt that he was to return to Japan, then sail for home.

After his term in Korea, Captain Beard was re-installed as a major, his rank of captain being a temporary measure, and he took up a post as Officer-in-Charge (OC) of a small transit hospital in Tokyo. Upon arrival he happily sewed the golden crowns on both shoulders of his uniform. By that time the sacked General MacArthur was back in Tokyo, still residing at the Emperor's Palace. There was a golden rule for all military personnel who happened to drive a vehicle past MacArthur's 'residence', slow down or suffer the consequences. Within days Major Beard was booked by US military police for speeding past the Emperor's Palace in his army jeep. General Douglas MacArthur saw himself as some sort of war god, the veritable 'Emperor of Occupied Japan', and speeding past his palace was something akin to a 'crime against the greatest'. By General MacArthur's decree, the guilty one's punishment was to be meted out by his commanding officer. As it turned out Major Beard was the CO and he had to punish himself. With a hilarious parody of pomp and humour, Major Beard and his Regimental Sergeant Major collaborated to ensure that General MacArthur's order was carried out to the letter.

Major Beard marched into the CO's (his) office, saluted the empty chair and the RSM read the charge. Major Beard then resumed his seat as CO and ordered that the defendant stand and listen to his fate. The Commanding Officer, Major Beard, then sentenced Major Beard to provide his troops, in each medical unit, with a minimum of three cases of beer. The US Military Police were then informed the officer had been found guilty – as charged – and an appropriate penalty awarded.

Conditions in Tokyo were much better than in Korea, but Major Beard still had about 50 hospital patients with all sorts of problems, including haemorrhagic or Manchurian fever, which he investigated.

'One night a Korean casualty became acutely disturbed, arming himself with a butcher's knife with which he threatened hospital staff in the ward,' he said. In his calm way, Major Beard approached the man with the knife, sitting next to and reassuring the disturbed patient until he was able to disarm him.

While in Japan, he spent a few days with a US archaeological unit in the Hokkaido Mountains to investigate if there was any relationship between the Australian Aborigine and the indigenous Japanese Ainu.

'None was found,' he said, 'but it was a fascinating expedition.'

For now, in December 1951, Captain Dr Donald Beard's time as 'Digger Doctor' was over. He flew home and in the hold of the SS *Taipan* was a big, black Dodge motorcar, which he had purchased with the help of an American friend in Korea for the sum of £700. There was a catch to his purchase. The Doc had to pay an extra £500 in duty (refundable after three years).

As he flew to Adelaide, he looked forward to working in peaceful surroundings, getting back to his cricket and baseball, a swim and taking a girl to the pictures. He would never forget Korea, the battles, the men, and from that time to the present day he maintains great admiration for the courage of the Australian soldier.

'The enemy were good soldiers but did not have a reputation for the good treatment of POWs.'

Every war has its heroes and every war breaks our hearts. During the Korean War, 29 Australians were taken prisoner. While in captivity they were treated badly, offered meagre food, deprived of sleep, and kept in appalling conditions where lice thrived and disease reigned.

'One Australian prisoner, Private Horace Madden of the 3rd RAR Battalion, died from malnutrition and ill treatment. Private Madden was a signaller, attached to 3rd RAR Battalion headquarters.

'He was captured at the Battle of Kapyong on 24 April 1951. His Chinese captors hoped to break his spirit by depriving him of his basic needs, mostly enough food. But Madden was defiant right up to the day he died on 6 November 1951. Private Madden was posthumously awarded the George Medal for his bravery under interrogation and his generosity in how he looked after his fellow prisoners. The surviving Australian prisoners of war were repatriated a few days after the armistice was signed on 27 July 1953.

'I left the Battalion with mixed feelings. In my time with them I had grown up and I became a proper doctor, whose aim was the complete care of the soldier, an aim that for me was both rewarding and humbling. The Australian soldier is magnificent. In 2011 they were deployed to Afghanistan where they upheld their great tradition.'

In April 2001, Don Beard was among a small commemorative military mission to visit Korea to pay homage to the fallen in the Battle of Kapyong.

'It was an emotional experience to visit the War Memorial, the war graves and cemetery in Pusan. Climbing the hills of Kapyong in the old 3rd RAR positions and to wonder how they could have held the Chinese advance. It was such an emotional journey.'

In July 2010, Don Beard asked if I would like to join him on a bus with a group of Korean veterans to commemorate the naming of five bridges built as part of the joint State and Federal funded $564 million Northern Expressway, linking Adelaide to the Barossa Valley. The bridges were all named after famous battles in Australia's war history: Hamel, Tobruk, Kokoda, Kapyong and Long Tan. The then South Australian Premier, Mike Rann, said: 'They were sacred places for all Australians, having helped shape the very future of our nation. They remain etched in our history forever.'

Attending the official opening of Kapyong Bridge were a few busloads of veterans and their wives, politicians, the press – and the author absorbing the atmosphere, watching those veterans proudly displaying medals on their chests, standing to attention at the speeches, many misty-eyed at the thought of battle and their mates who didn't make it home.

Colonel Dr Donald Beard gave a great speech. He was a little nervous as he is when delivering a speech, but he always does his homework. He has his speeches typed, double spacing, and religiously carries the typed speech with him, be it an important medical conference, or a local Rotary Club function. Don Beard stood tall, looked squarely at the gathering of people, completely ignored his typewritten speech, and spoke from the heart.

He charmed his audience with well-crafted words in a way any writer would love to engage their readers. Like the gentle Sikh medical orderlies who served on the front line in Korea with the 60th Indian Parachute Field Ambulance, Don Beard has a calm gentleness about him. Through kind eyes he looked at his audience and within seconds he had them eating out of his hand. He spoke with passion of the men involved in some of our most famous battles, especially the Battle of Kapyong. For a time we were all transported back to that epic battle.

Lest we forget.

Two

Early Days

The gardener spotted them as they were clambering back over the wall and he raised his shotgun loaded with saltpetre, and let fly with both barrels.

Donald Beard

Donald Douglas Beard was born at home on 22 February 1925; birth day of many celebrated people including George Washington in 1732. Home was near the city of Adelaide at 25 Marleston Avenue, Ashford, a stone's throw from Ashford House, now the site of Ashford Hospital, and Keswick Army Barracks – significant landmarks in Donald Beard's life for he would one day become a leading surgeon and a Colonel in the Australian Army. Donald's proud father, Harold, kept a meticulous record of all income and expenses associated with his son's birth. He did not miss a penny, detailing the cost of medical help, medicines, midwives and baby clothes.

At that time Ashford House belonged to a man named Ackland and when Donald was about five years old he and his friend, Leith Hamlyn, would run a stick along his galvanised-iron fence, making a deafening noise that agitated Mr Ackland's six wolfhounds, provoking the neighbour to chase the boys down the street. The Beard family fence also suffered. There is a notation in Harold Beard's little black book: 'Jan 1, 1929. Reimbursement from J.W. Anderson for damage to fence, £2.' The money was in restitution for his having run into the Beard house front fence in his motorcar on Christmas Day.

Harold's younger sister, Myrtle, lived opposite Donald and Beryl's grandparents in Marleston Avenue, Ashford. During visits to the family home, Harold began to take notice of a girl in the house opposite, a girl with stunning hair. Beryl explained: 'At the time my mother, then Alison Wright, worked down in Glenelg in a lovely home belonging to a Mr Crosier, a well-known grazier. She used to come home every fortnight on her day off and she always had beautiful hair and liked nice clothes. Harold used to watch this girl closely. Eventually he met her and they had a courtship of many years from the time they met in 1915 until the time they wed in 1920.

Early Days

'My mother's people were very much against my mother marrying my father because they said he was kinky ... another way of them saying they considered Harold Beard to be eccentric. My mother was told in no certain terms that she should not "marry out of her station". But my mother was a determined girl. She told her parents that she was going to "marry Harold Beard whatever they thought".' Harold was then working as a military pay clerk at Keswick Army Barracks and was keen to marry.

Harold Douglas Beard married Alison Mavis Wright at St Matthews Church, Kensington, on 28 February 1920. Arriving next day in a two-horse-drawn white carriage, she went to the family and showed them her wedding ring. 'I'm Mrs Beard,' she announced.

Beryl continued: 'Mother had two sisters, Henrietta and Charlotte, both of whom were "a bit grim". Charlotte said, "We'll see." And 12 months later, on 11 March 1921, I was born.' Life at Marleston Avenue holds many fond memories for Donald and Beryl. During school holidays the children and their dog would go out on a picnic.

'My poor mother used to watch the Schultz family go off for a Sunday drive in their Essex motorcar. Donald used to say, "Let's make out". So we fashioned a make-believe car out of branches left on the path from pruning. My mother and father had pruned the hedge and there were lots of cuttings available to us, perfect for Donald's imaginary car. "We'll need a steering wheel," Donald said, grabbing hold of a suitable branch. Donald sat in the front seat as the driver.'

Both Beard children had vivid imaginations, a gift granddaughter Sophie Beard inherited. At the age of 10, Sophie made a Christmas tree and the decorations that adorned it, plus the boxes of make-believe wrapped presents at its base. What Beryl and Donald did not have they made up and their creativeness and ingenuity gave them tremendous fun. 'Other times we'd make out we were at the butcher shop,' Beryl remembered. 'Donald was the butcher wrapping up all manner of things, such as a Mallee root which doubled for rump steak, and a rock for a porterhouse. We lived in fairyland.

'A highlight of the school holidays was to catch the Bib and Bub tram from the stop outside Keswick Army Barracks and visit our great-grandmother's cottage in Coglin Street, Brompton.' At Brompton the children played in the big pug hole, where they dug clay to make bricks. Children would lie face-down on bits of galvanised iron and slide down the slopes of the hole.

Dr Beard recalls: 'In 1930 we went to Moonta where Father set up a taxation business, but we had no transport from the stone home he had built at Port Hughes three miles away. Father rented a small room in Moonta for his office. While everyone wanted Dad's services, it was the middle of the Depression and his clients couldn't pay him. Also Mum did not like the country – she was lost and lonely – and she cried to Beryl to speak to her father. It was all very sad.'

Donald and Beryl do not recall a great deal about their primary schooling at Moonta, nor do they remember much about the sport they played in that small town. Their father was struggling financially because he wasn't being paid for his services and their mother was distraught about living in the country.

After the Port Hughes experiment, the Beard family returned to Adelaide to find their house occupied. A man of the cloth had leased the house for five years. The minister of religion had little means and could not afford to pay the rent. Evicting the minister would have been difficult at the best of times, but impossible during the Depression, so the man of the cloth Beryl calls 'an old devil' stayed and the Beards had to call upon the good nature of various relatives and friends to find suitable accommodation. Harold Beard was a dreamer and an eccentric. However, both Beryl and Donald will attest that he was a great teacher. He taught his children impeccable manners. He taught them to always do 'the right thing'.

'My father was quiet and proper. My mother was a feisty woman of Scottish descent,' Beryl said. 'She always said, "I will have my way."' Sadly she didn't have her way with the money.

'Father's dream home in Port Hughes soaked up half his earnings. In his little black book there are dozens of notations for land tax, payments to builders, carpenters, council rates and taxes. It was never ending. However, on the home front he was a loving, caring man. And he was very ambitious for us. Woe betide if we came home at the end of the week and we had not excelled in the weekly exams. If you had three 10s in reading, writing, arithmetic you were fine, but if you didn't get top marks he'd want to know the reason why.

'It was an odd relationship with my mother and father. My father didn't marry until he was 35 and my mother was 25. However, they loved each other very much. I still live by a little quote that I think was written by Oscar Wilde when he was in jail. *There will always be stars through the window bars, if we only look to see them shine.*

'Years later Donald used to take care of my mother and father. He took them on drives after he got a car, a big, black Dodge. One time, coming back from Victor Harbor on a cold, windy day, he saw a man on the side of the road selling cauliflowers. "Oh, look at that poor old man," he said, and stopped the car and went to the cauliflower seller and bought his entire stock. Donald filled the boot of his car with cauliflowers. That night all our neighbours had cauliflower with their evening meal. And my mother was busy for days pickling cauliflower.'

Many years later when Donald had rooms in South Terrace, Beryl arrived for an appointment. She noticed a young man walk into the doctor's room, then leave a little while later.

'When I entered the room I noticed Donald was wearing a sad expression. "Did you see that young fellow? He's just come out of Yatala Labour Prison, where he's had a rough time of it. I gave him a few bob for a meal and a bed."'

Upon their return to Adelaide, the Beards stayed with their mother's parents for up to eight months, then with Uncle Charles at Blackwood. Donald attended Blackwood Primary School. He recalls the time: 'There was a back veranda for me and Beryl, use of the kitchen, one bedroom for Mum and Dad and that was it. One Saturday morning a boy and I blocked up all the gutters in the school yard and turned all the taps on, made pools of water which we scooped up and threw at one another until one of the teachers found us and we got into trouble.'

During Donald and Beryl's growing years the Beard family moved house often. They moved from Ashford to Moonta, back to Ashford, then Blackwood, Maylands and Parkside, after which there were two rented rooms in Edmund Avenue, Unley, before the family settled in another house in the same street.

The Beards moved from Aunty Maud's and Harold Beard found that another two single sisters – the Misses Martin – living further down George Street, Parkside, could accommodate the parents and Donald, so he could complete his primary schooling, but not his sister, Beryl.

'I was distraught,' Beryl confessed, 'it was very traumatic to be separated from my brother. We were very close. I went to live with Aunty Olive, but I wasn't happy and often wished I could go home.' After attaining top marks at Richmond Primary School, Beryl was among 300 elite students to win a place at the coveted Adelaide Technical High School. At the age of 12, Donald was attending Parkside School and he ventured down to the Park Lands one Saturday afternoon hoping that a team might be short a man so he could get a game of cricket. Happily he found such a team, the Parkside Methodist Church eleven. '"Where do you go to church, young man," the team captain asked me. "I attend St Augustine's in Unley," I replied. "Oh, to play for this team you have to be a member of our church." I was converted on the spot! The team captain was Gordon Brown, the superintendent of the Parkside Methodist Church Sunday school. He was the father of Dean Brown, who later became State Premier.

'And so I became a Methodist for a couple of years. There were occasional visiting preachers and I recall one of them telling us that English is such a beautiful language that the words are more expressive than swearing. I take his advice to this day, except, perhaps, the odd expletive in distress. I do not like swearing particularly the four-letter words in conversation or at the theatre or on television. They are often used over and over and are unpleasant and lack expression. There is a man in my bowling club who swears all the time. No one else in the club likes it.'

That same summer, Donald and a friend used to slip away from school at lunch or after the school bell rang and run down to the Parkside Mental Hospital to load up with apricots, plums and nectarines. All they needed to do was climb over the wall. The idea was to negotiate the wall with stealth and speed, rush to the trees, load up with the stolen fruit and rush back over the wall to safety. However, one day they weren't so lucky. The gardener spotted them as they were clambering back over the wall and he raised his shotgun, loaded with saltpetre, and let fly with both barrels. Did it hurt?

'You bet,' he said. 'We copped the saltpetre in the bottom and in the backs of our legs. Boy, did it hurt. When we got home we had to lie face down and have bits of saltpetre extracted with forceps – one by one. We certainly didn't call a doctor. In those days you only consulted a doctor if you were dying.'

Dr Beard remembers that by the year 1934 'near the end of the Depression, good teaching commenced'. Donald started with Wellington Road School (now Trinity Gardens School).

'Wellington Road School had some very good teachers, one was a Mr Moulds, the other Mr Phillips,' he said. Young Donald loved the teaching environment and he embraced the teaching and learning. He has since been back to the school to speak at the school's centenary celebrations. Coincidentally Don and Margaret's grandson attended the same school and the Beard seniors stood in the same courtyard as Don knew so well in the summer of 1934–35. In 1935 Donald played his first game of cricket for Wellington Road School against Rose Park. 'We had to walk three kilometres from Wellington Road to the Victoria Park Racecourse, at the centre of which was the Rose Park cricket pitch,' he said.

'A master accompanied us as we walked to the game. We carried the team kit in a bag – two bats, one pair of pads for each batsman and a ball. Once a month during summer we were given a special treat. We'd catch a special tram to Henley Beach for swimming lessons in the beachside pool. Then we had a half hour's swim in the sea. On the return tram journey we were given a bush biscuit, which we happily devoured. And all of this for threepence. They were indeed halcyon days.'

The family moved to Aunty Maud and Uncle Ern's home in George Street, Parkside. The same conditions prevailed. Donald and Beryl had a bed each under the shelter of the veranda and their parents occupied a bedroom. The family had use of the kitchen. Donald well remembers Uncle Ern riding his old belt-driven Douglas motorbike and he enjoyed the times when his father bowled to him in the backyard. At Parkside School, Donald excelled in his studies, even in the school gardening projects.

'I recall each student was given a patch of ground to grow vegetables and I specialised in radishes. In fact, I won first prize and was presented with a copy of *Yates Home Garden Guide*. But I wasn't immune from the cane. I had four cuts of the cane across the palms of my hand on a couple of occasions and the punishment was probably deserved. I enjoyed Uncle Ern's stories of his sailing days on clippers, at one time being shipwrecked on an island south of New Zealand and surviving there on a diet of fish and penguins. My favourite subjects were English, history and geography.'

One day Donald and his friends were wandering down the main road heading towards the Park Lands to play cricket, when they passed a man standing at his front gate. The man smiled and asked Donald where they were heading.

'"Well," he said, looking at our battered cricket bat, "You can't play cricket with that piece of equipment. Wait on." The man went back inside his house and returned with a beautiful cricket bat, which looked as if it had never been used. '"Was my bat once. Too old for it now," he said, handing the bat to me. "Here, take it and use it well. I've no use for it these days."' The boys' benefactor turned out to be famous South Australian businessman Sir James Gosse, director and chairman of a number of boards including the Adelaide Steamship Company, the Bank of Adelaide, News Ltd, G. & R. Wills. Sir James was a stalwart of the Adelaide Club, president of the SA Chamber of Commerce, the Boy Scouts' Association and St Peter's Collegians Association. In later years, his nephew Alexander Downer entered Federal Parliament and his son, George Gosse, won the George Medal for delousing mines in the

English Channel. As fate would have it Donald Beard and George Gosse travelled together on the aircraft carrier *Sydney* to attend the coronation of Queen Elizabeth II in 1953.

For Donald Beard cricket and study were intertwined. It was very much like that for his entire working life. But mischief sometimes got in the way of his cricket at school. Donald had been creating havoc among the female students by dipping a girl's plaits into the inkwell during geography class. Mr Colebatch was unimpressed and decreed that as punishment Donald would have to stay in after school and clean all the inkwells. He will never forget the moment: '"But Mr Colebatch, I have to play cricket this afternoon," I pleaded.

'"You should have thought of that before you caused this trouble."

'"Sir," I said, thinking on my feet. "If you asked me any question on geography and if I got it right could I go to cricket?" The teacher thought about it for a few seconds, then smiled. "Right, Beard. What is the name of what is called the fire mountain of the Antarctic?"

'"Mt Erebus," I answered unhesitatingly.

'"All right," he said, with just enough pride in his voice for one of his students. "Beard, I think they've already gone. You'd better run to catch them!" Teaching by the headmaster, Mr Cattle, and Mr Colebatch was excellent,' Dr Beard said with conviction. 'I tried very hard because I wanted to get sufficient marks to follow my sister into Adelaide Technical High School.' Donald played cricket and football against Sturt Street, Gilles Street, Glen Osmond and Highgate schools; the matches were always tough, especially matches against Sturt Street.

'One of the girls in my class was the daughter of a racehorse trainer, whose stables were on the edge of the Park Lands,' he recalled. 'One day she invited me to have a ride. I couldn't lose face, so I clambered on my steed. The horse obviously sensed that I couldn't ride so he bolted across the park to trees with low overhanging branches and I was immediately swept off the bolting animal. I have never ridden a horse since.'

In preparation for a parade during the visit of the Duke and Duchess of Gloucester, he was among dozens of boys training on the Adelaide Oval. (Among the boys training that day were the notorious Lik Lak Cahill and Jack Broadstock. Years later, a West Adelaide and State footballer, Broadstock was warned off every metropolitan racetrack in South Australia.) At the end of the training Donald and his friend, Ray Kelly, decided to miss catching the tram home. Instead they ventured down to the River Torrens to try their hand catching yabbies. Eventually they wandered up to King William Street, where, by sheer coincidence, Donald bumped into his father. Later that evening, at home, he received a severe reprimand.

Donald had lots of energy and he loved being active. In town one day he had been to the children's library and on his way back along North Terrace he had fun jumping over the metal hoops circling the lawns.

'I ripped my shin on an unturned twist of wire and took myself straight to the Royal Adelaide Hospital where the laceration was sutured and dressed. I went home with my sock pulled high on my leg to hide the dressing and said nothing about the incident. Later the sock slipped and my father saw the top of the dressing. There was a reprimand, then an appropriate period before I received some parental sympathy.'

He was part of the school choir that sang at the Centennial Hall with the Thousand Voices Choir – a group representative of schools from throughout South Australia. School for Donald was mostly lots of study and great sporting fun, but there were times of great sadness. Two of his friends became sick with bad colds.

'They had contracted tuberculosis and died,' he said. 'At school we were all sad, but we didn't know the cause of the boys' deaths. We did not understand TB. It was not until 10 years later when I graduated that a cure – antibiotic streptomycin – was found for tuberculosis.'

The day he finished grade seven, the school headmaster, Mr A.C. Cattle, walked with him to the main gate of the school. 'I remember it now, as if it was yesterday. The headmaster stood there and said, "Well, Beard, you've done quite well. Pity you spoil it sometimes with practical jokes. But you are going to do well in the future, so work hard and play hard and good luck." It was a wonderful thing for a headmaster to tell a 12-year-old boy. A few months earlier I had wanted to be an engine driver. My grandfather, who lived nearby, was an engine driver and his two sons carried on the trade. One day one of his sons asked, "Do you want to come with me for the day in the steam engine?" So there I was, about 12 years old, shovelling coal for the engine driver on the Adelaide to Willunga run. Again, I kept this little adventure a secret from my father. Both my grandfather and his two sons were 6'4". I was determined to beat them and I eventually did, by about half an inch.'

Donald's impressive school results won him a place at the Adelaide Technical High School. As with all schools in the Adelaide metropolitan area, there were no classes for the first term due to the 1938 poliomyelitis epidemic, and study was by correspondence.

At the time he began high school, he hoped to become an architect. 'I enjoyed design, but I was the world's worst at line drawing.' Donald grew to be inspired by his uncle, Roland Beard, a World War I hero who served at Gallipoli, Egypt and France, and later specialised in obstetrics and gynaecology. He was assistant to the Professor of Midwifery and Gynaecology in Birmingham, England, then gynaecologist at the Royal Adelaide Hospital and tutor in obstetrics at the University of Adelaide. 'His name in Adelaide was held in high esteem. I said to myself if you can do that sort of work and be appreciated for it I think I'd like to do that. I decided I wanted to do medicine,' he said.

'So I told my father. I didn't have any languages. Latin was no longer a requirement. You could learn enough Latin for medicine. I did French Intermediate at the night School of Mines then I had to do leaving honours at Adelaide High School, where I studied German. Strangely enough, German was a popular subject in the middle of the war.

'I was reading the *Sunday Mail* Possum's Page and they listed people you could write to as a pen friend and I picked one out, a girl named Brenda Mills, 14 Graham Road, Eastern Bristol 5, England. So we used to write to each other. From 1941, I continued to write to Brenda until the end of the war. We sent food parcels to the Mills family home in UK and we received replies from them describing the terrible conditions that prevailed in England.

Eventually I got to England for study and a colleague, Peter Harbison, lent me his car to go round England to say goodbye to everyone. I got round to Bristol and called on this girl. She was married. I stayed with them the night and the next day she took me to the Gloucester burial place of England's cricket legend, W.G. Grace, and I think our visit created suspicion among the neighbours.'

Don was interested in cricket and history and William Gilbert Grace was called the 'Great Cricketer'. In 869 first-class matches Grace scored 54,211 runs at an average of 39.45. He hit 124 centuries and took 874 catches. As a bowler Grace took 2808 wickets at an average of 18.15 with a bowling best of 10/49 for MCC versus Oxford University at Oxford in 1886.

'As pen pals, Brenda and I used to write an aerogram, which you could buy for sixpence. They would photograph it and send 200 letters on a tiny roll of 35mm film. The roll of film was printed in England. What a novel way to cut down the use of paper.'

Sport, especially cricket, was ever on the agenda for young Donald Beard. 'My first game of cricket on turf was against Rostrevor in 1941. Les

Ziersch, who had come to Adelaide High School from Concordia College to do leaving honours, opened the bowling with me. We were being coached by Clarrie Grimmett down at the Adelaide Oval No 2 ground, because the school didn't have its own oval. Clarrie always told the bowlers to maintain a good line and length and "don't bowl down the leg side". Rostrevor didn't make too many. I got 5/25 and Les Ziersch 4/9, with one run-out. Much the same happened in the second innings and Clarrie was happy I had taken his advice.

'Poor Les Ziersch. When he left Adelaide High School in 1941 he joined the Air Force and within a year he was shot down and killed. He was a great man and a good friend. West Adelaide football star Bob Lee went to the school, also Jim Thomas, who should have been a Rhodes Scholar, but was bowled out through his addiction to gambling.

'A few years later, when I was playing for University against Adelaide, I came in last to join our captain, Chester Bennett, who was not out 98. "Let's see if we can get a few more runs," Chester said.

'I was in my element. How lucky was I? Here on the Adelaide Oval facing one of the world's greatest bowlers, Clarrie Grimmett. Clarrie came up to the crease and tossed the ball in the air. It was hissing – I'm sure I could hear the ball hiss – then it hit the ground, and it spat at me! I had no idea where that ball went. I played forward but somehow the ball got past my bat and the stumps were all over the place.'

Chester Bennett, who became coach of the Chappell brothers at Prince Alfred College, remained 98 not out.

Donald Beard bowled Grimmett 0

Grimmett 8/72

At school during a match against Sacred Heart, Donald was hit 'a painful blow to the "groin area", as the commentators say'. He was not wearing any protection and there he was writhing about on the pitch when the wicket-keeper noticed he was out of his ground and promptly stumped him. The Catholic Brother, who was standing as an umpire at square leg, made no allowance for the fact that the batsman was severely inconvenienced and he gave Beard out!

'I was a Protestant!'

Beryl took a different path in life to her brother. She gained entry to Adelaide Technical School with better marks than her brother who followed four years later. But despite her success Beryl had to leave her studies after two years due to financial problems at home.

'Because I wanted to become a cadet journalist, I applied to the *Advertiser* in December 1936 and got a letter to say "thank you, we'll keep you in mind",' she recalls. Beryl was kept in mind for the *Advertiser* alerted her to a good opportunity at Radio 5AD, which in those days was owned by the newspaper.

'I got the job at 5AD, but my job in the record library was mundane. That was the time of some famous Adelaide radio names – Jack Burgess, Dick Moore and Charles Norton. They would wear dinner jackets to read the news at night. It was very funny.'

In 1942, Radio 5KA offered Beryl a position as 'night announcer'. 'My father certainly did not have the money for both Donald and I to go to university. I was a little disappointed in my parents, whose attitude towards me seemed "well, Beryl can look after herself".'

Beryl looks back to the time when Donald was living with the two spinsters – Amy and Lilly Shepherd – at Maylands. There was many a time Donald got up at 5 am to help the local greengrocer with deliveries, which were carted by a wagon drawn by two horses. Not only did the money he earn help the family budget, he also delighted in bringing home scraps of old vegetables, which his mother tossed together to help make a stew.

Donald also helped on a bread round for Opie's Bread. At one particular house the baker would alight and go to the front door, whereupon he was ushered inside. Donald was told to finish his deliveries down the road and around the corner. The Doc smiled: 'I'd wait with the horse and cart and the baker would rush out somewhat flustered. How many of those liaisons occurred with all sorts of tradesmen in those days … and probably still do?'

As for Donald and Beryl's mother and father. 'They loved one another,' Beryl said. 'My mother loved him. He loved her. My father would often say in our mother's hearing, "Oh, Alison, with all your faults, I still love you."'

Harold Beard could well have been the sentimental bloke C.J. Dennis wrote so passionately about. Harold knew the Dennis family at Bungaree Station.

'The "Tech" was a great school with a severe disciplinarian headmaster, Sydney Moyle, whom the former students recall with affection. He had a staff of wonderful teachers who were always making us "try a little harder" and, thanks to their encouragement, we did try harder.

'One of them, Mr Haskard, rewarded the two students who tried the hardest during the week to accompany him to country football matches, which he umpired. These were great trips. Years later I looked after his daughter who was suffering from an aggressive melanoma of the leg.

'There was one particular rule of the headmaster's, which did not sit well with the boys. Mr Moyle told all students that there must not be any fraternisation between the boys and the girls and that ban applied to the annual picnic at Belair National Park. We even had to use opposite sides of the staircase at school.

'Although we sometimes transgressed, we usually adhered, because to disobey the rules meant "six of the best".' The Doc smiled. 'I got a couple.'

Today Dr Beard is patron of the school's Old Scholars Association. He has never forgotten 'those years of wonderful learning'. 'After I decided I wanted to become a doctor, I went to Adelaide High School to complete my matriculation.'

At Adelaide High School Donald again had good teaching and he enjoyed his sport, especially baseball and cricket, with the team being coached by ex-Test spinner Clarrie Grimmett.

'A friend, David Craker, got into some minor trouble and had to be reprimanded by our leaving honors teacher, Mr Nietz, who did not realise that David was seeing his daughter after school. At the end of the year David joined the Navy, but when the war ended he married Mr Nietz's daughter.'

Harold Beard was delighted with his son's progress at the Adelaide Technical High School and in December 1938 he wrote to the headmaster. It reads (in part):

Dear Mr Moyle,

As Donald's parent I feel it incumbent upon me to accord you at least a little recognition of those services accorded by yourself and the members of your excellent establishment of learning. Knowledge is just as great a power today as when I used to write of a maxim to such effecting my own distant school days away back in the times of Inspector Hartley!

Ever since my daughter passed through ATHS taking her Intermediate two years ago, I have held your school in high esteem, so it was with gratitude that I found my son Donald was accepted as a scholar at the beginning of the current year. His excellent position – 3rd with distinction in English – was largely obtained by virtue of his excellent tutors, and their persistent and patient zeal.

With season's greetings from us all to your staff and with best wishes for a restful and rejuvenating vacation.

Yours faithfully,
Harold Beard

Without doubt Don and Beryl were strongly influenced by their father, who left school at the age of 12 yet became a well-read man with an excellent command of the English language. During the Depression when jobs were at a premium and money was tight, Harold Beard negotiated the continuation of a regular column he had been writing for the *People's Weekly* at Moonta since 1927.

> Renshaw's ramblings. A contributor named Renshaw wrote a regular column for the *People's Weekly* from July 1927. His commentary covered a variety of topics. In the years before the Second World War he took a more philosophical line. From the period of the Second World War, the writer included news of local people and obituaries. The column was suspended from December 1944 until June 1945, and again in 1947. From the 1950s the column was only occasionally published. It ceased in October 1960.

No one seems to know the source of his *nom de guerre*, Renshaw, but the quality of Harold Beard's writing belied his lack of education, and was a great celebration of the way he researched and interpreted information. The following is an example of his work for the *People's Weekly*:

> In life a precarious gamble with luck or fate, as we call it, or are we allotted a definite existence by those higher powers which govern our entry and exit to and from things terrestrial? We read of a very active old lady, whose age runs to three figures, having visited old friends at Moonta quite recently, and whose interest and grip on life is so firm as to permit the taking and enjoyment, a few days ago, of an aeroplane flight. The illustrious William said that 'there is a Divinity which shapes our ends, rough hew them as we will'. An eminent London physician recently remarked, in a whimsical mood, that it appeared to him we lived by accident these days. Many die by accident; but with so many perils confronting us from day to day, it certainly would appear that a great number of us do live by chance. How many of us reach the goal of our ambitions? A very large proportion regard life in general as a bitter disappointment to their hopes …

His piece was largely philosophical in the years leading up to World War II, but readers discovered that Beard could build a convincing argument. Recognising the power of knowledge, he dearly wanted his son to have the highest possible level of education.

For Donald Beard, a chance to study at the University of Adelaide loomed.

Three

Fail and You're in the Army

I turned 18 in second year medicine and became liable for army service, but by doing medicine we were excused as long as we passed our exams. Fail one day and you would be drafted into the army the next.

Donald Beard

While the war raged and the people held fears of a likely Japanese invasion, Don Beard enrolled at the University of Adelaide. Initially, however, lectures were deferred. For the first two weeks of 1942, Donald and his fellow students spent their days digging slit trenches at the foot of the statue of university benefactor Walter Watson-Hughes, who had donated £50,000 to fund the building of the University of Adelaide. For Donald Douglas Beard, his dream of becoming a fully-fledged doctor would be determined by just how hard he worked at university. He needed good marks to get a place and he knew full well that he would need to study hard to pass his examinations at every single step along his academic journey. When he began university life, there were no clubs and societies nor inter-varsity sport; 1942 was one of the darkest years of World War II. Students were expected to work hard and study hard. There was no room for play. If the war was not enough to worry the toughest soul, Don's father Harold had to 'scratch and scrape' to gather sufficient funds to pay his university fees. On 15 February 1942, a shiver went down the Allied spine. On that day Singapore fell to the Imperial Japanese Army. In the wake of the British and Australian forces surrender, the Japanese began their terror campaign in the occupied Singapore. Rubbing salt in the wounds of every Australian and British soldier on the island, the famous Singapore Cricket Club became the Imperial Japanese Army's officers' club. Prime Minister John Curtin, told the people:

> The fall of Singapore can only be described as Australia's Dunkirk ... [The] fall of Dunkirk initiated the Battle for Britain. The fall of Singapore opens the Battle for Australia ... What the Battle for Britain required, so the Battle for Australia requires ... Our honeymoon has finished. It is now work or fight as we have never worked or fought before.

Meantime, 17-year-old Donald Beard was studying hard. He passed first year in physics, chemistry, botany and zoology.

'They all gave you a solid basic scientific start,' he says. 'But now these wonderful subjects have been deleted from the curriculum. More's the pity!'

Among the university's legend of brilliant teachers was Professor Douglas Mawson. 'A man', Donald maintains, 'who inspired you. A tall man, I can see him now in my mind's eye, striding down the road between the university buildings, his sandy hair flying in the breeze. He cut a great figure.'

Donald Beard didn't study geology so he wasn't in Mawson's class, but 'those boys who studied under him did not consider him a great teacher. He was more an inspiration'. The fellow who did well in teaching and research in geology was C.T. (Cecil Thomas) Madigan. During 1911–14, Madigan, B.Sc., Rhodes Scholar, geologist and explorer, was a member of the Australasian Antarctic expedition. Mawson, of course, is world famous. Donald was thrilled to discover that in March 1908 Mawson was one of the first explorers to climb Mount Erebus: the same Mount Erebus – 'the fire mountain of the Antarctic' – Donald's teacher Mr Colebatch had quizzed Beard about that day he wanted to join his cricket team against Sturt Street School.

In 1921 Mawson was appointed professor of geology and mineralogy at the University of Adelaide. He quickly established an effective teaching and research department and insisted that his students join him in geological fieldwork. His research covered a wide scope and he continued vigorously until his retirement. His stature as a famous adventurer and geologist enabled him to draw widely on the assistance of specialists throughout the world in describing rocks and fossils collected in Australia and the Antarctic.

The Flinders Ranges in South Australia held a special fascination for him. He spent many years studying the 'Adelaide System' of Precambrian rocks. Mawson concentrated on Proterozoic stratigraphy and Precambrian glaciation, showing that glacial beds extended for 1500 kilometres and that glacial conditions existed intermittently over much of Proterozoic time. His extensive fieldwork was carried out by foot, by horse and cart, camel and motorcar. On research expeditions, Mawson was usually accompanied by students, who learnt more from their university lecturer than geology. They learnt about camping and survival in the bush. While Douglas Mawson inspired his students by his adventurous spirit and his legend as an explorer, physics teacher, Professor Kerr Grant, was admired for his sterling leadership.

In 1922 Kerr Grant conceived the idea of constructing a high power siren, in which vibrations were excited in plates or membranes by utilising

Bernoulli's principle. At the outbreak of World War II, Kerr Grant was asked to give his opinion on an air-raid siren that had impressed the civil defence. 'You know,' he said at the time, 'a Swedish firm had come along with my hooter.'

However, Donald and all his fellow students knew that most of the research in the university physics department was done by two men, Dr Roy Burdon and George Fuller.

Dr Burdon inadvertently helped change the course of history, for it was Burdon who, in 1919, influenced the young Adelaide University physics student Mark Oliphant to become a physicist by showing him 'the extraordinary exhilaration there was in even minor discoveries in the field of physics'.

In December 1941, just after the Japanese attack on Pearl Harbour, a time when Donald Beard was eagerly looking forward to starting at the University of Adelaide, Oliphant was invited to go to the US and join a special team in a secret mission dubbed the 'Manhattan Project'. Oliphant and his team developed the atom bomb. Years later, Sir Mark Oliphant praised his university mentor: 'I was lucky in having a very good teacher in physics in Adelaide, a man named Burdon, Dr Roy Burdon, who started me off with enthusiasm on this subject and who weaned me away, I think, from my ideas of being a chemist.'

Donald Beard got to know Dr Roy Burdon's son, Ken, who studied medicine with him and later became a well-known doctor in Port Pirie. However, late in his career, Dr Ken Burdon was none too taken when the South Australian Health Minister, Dr John Cornwall, turned up one day and started to lecture him about how to treat lead poisoning.

Dr Burdon had been treating patients suffering from the ailment in the Port Pirie area for 40 years and 'he didn't need to listen to this fellow telling him how to manage the lead in the air in the district'.

'He was so jack of him,' Don recalled, 'that he asked him to wait a minute. He went inside the hospital and emerged with his medical registration certificate, handed the rolled-up scroll to the minister and told him where he could shove it.' Dr Ken Burdon was then aged 65. It appears it is not all peace and quiet behind the stethoscopes and hushed voices in the medical world.

Don knew of another case, famous within the inner sanctum of the world of obstetrics, whereby the Professor of Obstetrics drove out to the Queen Victoria Maternity Hospital to give the medical superintendent, Dr Reg Hamlin, a dressing down.

He continued: 'As the professor launched into his tirade, Dr Hamlin stepped back and let him have it, right on the jaw, and the impact knocked the professor down the steps. A month later the medical superintendent bobbed up in Ethiopia.'

As it transpired, Dr Hamlin and his wife Catherine, also working as a gynaecologist, were thinking about going there anyway. They set up a hospital in Ethiopia to treat young girls who suffered damage during childbirth because their pelvises were too small. The doctors Hamlin taught the Abyssinians how to minimise harm by operating on fistulas as recorded in their book, *Hospital by the River*. Officially Catherine Hamlin was not a qualified doctor, but she learnt to do the operations. The Hamlins successfully operated on more than 5000 women at the Addis Ababa Fistula Hospital, which they established in 1975, and it has become a major teaching institution for surgeons throughout Ethiopia and the developing world.

When Donald Beard first began his university education, money was extremely tight in the Beard household. As Donald's second year loomed, Harold was worrying about how he could fund his son's second year of university fees and he feared his son would have to leave university. Prime Minister Curtin could foresee the inevitable brain drain among Australia's youth, given that most able-bodied youngsters over the age of 18 had joined the armed forces.

As the war dragged on, a greater volume of casualties was inevitable, so too the brain drain. Curtin saw that it was crucial for the nation to produce bright young minds, a new crop of doctors, engineers, lawyers and officers of the armed forces. So, in 1943, he announced the abolition of university fees. The announcement lifted a huge burden from thousands of parents throughout the land, none more so than Harold Beard. The family would still have to raise money to pay for books and other essentials, but, by far, the greatest cost was the fees. At a dark time in our history, Prime Minister Curtin had brought a ray of sunshine to many Australian families.

'I turned 18 in second year medicine and became liable for army service, but by doing medicine we were excused as long as we passed our exams,' he said. 'Fail one day and you would be drafted into the army the next. University life was very restricted, courses were shortened and many students departed to join the services.

'So we put our heads down and had the best pass rate there ever was. They cut the course back, reducing it in length. They cut out Christmas holidays. Instead of three-weeks' term holidays, leave was cut to one week and that time was used to find work fruit picking or pulling onions. The university was for study and during my time there, not one teaspoonful of alcohol was allowed on the university grounds, except for study purposes.'

Beard and his fellow students made their own fun. At weekends they'd pack sandwiches and a bottle of water and ride their bikes to the Adelaide Hills for a picnic. By third year, which Beard passed, they had reached the 'business' part of their studies. They dissected bodies but, as Donald explains, there was never too much blood to contend with, as the bodies were full of formalin.

'This proved to be very helpful to our study,' he said, 'They (medical students) don't do it now. At the end of 1944 we went across to the Royal Adelaide Hospital, training as clinical students. That was good work and we thought we were little doctors. If you were going to take a girl out to the pictures, you'd sprinkle a bit of ether on your coat before you went; we found that had a positive effect. We worked a lot with the patients. We assisted in operations, helping the surgeon. We inserted drips, put plasters on arms and legs, duties that today are carried out by an intern. Students performed those duties and it was invaluable training. Today there are legal implications attached to students carrying out such duties. In my time there was so much work to be done and precious few doctors to do the job.'

On 28 February 1943, the RAF bombed Berlin in their first daytime raid. It was round that time that Donald learnt the sad news that two of his cousins, brothers in the same family, had been killed. In conflicts a world apart, one brother, a Lancaster bomber tail gunner, was killed in the raid over Berlin. The other, a member of an artillery regiment, was executed in Rabaul.

'I corresponded with many cousins and friends, but one by one they were killed,' he recalled sadly. 'However, Jack Dowling, the brother of the two whom I mentioned previously, survived as a wireless-operator air gunner. They came from a broken family and were brought up in a Salvation Army boys' home until they left, and soon after entered the services – Jack to the RAAF. Upon his return from war, he went on to complete an electrical engineering degree at the University of Adelaide and went to Woomera where his radar training equipped him in tracking rockets. On a visit to Woomera NASA space experts recognised Jack Dowling's ability and they invited him to Cape Canaveral, Florida, where he worked long, hard hours and, as director of the tracking stations, his team tracked the first manned spacecraft to the moon in 1969. Don says of his cousin: 'Not bad for a boy from a broken family who was brought up in a Salvation Army Boys' Home in Adelaide. Later my wife Margaret and I visited him at Cape Canaveral and watched a launch. I was very proud of him.'

Jack Dowling, Donald Beard's first cousin, eventually became the Director of Operations at NASA. He married five times. His second and fifth marriage was to the same girl. Family life at the Space Centre was disjointed. 'They sat in front of their tracking screen and had behind them a stretcher to grab occasional sleep.'

In the dark days of wartime 1943, Donald found the conflict very confronting. He continued to write to family and friends who were involved in the various war zones. Donald felt guilty. He felt that here he was, studying in safe Adelaide, while they were living the horror of war, risking death every moment. Word of the Nazi atrocities was beginning to filter through to the free world. In April 1943, news of the Warsaw Ghetto Uprising and subsequent massacre of the Jews by SS troops horrified all Australians. In May the RAF 'Dambusters' bombed the dams of the Ruhr Valley in Germany.

There was a huge manpower shortage and early in his course, Beard and his friend Maurice Page, an engineering student, rode their bikes to Mildura to pick grapes. They were paid 10 shillings per 100 25-pound 'dip tins'. On Friday nights Donald and his friends cycled 10 miles to Cardross, a small town near Red Cliffs, where they were working. The local dance was so popular there was barely room in the hall to dance. Those not dancing were standing outside. Anyone lucky enough to own a car got the girls. Beard and his friends rode their bikes home after the dance. He was playing club cricket in Mildura, but in one match the match was cancelled because of a wet wicket – the malthoid surface had literally melted in the wake of a week of daily temperatures topping 110° F.

The jobs Donald found during the holidays and at Christmas helped supplement the funds required to pay for university extras, books and stationery. With his friends he picked cherries, pulled onions and swept the streets, before they finally found work harvesting salt along the vast salt lakes at Lochiel at the head of St Vincent Gulf. At the height of summer, temperatures on the salt lake reached 150° F. The students slept on straw mattresses in unlined corrugated-iron sheds and despite the oppressive heat they were not allowed a beer at the nearby Lakeview Hotel because they had not yet reached the age of 21.

Don looks back fondly: 'We again found a local "hop" or dance at Nantawarra, some 12 miles away. Usually we rode our bikes, but sometimes we hired a car from the local mechanic. The car ran on Producer gas. A coke burner, lashed to the rear bumper bar, produced gas to fire the engine.' The car not only saved their legs, it was a status symbol among the youth.

Despite the war, a modified form of district cricket was played in Adelaide and whether Beard was in town or in the country he wasn't going to miss playing the game. He worked the Friday night shift, from midnight to 8 am. As soon as he knocked off he rode a borrowed bike six miles to Bumbunga Railway Station and caught the Snowtown train to Adelaide. He had stashed his bike in the unlocked baggage van and when the train stopped at Adelaide he collected his bike and rode to the cricket match. The game might be at Prospect, Glenelg or Alberton – no matter, he rode his bike wherever, keen to get a game of cricket. The match finished at 6 pm and he made the return journey. It took six hours for him to get back to his bed of straw under the corrugated-tin roof shed at Lochiel, but it was always well worth the trip. By midnight he had hit the hay. When they worked on the salt lake, Donald and his mates always discarded their shirts in the oppressive heat and by day's end, their bodies were encrusted with salt.

They were paid £5 a week for their labours and 25 shillings was deducted weekly for their 'board'. Because the town was in such an isolated part of the state and there was little opportunity to spend, they managed to save a few pounds from the experience. Donald's sister Beryl kept a letter written by the two unmarried Shepherd sisters with whom they once lived. The sisters were taken by Donald's development and Beryl produced a two-pronged letter, one section written by Amy Shepherd, the other by sister, Lilly. By December 1943, the women were living together in Sydney:

> Fancy being in your third year, Donald. The coming year will require a lot of study I'm sure. And when it comes to human life, it will need the best knowledge possible, and that is what you intend acquiring, isn't it Donald? Your aim is to alleviate suffering humanity.
>
> We were very pleased to hear of Beryl getting on as well. Sorry we haven't got a wireless, we might hear Beryl sometime. It would be quite a thrill. I suppose the potato shortage has helped mother keep her schoolgirl figure, eh? I am glad you like sport.
>
> I should think it very necessary for anyone in your profession. You would certainly score a victory if you bowled Don Bradman for a duck. I can see you are going to be a ladies Dr with your pretty speeches. Always be the happy Donald we know and you will always be loved.
>
> Yours sincerely,
> Amy Shepherd

Donald continued to do well at university, passing all his exams, albeit in the 'lower end of the field'.

'The bombing of Hiroshima was a terrible thing, with some 100,000 people being killed, however, an invasion of Japan would have been even more ghastly,' he said. 'I could see the end of the war was imminent when I began to start arrangements to play some intervarsity cricket and baseball with Melbourne and Sydney.'

Outside of his love for medicine were two sports: cricket and baseball, he was a fast bowler and a pitcher. Although he loved playing cricket in summer and baseball in winter, his all-consuming passion was studying medicine. He was committed to becoming a doctor. All intervarsity sports events were suspended during the war, but Don envisaged the end of hostilities was not too far away, so he began to organise matches. He loved baseball and the camaraderie that went with it. He captained the Adelaide University baseball team in the 1946 carnival (Adelaide versus Melbourne universities) in Melbourne. That year Queensland joined South Australia, Victoria and New South Wales for the first time in the carnival. Future Test opening batsman Ken Archer, brother of champion all-rounder Ron Archer, was in the Queensland side. But South Australia and Victoria were the standout teams.

In the final innings of the final match between Adelaide and Melbourne, the Melbourne bases were full. We replaced our pitcher, Laurie Smart, with Vic Ross, a POW who had escaped from the Italians and walked across the mountains to Spain.

'In walked a giant Victorian batter, a good hitter. The first pitch found the very middle of his bat and the ball soared over centrefield,' Don said. 'I thought we'd blown it, for a home run would have brought four runs and a win for the Vics.'

The ball seemed to be way out of reach for centrefielder Peter Brokensha, but the university star athlete turned and ran with the flight of the ball. A left-hand thrower, he stuck out his gloved right hand and the ball stuck. SA won the game and the carnival.

After the win, some of the Adelaide baseballers were keen to go straight to the pub to celebrate winning the carnival, but Don intervened. 'No, we'll duck home (they were staying at the Coffee Palace, owned by the Salvation Army) get dressed and get back to the Federal Hotel to drink free beer on the Victorians.'

It all made perfect sense for the SA players, so they followed the skipper's suggestion to the letter. They were committed to attending the end-of-carnival dinner at the Federal Hotel in Collins Street, and they were eager to down a few cold ones. When the players arrived, waiters emerged with trays of orange juice and ginger pop. Don politely declined the soft drinks, saying, 'No, no thanks, we'll have a beer.'

'There's no beer,' the waiter replied.

'Where can we get a beer?' Don asked.

'Well,' the waiter mused, 'you might get a beer with dinner.' Alas, no beer appeared.

After the main meal had been consumed, Mr Ernie Austin, president of the University Sports Association, stood to say a few words. He began: 'It's a wonderful thing to see a fine body of young university gentlemen enjoying dinner without alcohol.'

'With that, the Sydney players got up and left the room,' Don said. 'They got into trouble over that … As they passed the South Australian players' table the Sydney boys said, "We'll see you at the Cecil."

'Now the Cecil Hotel was a pub of somewhat doubtful repute. It was just up the road. As soon as we got through the meal we joined the NSW and Queensland teams at the Cecil … and the Vics went home.'

There was a lot of barracking between teams and players would shout derogatory remarks at the opposition, but Don maintains that it was always 'good-natured banter; unlike the sledging of modern cricket which is unpleasant'.

'Most of the games in Adelaide were played along the South Park Lands and University Oval and we'd meet up after the game at Bernie Moore's Brecknock Hotel. There we'd have a few drinks and we'd always buy the barman a drink. In winter we'd dry our uniforms in front of a huge fire.'

That summer of 1946–47, Don Beard was in line for a place in the SA State Cricket side to play the visiting MCC team. At State training he arrived to see the practice wickets were green and he was itching to have a bowl to Don Bradman.

'It was a good chance to further impress our captain before State selection,' he smiled. 'The wicket was green and I reckon I could have got the odd one to do something different. But I never got the chance to bowl to him because Bradman had asked the State coach, Arthur Richardson, if he could face only the spinners this particular training session. Richardson approached me and said, 'Braddles wants to face the spinners in this net, Don. Do you mind having a go in the other net?'

The chance to impress Bradman that night was lost, but Richardson did add that if he managed to take five wickets in the coming intervarsity match in Victoria 'State selection was a real possibility'.

'Well, I did far better. I got 10 wickets in the match and with that performance on the strength of my record in grade cricket, I thought I was in the side.'

Don knew the team would be announced in the first edition of Adelaide's morning broadsheet newspaper, the *Advertiser*, so he caught the tram to the newspaper office, where, in those days, you could buy a newspaper hot off the press, long before it hit the streets. Alas, the name Don Beard was not among the team list and the 21-year-old fast bowler wandered home a dejected man.

England scored 577 in the first innings of the game that Don missed selection; Wally Hammond hitting a masterful 188 and John Langridge, 100. Some inferred that Don might have been lucky to miss that match, given the England batting onslaught, but he dismissed such talk, saying, 'I'd have loved to have bowled for SA against England, whatever the outcome.' Today, Don puts down his non-selection for that match to his wristy action, which didn't always please the purists, and the Australian cricket hosts did not wish any controversy to befall the visitors in the first Test series between England and Australia since 1938. Ironically South Australia's medium-fast bowler Geff Noblet had a similar wristy action to Don Beard. Noblet got the nod, Beard missed out. Don Beard's cricket career spanned more than 50 years, including his playing for Parkside Methodist, University, Sturt, St Peter's Old Collegians and the Services teams, yet he was no-balled for 'throwing' twice: once by Perc McCullum during the war years and many years later by an opposing player umpiring in an Adelaide Turf match. In those games it was the usual practice for the opposing team to supply one of the umpires. Only the captain could object to a 'player-umpire' and after Beard was no-balled his captain Bill Whiting raced to the wicket and demanded that the opposition team change the umpire!

In the wake of the disappointment over missing State cricket selection, Beard's 1947 winter included an intervarsity baseball carnival in Sydney. His medical studies were over. All that hard work, and now a couple of weeks in Sydney, playing the winter game he loved and enjoying the hospitality of the Sydney baseball players and their friends.

'I was pitching against Sydney University on the Sydney University Oval and SA was cruising to what should have been an easy win. There were just two innings to finish the match. As I struck out the third batter in the top of the seventh, I noticed a telegram boy ride up on his bicycle and hand one of the players a telegram.'

Fail and You're in the Army

The telegram was for Donald Beard. It read:

Sorry, failed surgery. Supplementary in December.

Adelaide University

'I was distraught. All of my concentration for the baseball game was lost and I blew the match. I had failed my final examination.

'Well, despite our losing the match, the Sydney boys turned on a great time for us and we returned to Adelaide via Wagga Wagga where we played two more games and then I threw myself into my study. In a way, failing the surgery examination was a good thing for me because I worked so very hard to pass that during that process I decided that I was going to become a surgeon. For the rest of the year, 10 of the medical students who had failed, including me, had to sit a supplementary exam and were given experience as house surgeons (interns) at Royal Adelaide Hospital.

'I had a wonderful year as a house surgeon. One of my assignments was at Parkside Mental Hospital, where they had 1700 patients. In 1948 there was no treatment for schizophrenia and many other psychiatric illnesses, but most patients were happy to live in this environment where the hospital was more or less self-sufficient. It had a butcher's shop, market garden, dairy and a very good library. Patients were integrated into this little society and most of them seemed very happy there.'

Doctor Beard was involved in what is now a controversial method of treating the mentally ill: electric shock treatment.

'We used a lot of shock treatment,' he said. 'We used an electric machine which had been made by the hospital superintendant, Dr Hugh Birch, and occasionally it used to fire off unexpectedly and you'd get a shock yourself. My friends suggested it did me a lot of good.'

Medical staff also used insulin coma therapy. The patient was given an increasing dose of insulin in the morning sufficient to cause unconsciousness. At about 11 am the doctor would run glucose through a tube in the patient's stomach and he would regain consciousness. When the patients awakened the doctor would talk to them in their state of sedation, another form of shock treatment. The hospital had its own operating theatre and Doctor Beard got invaluable surgical experience with a variety of emergencies, from appendicitis, to broken bones.

Later in 1948 he was invited to work in what was called the 'receiving house' at Enfield Mental Hospital. He would ride his bicycle from Northfield

Mental Hospital to Enfield where patients would literally line up to undergo ECT, electro-convulsive treatment.

'There was always a long queue of patients outside the door waiting for their turn,' he recalled. 'Patients were strapped on to the table and held down by a couple of strong orderlies. There was no anaesthetic. But a patient needed to be restrained in this way because when you went into shock there were violent movements with the potential to dislocate your hip or your shoulder. It was just a zap, several seconds. But patients went into a fit and they were usually put to bed to recover after treatment.' Patients would receive a number of shock treatments each week.

'I believe shock treatment helped people, especially those who were very aggressive. At the time an operation on the brain was developed to help with forms of mental illness, including severe depression. The operation involved cutting pathways in the frontal lobe of the brain that was thought to be stimulating this bad behaviour. In fact, an Adelaide physician had the operation and he recovered fully.

'Treatment for mental illness not so long ago was simple, whereas today the development of certain drugs has enabled a lot of patients to leave the hospital. It is, I think, an unwise policy because many mental patients preferred the security of the institution and found they could not cope on the outside and got into trouble. The authorities pulled down the wall of the hospital, because having patients behind the high wall was bad for them. Later, I went back to the hospital as the resident doctor. I was thinking about taking up psychiatry. I found it fascinating talking to patients. It did help me in later years when talking to patients in peace time and to soldiers on the front line in Korea and Vietnam.

'We treated patients at the hospital with diluted Pentothal, the drug which puts you to sleep, and while the patient was drifting off I'd talk to them about their problems, how they might have been abused as a child, their upbringing and all the problems they had been hiding. All of this would come out during the patient's sedated state. Today they no longer use this form of treatment.'

That year was destined to test Don Beard in another way. In 1948 he suffered a bout of supraspinatus tendinitis in the shoulder from pitching. His shoulder became inflamed and during the cricket season he was unable to bowl.

'So I played for University Bs, strangely enough as a batsman. By then, I was the captain of the side. I was treated by Dr Ivan Jose and by physiotherapist Rafael Cilento (father of movie actress Diane Cilento) with potassium iodide. What they did was to put one plate behind the shoulder and a plate in front. They'd soak the front plate with potassium iodide, ostensibly this stuff was supposed to be going through to the other plate. It didn't happen as it was supposed to happen, but by the end of 1948 I had recovered.'

As a cricketer batting was never his forte. When he was RAH surgical registrar and playing for Sturt, the club captain Gil Langley rang Donald and said, 'Doc, we won't need you on Saturday because we are batting and it's running pretty well. We have this game all sewn up.'

'It was a match against Woodville, that club's first year in the competition. About 5 pm I received another call from Gil. "Doc, can you get down here quickly? We were about 6/150, chasing 210. But we've lost a couple of wickets, so please get down here fast." By that time I owned a car, but I didn't get there until the end, they were walking off the field. We'd lost by two or three runs and on the following Monday, *Advertiser* cricket writer Keith Butler wrote: 'Beard – absent 0'. But it probably wouldn't have made any difference. Woodville won by two runs and Beard's average for the season was 1.5.'

Don loved every minute of his intern year. He enjoyed the camaraderie among the young doctors. They all lived in and because they did not want to risk missing dealing with an interesting patient, they scarcely left the hospital.

'These patients were brought in by Joe Myren's private ambulances or the Hindmarsh Volunteer Fire and Ambulance Brigade, for which we were all on a volunteer roster to give lectures and demonstrations in early management of emergencies,' he said.

'We lived together and we played together. If we went out it was usually as a group to the theatre or a bike race or the Royal Show. When we went to a private party it was on the understanding that we would like to bring a few friends along. Sometimes we held parties in the hospital with dancing to records played on an old wind-up gramophone. If occasionally the party got a bit out of hand, such as tobogganing down the corridors on large blocks of ice, then we'd be "on the mat" next morning in the office of the Medical Superintendent, Dr Rollison, and later Dr Nicholson. We would either be fined and pay for any damage or our meagre salary was docked. But we never neglected our patients.'

Sometimes a group of house surgeons (interns) would clamber over the fence adjoining the Adelaide Botanic Gardens and capture a swan to release in the room of some unsuspecting colleague. Although nurses were strictly forbidden in the residents' quarters, the interns always looked for ways and means to 'smuggle' them in and, at times, their schemes proved successful.

'During the year we learnt a great deal,' Don continued. 'We helped each other and, after gaining patients' permission, we would discuss them and demonstrate them to our fellow interns.'

Don found the consultant physicians and surgeons to be very helpful. With the help of the consultants and a medical, surgical and gynaecology registrar, the young doctors were taught to perform many procedures. Today at the RAH, interns do not have the opportunity to do as many procedures as they did when Don was an intern.

'I hear that today interns often complain about inadequate salaries and the long hours. These factors were never a consideration to us, but times have changed in keeping with the rest of society. However, that doesn't mean it is all good.'

Four

The Road to War

We played cricket against the navy and air force and other teams about the base. We were virtually confined to the base, as General MacArthur ruled there was to be no fraternisation allowed with the Japanese population.

Donald Beard

Doctor Beard's very first operation came on a Saturday, the day Adelaide University took on Prospect in the Adelaide district cricket season opener. As usual he reported for work at the Royal Adelaide Hospital, worked for a few hours, then left work riding his bicycle from Adelaide to Prospect to play in the match. Just before he was about to leave the hospital, RAH registrar Dr Lance Bonnin said to him: 'Don, a patient came in this morning with an appendicitis. I'd like you to operate on this chap.'

'But I'm playing cricket, Dr Bonnin.'

'No worries,' the registrar smiled, 'you can start the match, get back here, do the operation and return to the game.'

Completing the task that Saturday involved a lot of cycling, some bowling, probably no batting and doing a good job on the appendectomy, his first operation as a surgeon. The operation took the Doc about an hour.

'Lance Bonnin was a wonderful surgeon. He came from a medical family. My mother worked as a maid for them in their father's house and surgery at Hindmarsh. Lance was a paediatric surgeon and his brother Jim became head of the Institute of Medical and Veterinary Science. Another brother, Noel, was a urological surgeon; another, Mark, a physician. Lance died from a cerebral haemorrhage at the age of 40.'

During 1948, as house surgeon at RAH, the Director of Army Medical Services J.M. ('Barb') Dwyer visited the hospital and spoke to the young interns, strongly suggesting that they join the Citizen Military Forces (CMF).

'"You didn't do anything doing the war, so you can join up now," Dwyer told us. There's no doubt many of us felt guilty about not joining up during the war. Our guilt was all about being in safe Adelaide studying medicine, while young men our age were putting their lives on the line in the battle zones. Dwyer made a valid point and a lot of us joined the CMF.'

Next Dwyer said that medical officers would be wanted in the British Occupation Force in Japan and 'that would be just the ticket for you men when you finish at the hospital, just the job before you go out into general practice or start your post-graduate training'. Don discussed the opportunity to serve overseas with his colleagues and most agreed it would be a terrific work and life experience for them. 'Six of us applied to serve in the occupational force,' he said, 'but only four were required.'

The six potential recruits were asked to attend J.M. Dwyer's rooms on North Terrace, where a final selection was to take place. 'Barb' Dwyer decided that the best way to decide was to do a very Australian thing: they'd draw straws. It is universally acknowledged that to draw the short straw is to miss out. Straws of various lengths were placed in a hat and passed around. Don drew the first one. To his horror it was a short straw.

'I thought I was gone. I had the short straw, but when I looked at Barb Dwyer he beamed, saying, "Okay, Beard's in ... now who else?" I have a feeling that Barb acted swiftly to ensure I was in the mix. He was a baseball mentor of mine; in fact in 1922 he played alongside Norrie Claxton, after whom the Claxton Shield is named. Claxton was also president of the North Adelaide Cycling Club. The four young doctors chosen – Hugh Douglas, Brian Cornish, Graham Wilson and Don Beard – all became top men in their field. Douglas became a paediatric surgeon, Cornish an orthopaedic surgeon and Wilson, like the Doc, a general surgeon. They were issued with their smart new uniforms and felt on top of the world.

'We left Adelaide on the *Westralia*, a ship bound for Kure, on the south island of Japan, to work at a hospital there under the banner of the British Commonwealth Occupation Force (BCOF).

'We thought we were in for a leisurely cruise. But aboard ship was a person who contracted measles and because we did not wish to start a potential measles epidemic ashore we were confined to the ship at every port we visited on the way to Japan. We berthed in Port Moresby, Rabaul and Cocos Island but were confined to the ship at every port.'

Don said the foursome from Australia were a 'pretty straggly lot, only three months out of CMF training'. Their patients were all soldiers, in Japan supervising the country's virtual recovery from the war. 'Our base was previously manned by the British, but they returned home and it became an Australian base – army, navy, air force.

'Initially my role was to look after casualties evacuated from Korea by the RAAF. Air force Dakotas flew to Iwakuni and the injured were ferried by

The Road to War

Australian ambulance train to Kure where a resuscitation team awaited them for rapid sorting, loading onto ambulances and transporting to the British Commonwealth Occupation Force hospital.

'At the outset I was able to do this, but within a short time there were too many casualties too complicated with severe wounds and I was way out of my depth. There was no other surgeon in the Australian Army. By sheer coincidence the Director General of Medical Services, Major-General Kingsley Norris, saw Bill (E.S.R.) Hughes at the races in Melbourne. Dr Hughes had just returned from England. He had undergone a complete surgical training. Young and fit, he had not at that stage started his private practice, nor his appointment at Royal Melbourne Hospital. So he accepted Major-General Norris's invitation to volunteer for work in Japan and I then worked with him as his assistant.'

Dr E.S.R. Hughes, who began provisionally as the Lieutenant Colonel officer-in-charge of surgery, soon proved his skill as a surgeon and administrator, and his expertise in casualty management.

'Then 3rd RAR was deeply entrenched on the battlefield in Korea with Captain Gandevia the infantry battalion's medical officer, and I was safely back in Japan. I thoroughly enjoyed working with Bill Hughes.' Don's admiration for Lt Col. Hughes grew and he revelled in working on severe injuries with the man he called 'a great surgeon: Australia's greatest surgeon'.

'The 29th British General Hospital arrived and worked with us because the British forces had a brigade of units in Korea. They tried to take us over and run the place, but the Australians wouldn't allow it. There was a young surgeon who was my equivalent and I thought I'd give him some assistance and tell him how to do this and that. He took it quietly. But then I realised that he had already completed his surgical fellowship and had been called up for national service. So he knew a lot more than I did and later he became the president of the Royal College of Surgeons in England.'

On the battlefield in Korea the management of casualties entailed the injured soldier having his wounds dressed and the Company medical assistant administering morphia. He was then carried out by regimental stretcher-bearers, and by anyone else who could be spared, including padres and cooks. At the Regimental Aid Post (RAP), the Regimental Medical Officer (RMO) would adjust splints and dressings, then organise evacuation by the Australian Field Ambulance to the American Mobile Army Surgical Hospital (MASH), where initial surgery was carried out by wound excision for abdominal and chest injuries and the surgical management of head injuries.

When the casualties were stabilised they were taken by American ambulances to the airfield where Australian planes flew them to Japan. The majority of those soldiers eventually arrived at the hospital in Kure where quality medical treatment awaited them.

'When I arrived in Japan, I was allocated to the engineers. I didn't think much of the offer. Anyway I went out and reported to the Commanding Officer, Lt Col. John Bleechmore. He told me what my duties would entail and I saluted the CO and rather than doing what protocol demands, a proper right-hand turn, I did a left-hand-about turn.

'The CO said, "You're not a very good soldier, Beard, but I understand you can play cricket. Would you like to be captain of the Engineers team?"

'"Yessir, that would be fine."

'We played cricket against the navy and air force and other teams about the base. We were virtually confined to the base, as General MacArthur ruled that there was to be no fraternisation allowed with the Japanese population. Huge signs were placed outside the military bases.

**THESE AREAS AND PLACES ARE OUT OF BOUNDS
TO ALL PERSONNEL OF 67 AUST INF BN**

JAPANESE DWELLING HOUSES
PUBLIC BATHS
CINEMAS
EATING HOUSES
THEATRES AND PLAY HOUSES
HOTELS
RESTAURANTS
BROTHELS
CAFES
FACTORIES AND OFFICES
HOSPITALS
RELIGIOUS BUILDINGS
BANKS
FISH HATCHERIES
GOVERNMENT OFFICES
DANCE HALLS
BARBER SHOPS TRAMS TRAINS BUSES

'We weren't allowed to mix with the people at all – not even so far as to travel on their public transport, go to a restaurant, a museum or an art gallery. It was a big mistake. General Douglas MacArthur was strict with the occupied people and his own army.

'I like Americans,' Dr Beard continued, 'but sometimes they do strange things. MacArthur thought if we mixed too closely with the Japanese you couldn't be giving them orders or instructions. In a way he was correct, but it meant that we were denied the chance of advising the Japanese people that their nation's previous military tactics were strategically and morally wrong.

'So our life was work and sport. I would do my sick parades in the morning, see any sick and injured; men who had been hurt training, a broken bone or two, a man who developed a hernia and the like, and I'd admit these patients to the hospital.

'We'd start the day at 7 am, knock off about 4 pm and then we'd have sport – tennis, hockey, cricket and basketball. There were a number of good standard cricket matches played at Kure. The air force team was the champion. We got word that the air force, the team against whom I had bowled successfully during the season, thought they'd better stop me. So they took photographs and movie film of my action and sent it to the Australian Cricket Board of Control for International Cricket (now Cricket Australia) in Sydney to have it vetted.

'At that stage I bowled off a long run and came racing in. We didn't hear any result of the enquiry back from Australia before the grand final, in which I opened the bowling and, for the first time in three years, the air force was defeated. Having a drink after the game, we asked about the film taken of our fast bowler.

'"Oh, yeah, the film … we got a note back from the board which said 'doubtful pass'." They were, it seems, in doubt over my wrist action, but I passed the test.'

Soon Major Beard was looking forward to his return to Australia. The others – doctors Douglas, Cornish and Wilson – returned to Australia in December 1949. In June 1950 came the farewell party his friends had organised him on the island off Kure. It was during the party on the day of 23 June that they heard the ominous news that the North Korean army was massing on the 38th parallel.

The experience in Korea was an important chapter in Don's life. In January 2013, General Peter Cosgrove AC, MC, CNZM (retd) said in tribute to the Doc: 'His role as a doctor tending soldiers in combat is a byword in the Australian Army. At the Battle of Kapyong in 1951 his inspirational care and leadership contributed to the love soldiers had for this strong man of peace and compassion. His invariable good humour, stamina and great professional skill make him a wonderful role model for further generations of medicos in uniform.'

Five

Home from the Front

> *... families trudging south with a few miserable possessions on their backs and their children dying at their feet.*
>
> Donald Beard

Don Beard left the front line in Korea, replaced by Captain Bob Barnes, another medical officer from Adelaide. After two months back as OC Camp Hospital Ebisu in Tokyo, Don flew to Australia in December 1951. He arrived home with enough money in his pay book to fund his postgraduate training and he was eagerly awaiting the arrival of the black Dodge sailing from Japan aboard the *Taipan*.

'The good thing about Korea was that you couldn't spend your army pay,' he said. 'Everything was provided and it wasn't as though you could wander down to a shop to buy anything. The only Koreans were families trudging south, carrying a few miserable possessions on their backs with their children dying at their feet.'

The army pay he saved turned out to be vital for he could now afford his surgical training. In those days students had to pay their own way, most relying upon their parents to help them financially. However, Don's parents didn't have the means to help. He knew he had to provide for himself. The big black Dodge proved a fabulous asset. When the *Taipan* docked at Port Adelaide, Don was there to greet the ship.

'Mum was with me. I'd caught a taxi to the Port to greet the ship,' he recalled. 'I was pretty keen to take a look at my new car. They unloaded the car and I was very disappointed to discover there was a scratch on one side of the body and they'd snapped the aerial off.' Dockside hands rolled the Dodge off the ship and on to the wharf. The car was filled with petrol and Don and his mother were off. He had gained his driver's licence while working as a medical student at the Lochiel Salt Lakes.

While I was still in Japan I applied for a job as the outpatient registrar at the RAH and I was successful. The job provided me with invaluable experience as night emergency surgical registrar and medical registrar every third night. I started work straightaway.'

People were asking Don about his Korean experience. Generally Australians didn't know a great deal about Korea or what the war was all about. 'They didn't understand that there had been conflicts between the North and South for centuries,' he said. He had done his homework on Korea. He discovered that just as in Vietnam, the unity of the Korean people over the past 2000 years had been fragile. There was evidence of deep division and inter-tribal warfare. When the Chinese conquered the Korean tribes in 108 BC they divided the country into a number of administrative regions. As Chinese authority gradually diminished, three kingdoms were established in the north and the south. In AD 389 the northerners invaded the southern state using the Uijongbu Corridor which, during the Korean War, saw a lot of action, especially in the years 1950–51. Chinese influence has been with Korea for hundreds of years and it was little surprise for those who knew Korea's history that China became involved in the 1950–53 Korean conflict. The Republic of Korea was inaugurated on 15 August 1948 under the presidency of Syngman Rhee. Less than a month later, on 3 September 1948, the communist North established the Peoples Republic of Korea at Pyongyang under Premier Kim Il Sung.

'Both the Chifley and Menzies governments appreciated that security in the Pacific rested on the US,' Don continued. 'It was also believed that Britain could still play a significant role. However, it was also realised that in 1942 neither the US nor Britain had been able to give much support to Australia.

'The Korean War broke at a difficult time for Australia. The defence forces were slender. Most regular army personnel were needed at home for the national service scheme. Future plans for force expansion were already focused on Malaya and the Middle East. The government was torn between an over-commitment of existing forces to Korea and the displeasure of powerful allies, through making too small a commitment.'

In his book *The Korean War*, Max Hastings wrote of North Korea attacking the South by trooping across the 38th parallel. Shock waves slammed into the heart of America, and its top brass believed the war was the start of a worldwide communist conspiracy.

'So the invasion of South Korea (in June 1950) was seen as a fundamental challenge, which had to be met at any cost.'

The legendary World War II hero, General Douglas MacArthur, had become an utter menace, despite his brilliant strategy against the North

Koreans at Inchon, a battle that surely saved Seoul and ensured the Allies would eventually prevail. The man was 'impossibly vain, contemptuous of civilian authority and fanatical in his view of the struggle'.

'He was determined, at the very least, to destroy the North Korean regime, and at a meeting on Wake Island in mid-October (1950) he assured President Truman that his strategy involved no risk of Russian or Chinese intervention.'

Within months up to 500,000 Chinese soldiers emerged from the snow and, to the utter surprise of the Allies and the dismay of the Americans, they swarmed south like a well-drilled army of ants. It was not until July 1953, when Don Beard was sailing home on the aircraft carrier, HMAS *Sydney* from the coronation celebrations, that an armistice was signed at Panmunjom. At that time Dwight Eisenhower had replaced Harry Truman as US President. The US still had a monopoly on the atomic bomb and there were whispers in diplomatic circles that atomic weapons might be used to break the deadlock in Korea.

'I was pretty well received when I came back from Korea,' he said. 'I had a job, a car, the black Dodge and I was being invited to speak to a variety of audiences about my Korean War experience. I even addressed a mothers' club at Brighton,' he smiled.

Don had plenty of stories to tell. He would speak about the problems at the MASH where medical supplies were short and about the nurses.

'In Korea nurses were used on the front line for the first time in a major war. That brought its own special problems, including the need for separate ablution and accommodation blocks and keeping men and women apart.

'There was another problem, perhaps the toughest of all. Some of the US medical staff were intolerant and sometimes disrespectful to their regular army chiefs. Discipline in the army is paramount. The surgeons had been deferring their national service during medical training and they thought they would go straight into private practice, but suddenly they were swept up in the Korean War. They were dedicated to the care of the soldier, but not so dedicated to regimental discipline, which made it difficult for the commanding officer.

'I always found the Americans helpful and generous and good soldiers, but they were not always well led and some of their generals made costly errors. I knew and respected the rules and the need to have a disciplined fighting force and medical team.

'There were a few helicopters in Korea, but the 3rd RAR battalion was in the mountains and the early model was incapable of lifting casualties higher than 1500 feet (460 metres), and could not operate during bad weather or at night. How different to the war in Vietnam. Our commanding officer (Colonel Ferguson) took a tremendous interest in the RAP (Regimental Aid Post), the sick and the injured, and at all times he kept me fully briefed and conversely at these meetings he sought information about the health and well-being of the Battalion. The liaison between the CO and the RMO is vital at any time, especially on the front line.'

Often Don reflects on his time in Korea: 'I wonder what it was that made the Australians behave so magnificently under great stress. The casualties were mounting fast, yet the men went about their business; the fighters took the battle to the enemy and the medical team did what they could for the wounded. My admiration for the Australian soldier continues to grow. Korea was very much the "forgotten war".'

On 27 March 2011, just weeks before the 60th anniversary of the Battle of Kapyong, South Australian members of the 3rd RAR battalion were invited to the unveiling of a memorial on The Pathway of Honour at the rear of Government House. The 3rd RAR was based at Woodside Barracks from 1965 to 1981. Two special dates fixed the creation of the memorial in 2011 – the Battle of Kapyong's 60th and the 40th anniversary of 3rd RAR's second tour of Vietnam. Seven surviving members of the Battle of Kapyong were honoured with 3rd RAR life membership; among them Colonel Donald Beard.

Surprised to be acknowledged, Don said: 'I was very proud to be a part of the medical and surgical unit helping the Australians I grew to respect. When you are in action so many of the men around you are working to the same end and you grow together. There was a bond of friendship that you do not get in any other situation in life.'

When Don first returned from the war in Korea he began work as a junior surgical registrar at the RAH and studied hard for the first part of his surgical degree. In addition to his clinical work, there was the hard work studying the theory of anatomy, physiology and pathology.

But it was not all hard work and no play for him. In summer, there was cricket.

'I went to Unley Oval. Initially I played for Sturt in the Adelaide Turf team with Ken Webb who had been opening bowler for SA,' he recalled with relish. 'Ken was very fast, yet he operated off a very short approach, but he was completely legal in his action. We wreaked havoc on the other teams.

At one time we were reported for "dangerous and intimidatory bowling".'

Don lived across the road from Unley Oval. 'I played half a season of Adelaide Turf cricket, then mid-way through the 1951–52 season I presented myself at the Sturt nets. Len Darling was club coach. He was a good State player between the wars and he played in two Test matches during the 1932–33 Bodyline Ashes series.'

Darling scored 17 and 39 in his debut Test against England at the Gabba in February 1933, and 85 and 7 in the Sydney fifth Test match. He played 12 Tests, scoring 474 runs at an average of 27.88. Under Darling's coaching Sturt won five premierships after World War II – 1946–47, 1948–49, 1949–50, 1950–51 and 1955–56. In all Sturt has won 12 premierships. Don recalls: 'Len Darling's favourite saying always cropped up when you arrived after training had started: "Oh, you're late … have you been having a cold collation?"'

At the end of the 1951–52 summer Don won himself a place in the Sturt A grade side, having captured 32 wickets at 6.5 runs apiece in just half a season to win the H.V. Millard Trophy for the best bowling average in the Adelaide Turf Association. 'That's when Gil Langley said to me, "Doc, you've got an outswinger. That's all you need to get rabbits out." At one stage eight of our side had played for the SA State team.'

Don Beard was a man who knew how to make things happen, as evidenced by his ingenuity in having a car shipped to Australia in the early 1950s. During a lull in fighting in Korea, Don was sitting talking to an American gunner officer attached to the 3rd RAR. 'I told him how difficult it was at the time to buy a good car in Australia,' he said. The officer told him his brother had a key role where he worked for the Chrysler factory in Detroit, then a world leader in car manufacture. For an outlay of £700 the man's brother at Chrysler could convert a Dodge to right-hand drive and have it shipped to Japan where Don could organise it being taken to Australia. Work, study, cricket and socialising proved a good mix for Don and the black Dodge was an asset in two ways.

'The black Dodge got me about of course and it was a great help with regard to social activities because the girls liked being picked up in the Dodge,' he laughed. 'I always kept it highly polished and in good running order.' The black Dodge gained a certain notoriety some years later when a young doctor made mention of the car in her autobiography.

Life was pretty good and he studied hard, but Don sensed that his medical education needed a stimulus. He gleaned that there was not the sort of expertise among dedicated medical tutors in Adelaide that he could find elsewhere.

One of the exceptions among medical tutors in Adelaide was the celebrated Dr Russell Barbour.

'He was a brilliant trauma surgeon and later (1953–55) became director of medical services in the Australian Army. Dr Barbour was very good to young surgeons and gave them whatever time he had available. I suppose the best description would be that he was a bit of a "Weary Dunlop". Dr Barbour served in London hospitals during the worst days of the Blitz. He worked under extreme stress in that dangerous environment and learnt a great deal about treating trauma patients. When he arrived in Adelaide in the late 1940s, Dr Barbour was the best trained surgeon in the State. He was able in many disciplines, even gynaecology, but certainly in general surgery and particularly in orthopaedics.'

In 1957 Ludwig Guttman, who established the great spinal injuries unit at Stoke Mandeville in the UK, came to Adelaide. Guttmann was almost evangelical in his interest in the field and 'fired everyone up'. Dr Barbour took spinal injuries as his major specialty. He closed his orthopaedic ward, a section of the hospital with 32 beds, and went to the RAH board and said 'this ward is now the spinal injuries unit at the Royal Adelaide Hospital for acute spinal injury cases'.

Dr Barbour urged well-respected senior administrator Colonel C.C. Rankin, whose wife was a physiotherapist and acknowledged the problems with spinal injury cases, to set up a rehabilitation centre for spinal injuries as Northfield. The area had been used for tuberculosis cases but by the mid-1950s the disease was on the wane and here was a ready-made facility for the kind of rehabilitation centre Dr Barbour had envisaged. Northfield was ideal. It was at ground level, easy for wheelchair access and there was ample room for expansion.

Don's idea of going to England to learn from the best was suddenly put on hold. He received a phone call from Keswick Army Barracks informing him that they had word from Canberra. 'I'd been nominated as the medical officer for the coronation contingent to go to England to march with the Queen on coronation day. Could I get leave? The RAH superintendent was an Englishman and he was delighted that one of his young doctors had been granted such an honour.'

Don's official surgical studies were shelved for five months.

Six

1953: Marching with the Queen

Here I was at Buckingham Palace saluted by five-year-old Prince Charles in the presence of the future father of Princess Diana.

Donald Beard

Captain Donald Beard gave his army boots another good polishing before setting off for breakfast on board the giant aircraft carrier HMAS *Sydney*. He was part of an 100-strong contingent about to join other Commonwealth nations to escort Princess Elizabeth from Buckingham Palace to Westminster Abbey and then escort Her Majesty Queen Elizabeth on a triumphant 12-mile march around London. The coronation was scheduled to take place in London on 2 June 1953.

Upon docking at Southampton, the Australians were loaded upon a steam train and taken directly to Pirbright, a long-established military training facility situated midway between the towns of Woking and Guildford in the Surrey heartland, a 30-minute train ride from London. Pirbright is where the kings and queens of England have their elite battalion guards train and it proved an important training ground for British Army recruits throughout World War II.

'We were greeted at the station by a 40-piece Army drum and fife band and amid much fanfare we marched into camp,' Don recalled. However, it was not all plain sailing for the young medical officer. Regimental Sergeant Major (RSM) Brittain was a legend of the Pirbright Brigade of Guards training facility. He was there in 1940, throughout the darkest days of the Battle of Britain and the Blitz. Throughout that awful conflict and beyond, RSM Brittain's eagle eye glared critically at every turnout in the barracks. His idea of training the men was by the way of the toughest of tough love. If they came through for RSM Brittain they would be the best turned out soldiers in the army. RSM Brittain was still there at Pirbright in 1953 when Captain Beard and his men arrived. The RSM was, as the Australians soon discovered, as tough, as menacing and as uncompromising as they had been led to believe. RSM Brittain stood before his men, his staff tucked under his arm, his right arm ramrod straight by his side. His bark seemed every bit as menacing as his bite.

'Next morning as we marched out on to the parade ground for the officer squad training, I drilled confidently as a tall, fit young man,' Don said. 'RSM Brittain saw me and immediately declared, "Righto, Captain Beard, front rank, left-hand marker," which was a top spot, the coveted marching spot on Coronation Day. Because I was tall, the RSM thought I would suit the role.' But as Captain Beard marched past, RSM Brittain raised his eyebrows, his eagle eye having spotted Don's Australian Medical Corps flash: the badge of insignia worn on the shoulder. '"Excuse me, sir! I see you are in the medical corps."'

Captain Beard realised that RSM Brittain found himself in a dilemma. 'In England, medical officers are not renowned for their ability to drill and to march in formation,' Don said. RSM Brittain stood to attention and facing Captain Beard said with more than a hint of sarcasm, 'I understand, sir, things are different in Australia, sir!'

The RSM took his time, looking the tall young Australian up and down, perhaps trying to find a way, without losing credibility before his own charges, to ease the tall Australian medical officer out of the key role in the march at the coronation. Because RSM Brittain was an old-school type, a real stickler for the rules, protocol dictated that once he made the decision for Captain Beard to be 'front rank, left-hand marker' he could not immediately rescind the order.

'Do you think, Captain, you can cope with the position?' the RSM barked.
'Yessir!'
'Well,' he said, scratching his chin, 'we will see how you go.'

Captain Beard knew from the RSM's menacing tone of voice that he was in for a tough time.

'The RSM followed me about with his drill stick. It was a triangular stick that could be adjusted according to the step of the march and he'd walk alongside me, riding me, hoping I'd make a mistake. I thought, I'll fix you RSM Brittain.'

However, Captain Beard's determination to drill to a higher standard on the parade ground, good enough to satisfy the demands of the most ferocious drill instructor Pirbright had produced, could only be achieved by his working overtime. That night Captain Beard visited the sergeants' mess and asked, 'Have you got a good drill instructor here, someone other than RSM Brittain?'

'Yes,' a sergeant called from the group.

'I explained the problem and the sergeant agreed to help. So there we were – during the day RSM Brittain was doing all in his power to get rid of me and in the evening, at the end of the day, I'd be put through my paces in the forest clearing behind the barracks with this sergeant who was doing his utmost to save my spot for me.'

It proved a happy outcome. In the wake of solid and consistent training, Captain Beard came through with flying colours, becoming so proficient that RSM Brittain 'couldn't find sufficient faults with me' to rescind the order for him to occupy the key 'front rank, left-hand marker' post in the coronation march. It was a significant win for him and his mentor drill sergeant. All the extra hard work had paid off and later RSM Brittain gave Captain Beard the hint of a jolly well done. It wasn't outright praise, for that was never the RSM's way, but it was due recognition: 'Well, Captain Beard, you've maintained the standard I would expect of you and you can keep the position for coronation day.' Captain Beard had won his 'Battle of Brittain'.

A few days later, the men were drilling hard before the tyrant RSM Brittain on the parade ground when they spotted a corporal dashing towards them.

'Sir,' he said excitedly, 'there's a telephone call for Captain Beard.'

'Phone call? Beard? Phone call on parade? We don't accept phone calls on the parade ground, Corporal,' the RSM bellowed, his face like thunder. 'Leave the parade ground, now!'

'But, but, sir …' the Corporal stammered, 'the telephone call is from Buckingham Palace.'

'All right,' the RSM sighed, obviously taken aback. 'Well, Captain Beard, you heard, double off … but don't be long … we'll wait for you.'

Captain Beard was every bit as surprised as everyone else at Pirbright. Why would anyone of lower rank than a general be summoned to talk to a member of the Royal Household?

'John Althorp here, Don. I'm now with the staff at Buckingham Palace and I wondered whether you'd like to come up here for a drink sometime?'

John Althorp had been promoted as equerry (personal assistant) to King George VI and he held the role with the new monarch.

'John and I met in Adelaide and we became good friends,' Don recalled. 'Our first meeting was at University Oval for the annual Parliament versus Press cricket match. It was then we got into conversation. John was the aide-de-camp to the Governor of South Australia, Sir Willoughby Norrie, and I

1953: Marching with the Queen

found myself being invited to Government House for drinks, and later, to formal dinners.'

Thrilled to be asked to drinks at Buckingham Palace, Captain Beard readily agreed to John Althorp's invitation. When he doubled back to the parade ground, RSM Brittain might have noted an extra spring in Captain's Beard's step, and he was keen to learn the reason a member of the Royal Household was calling him.

'What was that all about, Captain?' RSM Brittain asked gruffly.

With as much humility as he could muster, Captain Beard replied: 'Oh, that was an old friend from Adelaide, Major John Althorp. He's equerry to the Queen and he's invited me to Buckingham Palace for drinks.' RSM Brittain stiffened, held his head high, barked an order and the drill continued.

John Althorp was to become the 8th Earl of Spencer and his place in history was greatly enhanced by the fact that he would become the father of Diana, Princess of Wales. We mostly remember the 8th Earl Spencer as the ruddy-faced man who led his daughter, Diana, with rather doddery pride up the aisle of St Paul's Cathedral that day in 1981. In his prime, when Don first knew him and when Frances Fermoy first laid eyes on him, Viscount 'Johnnie' Althorp was tall, debonair and, what Frances then firmly believed, desirable. Viscount Althorp, son of the 7th Earl, was heir to a 121-room stately home with 14,000 acres of rolling land in Northamptonshire, Warwickshire and Norfolk, including umpteen cottages, farms and villages.

When the time came for Captain Beard to visit his friend at Buckingham Palace, he caught the train from Pirbright to London and within a short time of alighting at Paddington Station, he was, via a London cab, at the gates of Buckingham Palace.

'I was ushered into a small, beautifully furnished room,' he said. 'Then, out of the blue, around the corner came a small boy in a toy car. The instant he saw me in uniform the little boy jumped out of his toy car, came to attention and saluted me, with a confident, "Sir!".

'Here I was at Buckingham Palace, saluted by five-year-old Prince Charles in the presence of the future father of Princess Diana.'

On the day before the coronation, the Commonwealth contingent, including Captain Beard, moved into dormitories at Earl's Court. 'My bunk was in row 80-odd, section X. There were three tiers of bunk beds and in each row hundreds and hundreds of us nervously awaiting Coronation Day.'

The Australians had spent hours pressing their new uniforms, made especially for the big day and the boots they polished so fastidiously on a daily basis during the long voyage to England in the HMAS *Sydney*, were given another good spit and polish. Captain Beard hung up his uniform carefully and his boots shone. He felt a sense of excitement.

'We awakened to the news that Edmund Hillary had conquered Mt Everest and had reached the peak – the highest point in the world. It was great news and it almost seemed Hillary had done it for the Queen. It is possible that he thought of Her Majesty as he struggled the last few hundred feet to the top. But we returned to the thoughts of the day in London. The weather forecast was bad, showers, with more frequent showers as the day wore on.

'We had breakfast and then it started to rain. It rained on and off during the day, but we scarcely noticed it, such was the high we were on.'

Throughout the night gentle rain had fallen on thousands of coronation campers, who had slept under an amazing array of raincoats and blankets along the proposed route. There was generous applause for the Royal Marines who gracefully negotiated a traffic island while marching line abreast, and the crowds watched in amazement as a young man in singlet, shorts and plimsolls rushed down the centre of Whitehall as if this early morning was like any other summer day in London; a time to train. The Australians formed up with the rest at Earl's Court; a marvel of organisation, planning and discipline. The men had a great sense of pride. Captain Beard stood tall, aware of his key role as 'front rank, left-hand marker', and they were soon on their way for an appointment with Princess Elizabeth at Buckingham Palace, on her way to becoming Queen. Captain Beard was at the head of the ranks of soldiers and he managed to get a good view of the Queen's golden carriage as it cruised through the gates of Buckingham Palace and down Pall Mall. The Queen sat on the right, the Duke of Edinburgh by her side. She wore a magnificent gown designed by Norman Hartnell, covered in beads and needlework. If Her Majesty wanted colour in her gown so that it did not look as if she had recycled her wedding dress, the young and radiant Queen was successful. The rose of England, the thistle of Scotland and all the other flowers representing Ireland and Wales – and all the symbols of representing the major colonies of the British Empire – were beautifully embroidered on her gown.

The gown was considered to have been one of the most magnificent pieces of needlework ever created by the Royal School of Needlework. The great robe was also embroidered for the occasion of the coronation and is still used today by the Queen for the occasion of the Opening of Parliament. The State

1953: Marching with the Queen

Royal Gold Coach, built by Samuel Butler in 1762, has been used by every British monarch since King George IV. Because of its great age, colossal weight and lack of manoeuvrability, the Royal Household is reluctant to use the coach in functions other than coronations, weddings and the jubilee of the monarch.

'It was magnificent,' Don declared. 'The Queen in the gold carriage, pulled by eight horses. We formed up behind her. As we marched out into London, people in their millions waving and cheering, lined the streets. From my position in the march I could plainly see her coach.'

The Queen's carriage led the procession. Her Majesty turned off into Westminster Cathedral and Captain Beard, along with the rest of the Commonwealth contingent, broke off into their respective groups, enjoying a well-earned rest in nearby streets and parklands, where they enjoyed sandwiches, drank water and chatted among themselves. The troops were issued with haversack rations. It wasn't glamorous but the War Office meticulously worked it out, apparently to the last one-hundredth of an ounce of pepper, which was considered to be a sufficiency. The ration comprised: a cheese spread roll, a bar of milk chocolate, a portion of fruit cake, an apple, and two ounces of barley sugar. In all, 30,000 soldiers participated in the Coronation Parade, marching or lining the route. Captain Beard was among the 1100 soldiers waiting in the parks and the streets while the Queen was in the Abbey. 'We neither saw nor heard the actual service,' he said.

Inside Westminster Abbey Queen Elizabeth II was crowned by the Archbishop of Canterbury in a ceremony that remained loyal to a centuries-old sacred ritual. All the implements of majesty were on show: the Orb, the Sceptre, the anointing oil and the great crown of St Edward. After the ceremony and the grand celebratory trumpet music written by Sir Arthur Bliss, the Queen once more made her way beside the Duke of Edinburgh in the State Royal Gold Coach. And again the Commonwealth contingent of defence personnel fell in behind the Royal coach on its long tour of London back to Buckingham Palace.

Those present saw their new Queen portray great natural dignity. She made the necessary responses during the ceremony in a cool, clear voice. Millions still lined the route. The people cheered and waved their flags. They reserved a special cheer for Field Marshall Viscount Montgomery, who was leading by a length at Horse Guards Avenue from the meticulously aligned row of field marshalls, which included Earl Alexander, Lord Ironside and Sir Claude Auchinleck, signalling the approach of Her Majesty.

Among the people in the crowd was 17-year-old Ian Craig, standing alongside some of his fellows, members of the Lindsay Hassett-led 1953 Australian Cricket Team touring England. Don Beard would have known most of the Test players through his role as medical officer with the South Australian Cricket Association. He spent many long hours at Adelaide Oval during Sheffield Shield games, the annual Test match, international and domestic one-day contests.

On Coronation Day the Commonwealth contingent of marchers covered more than 15 miles (25 kilometres) – the Royal route, plus the journey from Earl's Court to Buckingham Palace and return. By the time the men arrived back at their barracks there were lots of happy faces and plenty of tired, aching feet. But the exhilaration of the day was with them all. They now wanted to celebrate. 'We had the night off, we could do whatever we liked,' Don laughed. 'I teamed up with a couple of captains – Kerr and Mahon – and we wandered about London – Piccadilly, Regent Street, wherever. There were parties everywhere. All the hotels, from Hyde Park to the West End, were full of revellers.

For Captain Beard and his colleagues it was open house. 'We were made welcome everywhere and we didn't have to buy a drink throughout the night. They'd see us in uniform and say "come in, come in". The whole of London was one big party.'

The coronation had been a resounding success. The *Daily Express* produced a special 'gold' coronation edition in tribute to the new monarch. The entire newspaper was printed in brilliant gold lettering. 'Tanfield's Diary', published in the *Daily Mail* on 3 June 1953, wrote under the banner: 'Big Night Fun Went On Into The Small Hours.'

> What a night – and after what a day! It was the longest (and shortest) night I have spent in London since VE night. In every corner of the West End there was a glittering ball – and in between each one a jam-packed cheering, friendly, happy crowd that made it almost impossible to get from one place to another. In all, I slipped into about a dozen parties and a couple of theatres. Long, long before I left my car – just left it by the side of the road in the hope that I shall find it today – and made my way by foot. Hard to say what were the high spots. Noel Coward singing at the Savoy was wonderful; so was the quiet elegance of our best private party, Madame Massigli's at the French Embassy; so, differently was the fun at London's newest pub, the Lord Belgrave. But whatever it was it didn't matter. You took your fun as it came – and it came all along the line. As I expected the Café de Paris was jammed. Not a seat

1953: Marching with the Queen

anywhere at seven guineas a time. Noel Coward, of course, and lots of tall, dark, handsome strangers with American accents. Prettiest girl with whom I danced there was undoubtedly Lady Beatty, an American before her marriage to Earl Beatty. Also saw for a brief moment Sir Victor Sassoons – as young as ever. Do these cosmopolitans never grow old?

Don and his two mates eventually got back to their bunks in Earl's Court, but there was a problem finding them. Next day, 24 hours after the thrill of taking part in the coronation march, Captain Beard's group was given a week's leave and a railway ticket. They could travel anywhere in the UK, see what they wanted, do what they wanted. Don travelled to Inverness and took in the beauty of the Scottish Highlands and, of course, Loch Ness, then across Scotland and down to the Lakes District. After that enjoyable leave, there was a brief return to Pirbright where RSM Brittain said a 'well done' to his men, although Don detected a hint of sadness in the RSM's tone. Clearly the old warhorse would have loved to have been a part of the Coronation Parade.

The men were then ordered to travel to Portsmouth and report on board ship, where the HMAS *Sydney* was anchored at the Spithead, off Portsmouth, in time for the Coronation Fleet Review on 15 June 1953, the first postwar review of hundreds of ships – from aircraft carriers to battle-class destroyers of many nations. Ship reviews by the reigning monarch have been a Royal Navy tradition since the Battle of Trafalgar. The Queen reviewed the ships of the Coronation Fleet, including HMAS *Sydney* where all hands were lined up, resplendent in their smartly pressed uniforms and shiny boots. However, Her Majesty could not visit every single one of the 100 ships at the Spithead. That night, all the ships' lights were turned off before an hour-long fireworks display.

After the Queen's review, HMAS *Sydney* sailed out of Portsmouth, bound for the US and Canada. Captain Beard and all the defence personnel aboard were part of a world goodwill tour that lasted five months. Every day was very much an adventure, either at sea or on land. First port of call was Halifax, Nova Scotia. As their aircraft carrier came within 40 miles (65 kilometres) of port, a Canadian naval liaison officer flew in on a helicopter to help with arrangements for the crew's four-day shore leave. There would be much to celebrate the beginnings of Queen Elizabeth II's reign, a number of official functions, including dinners and a grand ball. Each officer aboard the ship was handed an envelope containing the name, address and contact number of the girl he would accompany to the ball.

'It was an "arranged date", but if you hit it off and wanted to remain friends with your girl for the rest of your stay in Halifax, you were free to do so,' he smiled. 'My date's name was "Spike" Hill, a dietician at the naval hospital. Well, we marched through the streets and we went to the ball. I had to play cricket against the Combined Services team the next day and we didn't get back to the ship until eight o'clock on the morning of the match.' For Don the game proved a great contest and all the better for his bagging a few wickets.

The ship sailed on to the US, anchoring in Chesapeake Bay. The men marched in an Independence Day parade in New York, then travelled to Washington where Captain Beard and company met a couple in the street that neither Don nor his friends knew and within minutes the couple invited them to dine that night at the Shoreham Restaurant.

Leaving North America the HMAS *Sydney* headed for the West Indies, specifically the island of Jamaica. Captain Beard again played cricket, this time turning out for the Contingent Team against Jamaica. He loved the Caribbean; the people, scenery, cricket and rum. Just as the ship began to move out of the harbour, George Gosse, son of Sir James Gosse, the man who gave 11-year-old Donald Beard and his cricket-mad mates his own cricket bat to replace the 'poor battered relic' they were carrying, joined him for a chat. Most of the officers had received a top-quality bottle of Jamaican rum at a mayoral function and George Gosse was offering to share his bottle of rum with the tall Australian doctor: a tot or two on the quarterdeck. Don readily agreed. As the HMAS *Sydney* sailed grandly into the glorious Caribbean sunset, the pair sipped rum and chatted.

George Gosse was a George Cross winner. All living George Cross and Victoria Cross winners were automatically invited to attend coronations. Gosse was a mine clearance specialist for the Royal Australian Navy. He won his medal for what was described in the *London Gazette* of 30 April 1946 as 'heroism displayed between May 8 and May 19, 1945 in the treacherous waters of Bremen Harbour, Germany'.

Gosse had dived into the harbour and reported sighting what appeared to be a new form of mine. On 8 May 1945 Gosse dived again and verified that it was a pressure mine known as an 'oyster'. He was given the task of recovering the device intact. Next day he dived to remove the primer and, with improvised tools, he rendered the device safe. During the delicate and dangerous procedure Gosse heard a loud noise, later found to have been caused by the detonator firing as the primer was removed. Gosse later defused two similar mines that posed a danger to shipping and on both occasions the detonator fired before the mine reached the surface. The George Gosse Ward at Hollywood Private Hospital in Perth was named in his honour. Vivian Bullwinkle, the lone survivor among Australian Army nurses killed in 1942 in a hail of machine-gun bullets at the hands of the Japanese on the beach at Banka Island, had a wing of the hospital named after her.

'George and I had time only for a couple of rums when an orderly from the sick bay came up to us and asked me to please come down to the sick bay. I said, "I am not on duty today, it's the naval surgeon's roster tonight."

'The man was persistent. "Oh, no … we need you, we need a surgeon to attend to the injured man."'

As it transpired, the chief petty officer sick bay attendant had been ashore during the day. He had dabbled in what the men referred to as a 'bit of black velvet' and the man was afraid that his Jamaican liaison might lead to his contracting an unwanted affliction. In his frantic attempts to ensure that no one must know of his indiscretion, he grabbed hold of a syringe full of penicillin and plunged the needle into his left buttock. However, in his clumsy attempts to withdraw the syringe, the man broke the needle in two, causing some two inches of the pointed end of the needle to remain deeply embedded in his buttock. Reluctantly, Captain Beard went to the sick bay.

'I locked the door of the small operating room and asked the man to lie face down and, upon examination, I concluded that the embedded needle did not pose any threat and could be left where it was … there was no need to operate.' But the man became agitated.

'"What if the needle gives me trouble and I have to report the incident," he said. I told him that in such an event an operation could be carried out at the time. But the man was very agitated saying, "Yes, doctor, but I'd be sacked if it became known that the petty officer sick bay attendant had injected himself with penicillin. We've got to get that needle out now!"'

Captain Beard had consumed a couple of George Gosse's rums but he agreed to operate. For more than two hours Dr Beard cut into the man's buttock, pouring more and more local anaesthetic into his patient to ease the man's suffering, until he eventually said, 'Well, I can't find the needle. I'll have to close up now.' And just as the doctor was in the process of removing the forceps he felt something metallic. It was the two-inch needle segment. He quickly extracted the offending needle, sutured the wound and said, 'Right, you are to report for duty first thing tomorrow. Don't show any pain, or limp in to work. And, under no circumstances, are you to call me early.'

Don had the time of his life on the world tour. The pageantry, tradition and excitement blew him away. Captain Beard was just 28 years of age at the time of the coronation – he had the world at his feet. He kept dozens of press clippings and photographs, enough to fill a huge black-covered book with 'Coronation Tour, 1953, Capt. D.D. Beard' emblazoned across the front cover in gold lettering. Former Kensington, Sturt and South Australian cricketer Bruce Bowley, who worked for a large stationery supplier in Adelaide, presented his friend with the gold-embossed folder. It contains a treasure trove of photographs, dinner menus, press clippings of Captain Beard's coronation year adventure, a veritable time capsule for the world of 1953: the year of successful US tests of Salk vaccine against polio, the ceasefire in Korea, Sir Edmund Hillary and Sherpa Tenzing Norgay's conquering Mt Everest, and the marriage of John F. Kennedy to Jacqueline Lee Bouvier.

In his scrapbook are numerous press reports, but there are also a few humorous, even risqué articles, such as the piece written in a London magazine, the source of which is now unknown. Under the headline 'They Done Me Wrong', and the pseudonym 'A Lady's Lament', London showed it could turn easily from tradition to humour:

> My name is Prudence. I was born in Birmingham in 1928 being a love child of one Lord Austin and I led a secluded life in North London until my 23rd birthday. Then I joined the Navy and became an officer's chattel. There were ten of them and they decked me out with jewels and flags, with Royal crests and ciphers, with kangaroos and rude cracks. I'm not one of those painted dames and not what you'd call well-groomed or smart.
>
> No one could possibly accuse me of being fast, but I must have something because those ten officers loved me dearly.
>
> I'm not an expensive dame either – it only cost those boys a fiver each to possess me body and soul.
>
> For six splendid weeks they took me everywhere – to the White Dart at Pirbright, to St James' Palace, to the Dig and Duck, to Buckingham Palace, down lovely country lanes to the Talbot And Ripley where Nelson wooed his Emma. Right across London town to the Dulwich Village where George Crago was wed. They took me everywhere in England.
>
> Coronation year was colourful and gay. Oh, so gay! I rested each day beside the triangular 'Square' in Pirbright Camp where my lovers forsook me to pay homage to a Guards Brigade RSM, but every evening they kept me fully occupied – usually to the wee sm' hours.

Seven

England

I saved money by missing lunch and pinching a dry roll from the breakfast table.

Donald Beard

After returning from the coronation tour, Don Beard was keen to pursue his studies and gain the necessary qualifications to achieve what he set out to do, become a fully fledged surgeon.

'I went to Melbourne and failed,' he said, 'so I came home and continued studying. However, I realised that the teaching in Adelaide wasn't very good and nor was the student. All the teachers here at that time worked in an honorary capacity.' While the 1953 coronation tour was a wonderful experience, it did interrupt his medical studies. He decided that to get the right surgical education he needed to look beyond Australia's shores. England beckoned. He thought hard about his decision, but instinct told him that it was the right career path. Don spoke to Dr Russell Barbour, the brilliant trauma surgeon and a medical professional for whom he had the greatest respect.

'I told Dr Barbour that I thought I'd go off to England to study full-time without having to work at a hospital.' Dr Barbour agreed. There would, however, be significant costs to the venture. Don would need to pay the cost of travelling to the UK and during his time there would have to support himself financially and pay for full-time courses. By the time he was preparing to leave for England he had enough funds to bankroll his study overseas for about two years. Don was fortunate in that he had managed to leave most of his army allowance in his pay book. His war service had provided money for his all-important medical studies.

Thanks to the recommendation of State cricketer Keith Gogler, who worked for a shipping line, Don managed to save the fare for the voyage by getting himself appointed as ship's surgeon on the Blue Funnel line's SS *Nestor*, a 14,500-ton cargo vessel, sister ship to the SS *Ulysses*. Three of his good mates – Jim Harris, Peter Harbison and Jim Mill – also decided to go to England where, as they all agreed, they would be taught well.

'Each of us got jobs as a ship's surgeon and we all hooked up in London,' Don said.

'We lived at Lincoln's Inn Fields – just north of Fleet Street, London. For £5 a week, my three medical colleagues from Adelaide and I were able to get a room in The Royal College of Surgeons of England. Our board money also entitled us to breakfast and an evening meal. I saved money by missing lunch and pinching a dry roll from the breakfast table.'

It was a different sort of education in that the students paid the teachers for each course. Tuition was all day every day Monday to Friday and at 5.30 each evening one of the teachers, Frank Stansfield, conducted anatomy classes in his own flat. 'If you passed the anatomy examinations you paid him £25, if you failed the course you didn't pay anything,' Don recalled with a smile. 'You then asked him if you could go to the next session, which lasted for three or four months. Now, if he liked you and you had shown enthusiasm for the subject, and were motivated to learn and you had the right attitude he would say yes, but if he thought you weren't good enough or not trying hard enough he'd say, "I think you'd better go away and do some study on your own for a few months, then come back and see me."

'Those fellas never got another run.'

Don studied hard and eventually passed his examinations in London and in Edinburgh, Scotland. The young medical men virtually ate, drank, slept and studied at the College of Surgeons. There was little respite, although they usually got to the pub of a Friday night.

'We had only one beer,' he laughed, 'it was all due to good timing. You see if we got to the bar at closing time we had no time to buy beers for others. Often there were members of the cast of the play *Kismet*, then on in West End. We'd find ourselves drinking and chatting to the cast until closing time.'

Every couple of weeks Don and his three Australian friends – all of whom became life-long friends – and a South African and a Welshman would go to a party as a group of six. 'If any one of us was invited to a party somewhere in London or Chelsea, you'd say, "Yes I'd love to come to the party, but I've got some friends at the college, would it be possible if we brought a few bottles and they could come too?" That way our entire group of six would always be invited and we went together, each armed with two bottles of beer. It was wonderful. We met all sorts of people in and around London.'

By the 1950s he had a long-established reputation as being a deft hand in downing a pint. 'At one party a fella put a pound note on the table and said, "Here's a quid to anyone who can drink a pint of beer faster than I can." We let it run, the money built up and then Jim Harris put a quid on the table. They said to him, "Are you going to drink?" He said, "No, my mate Beard is," because Jim knew I could knock off a pint pretty fast. We had a pint and it was a tie.

'And they said to me, "You'll have to have a re-run with this other chap." They said, "What are you?" I told them I was a surgical student. They asked the other fella and he said, "I'm a brewer's drayman from Brighton." I knew I was up against something here. So I knocked it off and Jim Harris swept £17 off the table. And we also swept up two girls and said, "We'll take you home." That was a great night.

'After another party, I left early and caught a bus, but unfortunately it was going in the wrong direction,' he laughed. 'At the terminus the crew shared a thermos of coffee and sandwiches and returned to the bus depot in East London, but on their way they drove me to the college – half a mile off their route.'

Don gained invaluable experience spending a few weeks at a time with the best surgeons in London. That opportunity was provided by Dickson Wright, an eminent surgeon at London's St Mary's Hospital.

'Mr Dickson Wright was the father of Clara Dickson Wright, one of the Two Fat Ladies, on the hugely successful (eponymous) cooking show on British television. The two female stars of the show would travel by motorbike and side-car. Mr Dickson Wright was called "smiling death" because he often grinned at students taking examinations and later failed them. He became interested in me because of our mutual love of cricket. He was a great cricket lover and he lived over the side fence of Lord's Cricket Ground. It is amazing how you can gain entry to a number of areas through sport,' Don said.

'Similarly, my army experience helped me meet Sir Neil Hamilton Fairley, who was director of the Tropical Medicine Institute in Liverpool. He was the man who did all the work on malaria during World War II in Townsville, which resulted in his introducing Atebrin, a drug which helps prevent the disease occurring.'

Don loved England – the people, the culture, the history and the cricket. It was a special mix that resonated with him and has retained a special place in his heart all his adult life. One of his mentors was none other than Sir Gordon Gordon-Taylor, one of the most outstanding British surgeons of the 20th

Century. The man lived a life that was the stuff of legends. Born in Aberdeen in 1878, Gordon-Taylor was educated at the University of Aberdeen, where he graduated Master of Arts in 1898. He gained his FRCS in 1906, but it was his exploits during World War I that established for him an enviable reputation. Gordon-Taylor held the rank of major and worked in a number of casualty clearing stations on the Somme, where he gained invaluable experience in the treatment of large abdominal wounds.

Gordon-Taylor became world-renowned for his successful multiple resections of the intestine. During his work as a consulting surgeon to the 4th Army in France, he worked with surgeons from Australian and New Zealand. In 1934 he travelled to Australia as Visiting Examiner for the Royal College of Surgeons and was awarded an honorary FRACS. He would later call the Australasian College of Surgeons his second spiritual home and the Doc considered himself indeed fortunate to come under his wing. Apart from their great passion for surgery, they shared a love for public speaking, dancing, the classics and cricket.

'Sir Gordon Gordon-Taylor was a wonderful man and mentor to me,' Don said. 'I was lucky. In England I immersed myself in surgery and played cricket wherever and whenever I could. I'd awaken on a Saturday morning, do a couple of hours study, then it was off to play cricket.'

His captain was Jim Workman, a good cricketer who played in the Victory Tests against England in 1945; a team led by the redoubtable Lindsay Hassett. Others in the side were the brilliant all-rounder Keith Miller, Bob Christofani and Keith Carmody, the man who 'invented' the umbrella field.

'After the Victory Tests, Workman stayed on in London to work. Our side, under Workman, played throughout the South of England against such teams as the BBC, Barclays Bank, Black Heath and East Molesey where I met Group Captain Lionel Cheshire VC, for whom I promised to work in one of his charity hospitals in India.

'We did not play for premiership points. Each game was played for itself; the enjoyment came with teams being evenly matched and the level of sportsmanship displayed on the field. At the end of the season, the captain would sit down, look at the fixture list and say, "I'll write to this captain and see if we can get a game." The other fellow would look at your club's results, and see if your list provided a good-enough challenge for them to play a match against you. The system had all the good sides playing against one another. It was a good system.'

Later the team was invited by the East Molesey Cricket Club to a mid-summer dance. 'Jim Hyde, another South Australian surgical trainee, and I took two girls, one of whom had a car. We danced all night, then had breakfast with the President and drove halfway across the South of England to Woking where we were due to play the Woking Club Xl. It was touch and go and the two opening bowlers arrived just as the Australian team were taking the field. Jim and I had changed en route and we suggested the girls drive straight onto the field. We were not well received. However, after the match we had the customary buffet and drinks and all was forgiven.

'Initially I failed my fellowship in surgery at the Royal College of Surgeons in England, but I went to Edinburgh where I was successful and returned to London in May 1957 and passed. The pass rate for both parts of the exam was about one in six.

'It then appeared the world was open to me. Sir Gordon Gordon-Taylor had arranged a job for me as surgical registrar. I would have the opportunity to visit theatres, art galleries, museums in London, because I'd not been able to do it while I was studying so hard.

'In addition I had just been picked in a combined Club Cricket Conference team selected from hundreds of cricket clubs throughout the south of England and I'd been picked to play against the MCC at Lord's. So everything appeared great. But suddenly the house fell in. A telegram from Adelaide arrived to say that my father was very sick and I should come home.'

Upon his arrival back in Adelaide Don had £5 in his pocket, and his trusty black Dodge, resting on blocks in the family home garage. Don knew that there was a position as senior surgical registrar at the Royal Adelaide Hospital. He believed a three-year appointment in this capacity at the RAH would prove 'just the ticket' to enable him to complete the surgical training his premature departure had not allowed him to finish in England. He was better qualified than any of the potential applicants in Adelaide, having surgical degrees from London, Edinburgh and Australia – and army war service.

'It was normal practice to report to the director of surgical studies in Adelaide, Mr Alan Lendon, before starting your work,' he said. 'He would tell you what to do. However, I didn't think I *needed* Mr Alan Lendon to apply for the position. I thought with all my war experience, plus my work in London and possessing three fellowships that would be quite enough … but I made a big mistake.'

Mr Lendon informed Don that the Australasian surgical examination was to be held in Melbourne in two weeks. He deferred his selection of the new registrar by three weeks to enable his registrar Keith McKenna to take the surgical examination and be qualified before the hospital selected the new registrar. Don Beard and Keith McKenna travelled together from Adelaide to Melbourne to take the examination. After sitting the second day of examinations on Friday, Don rushed to Spencer Street Station and caught the evening train to Adelaide. He was due to play for Sturt in the district cricket competition next day. He would return by train in time to take the crucial oral examination on Monday. Don found his examiner to be Mr Lendon himself and he was grilled with a barrage of tough questions. All Sunday night Don had sat in the train on his return trip to Melbourne and now his examiner was giving him a hard time.

'I think he was upset that I had not sought him out and asked for his help,' he recalled. 'Mr Lendon grilled me about arthritis of the shoulder. I told him arthritis was common in weight-bearing joints, but not so in the shoulder, especially in young people. Then he made a less than subtle reference to my weekend cricket activities in Adelaide, "What about fast bowlers?" Keith McKenna, who was a RAAF pilot during the war and became a wonderful surgeon, got the job. We remained good friends.'

Don was out on a limb. He had no money, no job and no rooms to practise in. 'I spoke of my problem to another young surgeon, Bill MacBeth, who was going to England in much the same way as I had done a couple of years before. He said, "Oh, I'll have a word to Ivan and see if you could have a couple of sessions in his rooms on North Terrace," and I agreed that would be good.'

Don didn't hesitate. He rang Sir Ivan Jose and asked Adelaide's top surgeon if he might have an appointment to come and see him. He was quietly confident. After all, Bill MacBeth had paved the way. Don shook Sir Ivan's hand and got straight to the point: 'I understand I might have the use of your rooms?'

Sir Ivan was a little taken aback by Don's approach. He bristled, but there was something about this tall, confident young man that led him to say, 'Yes, Beard, that would be all right.'

'Oh, Sir Ivan, what about rent?'

'Call it £5 a week and you can have the use of my secretary.'

Don was well pleased. He could never have conceived that his first meeting with Sir Ivan Jose, Adelaide's most famous surgeon, would bring an even greater benefit.

'As I was leaving Jose's rooms he said, "Look, by the way, I'm going to be away for nine months, would you like to do my locum and look after my patients during my absence?" Well, I nearly collapsed on the floor.' To Don this was the surgical training equivalent of winning the lottery. He would care for all of Sir Ivan's patients and get to pocket 50 per cent of the total income.

'The news of my new role would spread throughout medical circles. I had a brass plate made and put it up at Gawler Chambers. On the Sunday morning I drove into town to look at my brass plate and take a photograph of it.'

A day or so later Don ran into Bill MacBeth who said, 'Don, you haven't been to see Ivan?'

'Oh, yes I have, Bill,' he smiled. 'I'm starting work there on Monday. What's more he's going overseas for nine months and he said I can do his locum while he's away.'

Bill MacBeth stood and stared at him. He was speechless for a few moments, then he smiled broadly, 'Don, I was talking about Ivan *Magarey*. He's the man you were supposed to be ringing.'

'Ivan Magarey was a paediatrician and father of Bill's fiancée. I went to Ivan Magarey and told him. He laughed and said, "Well, you stick with Ivan Jose and you'll get on far better."'

No wonder Sir Ivan had been a little amazed at Don's confident and assertive approach. Sir Ivan Jose and Dr Magarey also had a good laugh about the matter. The opportunity was perfect for Don. He knew that on the strength of his qualifications and his working for Sir Ivan Jose, he would gain one of the registrar appointments at the RAH, scheduled to become available in 12 months. Don would work Sir Ivan's locum for nine of those months, the other three would be taken up working overseas.

'Thoracic surgeon Mr Howard Brown asked me to join his team to go to Papua New Guinea to do tuberculosis surgery on the natives,' he said. The Australian medical team faced a tough task for all of the patients and the blood donors were suffering from malaria, tuberculosis, hookworm and they were anaemic. While Don knew the work would be tough and there would invariably be long, arduous hours in theatre, he also knew the experience would prove of great value to his surgical career.

'We arrived in Port Moresby on a Friday afternoon and the instant I walked into the hotel foyer I ran into an old army friend, Major Don Patterson, who was posted there. He asked about my medical role, then said, "Oh, Don, could you play cricket for us tomorrow?"

'Well, I had packed my cricket boots. I've always believed if you have your boots with you when you go abroad you might get a game of cricket. As it turned out I played for the army team every weekend, except on the occasions when we flew north in an old Fokker aircraft across the Kokoda Pass to Goroka.'

There was a minor concern among the medical team because every night word would go out on the radio about every patient each member of the surgical team had operated on that day.

In pidgin English, the language peculiar to the natives of Papua New Guinea, the people would learn the outcome of every operation. Don did not then know that the indigenous population was far from happy. There was an undercurrent of resentment towards the white man, sentiments which became patently clear some years later when the indigenous people vented their anger with random violence and riots.

'I did not realise how much resentment there was: to me the indigenous folk were lovely people.'

By January 1959, Don was back working at the RAH engaged in extremely busy surgery as the hospital's senior surgical registrar. He was on duty every day and every third night and often operated well into the early hours. Arranging time with his medical colleagues to cover for him while he played cricket was always a challenge.

'One doctor would do my Saturday afternoon for me, but I virtually had to *buy* the time by offering to work a full day in exchange for his working a half day for me,' Don explained.

'I'd give them far more, to ensure they'd do it for me. One time in Adelaide there came a time when neither of my colleagues could work the full Saturday afternoon. So I rang my Sturt club skipper Gil Langley and explained to him that I would not be able to leave the RAH the following Saturday.

'"Oh, Doc, we need you Saturday. We have to win this match. We'll have a phone hook-up with the hospital. If you could come out to Unley Oval and bowl flat out for an hour, we'll have a car ready to take you back to the hospital if anything happens and you are needed."

'So I went and bowled. I bowled flat out for an hour and got a few wickets, then raced back to the hospital and relieved the surgeon who was doing my work. *Sunday Mail* got on to it and they had big headlines in the paper: 'Beard's Hour of Glory'. Monday morning the phone went and the medical superintendant said, "What's this about playing cricket?"'

The RAH superintendent at the time was Bernard Nicholson, a medical administrator who had the good name of the hospital at heart. In taking

Donald Beard to task over his playing cricket of a Saturday afternoon, Bernard was thinking only of the hospital and its name.

Don's love of surgery was almost matched by his love of cricket. One Friday night in the wake of a spate of horrific car crashes, he was operating throughout the night. Then in the morning he went on his ward rounds. After a sleepless night, he wound up in the trauma ward. It was 12.15 pm. Sister Fairfax had her eye on the exhausted Dr Beard.

'How are you going?' she asked.

The Doc looked up. He must have been running on auto-pilot.

'I've got to get to Glenelg Oval to open the bowling today.'

'Have you had lunch, doctor?'

'No. I don't think I'll have time …'

'Ah, but you have to have some nourishment,' Sister Fairfax said knowingly. She reached for a bottle of 'head' mixture. This was what Don remembers as a 'vile' mix of milk and vitamins, Vegemite and cream. Patients who were unconscious had the 'head' mixture run into their stomachs via a tube. This life-saving mixture was Sister Fairfax's idea of giving Don the sort of boost he needed for a hard day's fast bowling.

'Mr Beard, I'll put a tablespoon of brandy in it to take the taste away.' She laughed, 'And it will give you another yard of pace.'

Without a skerrick of sleep and boosted by the brandy-fortified 'head' mixture, Don sped down Anzac Highway in his black Dodge. He had less than 20 minutes to get to Glenelg Oval, so that meant changing his gear along the way. At each traffic light he frantically changed a piece of apparel. At one light he changed his shirt, at another his creams, then the socks. He left his boots until he arrived at the ground. As he was putting his boots on the Sturt players began filing onto Glenelg Oval. No sooner had he reached the wicket than Gil Langley tossed him the new ball. Within an hour's play, the Glenelg batting was tottering at 5/8. Beard had the figures of 3/0 and Bruce Bowley, his opening partner, had 2/8. Headlines in the *Sunday Mail* of 20 February 1954: 'Leaders Collapse For 65: Beard, 6/26'.

Sister Fairfax knew a thing or two.

'Thanks to the brandy and "head" mixture, I had never bowled so well,' he said. 'It is amazing what we can do physically if we really our minds to it. They talk today that modern surgeons get tired quickly and cannot be at their best when working too hard or for long periods. I was never aware of it.'

That same day Beard demolished top-of-the-table Glenelg, 18-year-old

Barry Jarman, who some two years later introduced Don to Margaret Dunn, hit 117 for Woodville against University; Colin Gurner scored a few (run out) in his first innings for East Torrens, and big Bob Mclean took 4/52 with his gentle leg-spinners.

Don Beard and his medical colleagues lived in at the RAH. Because they saw their work as a commitment to serve and make a difference in people's lives, they didn't look at their pay slips or complain about long working hours. 'We thought if we lived in at the hospital, we would get to see more patients and greatly enhance our surgical experience,' he said. 'There is no point in people from our time saying that is how it should be for today's young doctors. It just so happened that what we experienced was the norm for that era. It didn't worry us. The work was there and we did it without complaint.'

One night at the RAH when Don was on duty, he had a telephone call from the Theatre Royal. His mate, Johnny Selth, who later became the SACA catering manager, was on the line.

'Doc, you have to get down here; one of the nudes fell out of her basket,' Selth said, with a hint of humour in his voice.

Don explains: 'They called for a doctor and Selthy sprang into action. He was first across the footlights.' In those days nudes in vaudeville theatre shows could be suspended inside a cage, however, they were not permitted to move. They had to sit, stand or lie motionless. Somehow one of the naked women fell from her cage and crashed heavily to the stage floor. Beard had taught Selth a certain amount about being a doctor because the young doctors in their social group thought he would have liked to study medicine. 'We used to get him to come in to the RAH casualty department and he'd help us doing dressings and things. He'd often spend several hours at the hospital. Selthy was one of the mob.'

Don raced to the Theatre Royal. He gave the pretty and naked girl a thorough examination, including the injured ankle, and declared it not broken but sprained. 'But I think we'd better have another look at it tomorrow morning,' he told her.

The young lady lived with three other young women in an apartment at North Adelaide. 'The next day, Sunday morning, Selth and I went out to see the girl and then we invited them to a picnic up a hidden creek at Hardy's Vineyard with the thought of getting the girls to disrobe.' He smiled, 'But they came dressed in layers of shirts and jumpers and jackets, not one item of which was removed. What a waste of the sumptuous lunch we had turned on.'

In September 1960 Don was shocked and saddened to learn of his mentor's death in London. Sir Gordon Gordon-Taylor, who walked miles every day and nurtured a healthy dislike of motorcars, was tragically run down by a car outside Lord's Cricket Ground on 2 September 1960. His passing was mourned by the world of surgery. He lived long enough to see a portrait of himself by eminent artist Sir James Gunn. The portrait had been commissioned by his former student, Dr Donald Beard.

'I wrote to every postwar Australian and New Zealand surgical graduate asking for a donation towards the project and I received wonderful financial support,' he said. 'Sir James Gunn's fee for a portrait at the time was around £1000, but he charged us only half that amount.'

Sir Gordon Gordon-Taylor was taken by ambulance to his old hospital – The Middlesex – where he died just before his portrait was unveiled at a surgical conference in Adelaide by Beard. The portrait now hangs in the Hailes Room at the Royal Australasian College of Surgeons in Melbourne. The grand old man of surgery had taught him well.

Within a few months Donald Beard was to meet the girl of his dreams.

Eight

Margaret – 'The love of my life'

Whenever we have an argument, it's soon over. He never broods or holds a grudge.

Margaret Beard

Margaret Dunn and Don Beard met at the wedding of a mutual friend, Sue Morphett, in January 1961. One of Don's cricket mates, SA and Test wicket-keeper Barry Jarman, introduced them. Almost a year to the day after they met, Margaret and Don were married.

A year or so before she married, Margaret's dedication and care towards her sick mother so impressed her father Alexander Dunn that he gave her a 10-month long, round-the-world tour as a present. She was just 20 years old and enjoyed touring on the cruiser *Willhem Rhys*. Margaret was among nine girls in their group, including Sheila Scales, their chaperone. Among the girls was Melbourne-based Penny Lane, later Penny Smith. Penny and Margaret were destined to become life-long friends.

Margaret and Don were married at St Augustine's Church, Unley, in January 1962. Ian McLachlan was best man and long-time friend Dr Brian Peters was the groomsman. As a Sturt Cricket Club A grade team-mate of Don's, McLachlan, who took many an edged chance at first slip from the bowling of his fast bowler friend, knew a good catch when he saw one.

The Beards set up house in Marryatville. As was the way in the workforce of the early 1960s, Margaret did not resume work after she wed. Society was almost conditioned to all young married women leaving work to care for their families.

Margaret said: 'I worked at Verco & Gurner for about five years and I used to run the radiography department at Calvary Hospital when the nuns were in retreat. Memories of the nuns' special blend of coffee and morning teas flooded back.'

Don Beard dresses immaculately. In the early days, when he escorted Margaret to a ball or a dance he would always bring her an orchid. Unbeknown to Don, Margaret did not like orchids, especially those at the centre of a corsage.

'I think the time I finally told him about my dislike for the orchid corsage was during a big dinner for the AMA at the South Australian Hotel. We were all dressed up to the nines. They used to wear tails and all sorts of things in those days. I'm sure I had a long dress on and I think that's the time I sort of stuck the orchid on the side of my bag and Don said, "Why don't you pin it on?" I finally admitted I didn't like corsages.

Don Beard knew he married a special lady: 'It did not take long for me to realise that most of my ambitions and the good things I thought I was doing were encouraged and stimulated by Margaret, who was doing some wonderful work for Anglicare and St John Ambulance of Australia.'

She started with fundraising in the auxiliary and eventually became examiner and president of cadets and the Australian representative of St John Eye Hospital in Jerusalem. In October 2012, Margaret was given the high honour of being made a Commander of St John's, Jerusalem. On Friday 14 June 2013 Margaret Beard was invested at Government House in Adelaide with the Most Venerable Order of the Hospital of Saint John of Jerusalem. Donald could not have been more proud.

'At home she cared for the children, ran the house and did the cooking. She has been a fairy godmother to so many and a long-term blood donor. I am very proud of her.'

Margaret and Don have two boys and four grandchildren. 'When the boys were growing up I think they missed out on Don's time. His patients were always number one, because they had to be,' Margaret said. 'Even at the cricket Don seemed to give others more time than he gave to the boys. Matthew and Alastair would go to the cricket with their father and there Don would be talking to everyone he knew and the boys must have been thinking, What about us? There was Don's work, his cricket and sometimes he'd go off to army camp and be away from Friday to Sunday. I am convinced that Matthew and Alastair were turned off a career as a doctor because of Don's long absences.'

Matthew is a physiotherapist and Alastair a financial advisor to an energy firm in Melbourne. Both boys have two children, now teenagers. Matthew and Marie Beard have James and Sophie, and Alastair and Jennifer Beard have Phoebe and Julian.

Dr Beard regrets having been so domineering with his boys. 'I think I was too demanding with them, ordering them about too much and telling them what to do without thinking a great deal about what they wanted to do,' he said. 'I thought I was helping them, but I know now that I was not.

'Alastair had degrees in Commerce and Economics and sought to get a better job. This he did and passed further examinations in business administration. This meant very hard work and he succeeded and improved his work prospects. Alastair's wife, Jennifer, who had played violin in the Australian Youth Orchestra, now enjoys teaching the art.'

Don is so fond of all his grandchildren, but the tyranny of distance doesn't allow him to see Alastair and Jennifer's children, Julian and Phoebe, as often as he would like. 'We are still very close as a family,' he says. 'And Alastair's son, Julian, is a pretty good fast bowler. He is also a good footballer and he helped Scotch College win the premiership in 2012. Julian has also done well in his studies at the very school where World War I General Sir John Monash excelled.'

Julian Beard was picked for Victoria's Under-15 State cricket squad. He was presented with his State cap during a break in play during the 2011 Boxing Day Test at the MCG. However, he sustained an injury before the championships and couldn't play. This injury forced Julian from the Victorian team. In September 2012, Julian spent a few days in Perth working with Don's good mate, Dennis Lillee. Having missed State selection in 1947, Don knows how disappointing it must have been for his grandson. Julian has since fought his way back into the Victorian youth squad and in June 2012 he was chosen for his school team to tour England.

'Phoebe has made the most of her chances; her favourite subjects and her successes have been in the humanities and arts. In sport she has represented her school in rowing and she is captain of the swimming team. She has completed school and in 2012 she started her university studies in fine arts.'

Penny Smith, the Melbourne-based close friend of Margaret and Don Beard who met Margaret on the around-the-world trip all those years ago, is a remarkable woman. She's a superb cook and wordsmith who has written a number of fine books on cooking and travel. In her magnum opus, *A Ton of Spirit* (Allen & Unwin, 1990), 48 of Australia's 300 centenarians speak with her. Penny says unequivocally of Margaret and Donald Beard: 'Most people would aspire to have the marriage they have enjoyed. Margaret has always accommodated Don. She's put up with and appreciated everything in his life. Even the bad times when people have been critical. I think it is one of the best marriages that I have ever known.

'He's allowed her to be herself. He's been tough in many ways, coming home for dinner and expecting Margaret to put on a meal for 10 people. This happened on a regular basis, with dinners for cricketers, opera singers, doctors; you never knew who might be there. And Margaret, without complaining, would put on wonderful meals. He never said, "Would you mind?" It was a given. And that's not a criticism it's an era. I guess the payoff was that when Margaret said she wanted to go to Yemen or Kenya or Ireland – or anywhere else with me – he never said no. We'd go away together, as we did, somewhere each year over many years and we always went with his blessing.' Given Donald's inclination towards possessiveness early in his relationship with Margaret, Penny's words resonate to a large degree.

'Well. One time we were at Victoria Falls and the instant we got to our hotel room and put the bags down the phone rang. And I said, "That will be bloody Don!"

'"Where are you, what are you doing?"

'I said, "Are you checking up on us, Don?"

'We'd get on a plane with Qantas and there'd be flowers and champagne. He was so thoughtful, unbelievably considerate; he allowed Marg time off and never baulked at the cost. Don is full of praise, full of energy, driving you to improve, learn or experience. But the boys (Matthew and Alastair) have said to me, "You don't know how tough it's been to be his son."

'I do know because I have watched the boys since they were children. Don was one of those people who believed there was no prize for running second. You had to be best in what you did and if you were sick that was a weakness, if you were tired it was only in your mind. That's why it is difficult seeing him now, because Don's slowed down enormously and he's not applying the same philosophy to himself that he used to impress on others. As for Margaret we just clicked. I know I was the rebel. I came home from the tour to be her bridesmaid, otherwise I don't think I would have come home. We've travelled the world together. We very rarely have a cross word, we enjoy the same interests. Anything I know about gardens I've learnt from Margaret because I've always been a cook or a journalist. I do botanical art. We've learnt from each other.'

One time when Margaret and Penny were in China there was a drama unfolding in the Beard family back garden. 'I might have known straight away about Don's back injury, but my mobile phone didn't work,' Margaret explained. 'I'd never had a mobile before. I borrowed an old one of Marie's. I discovered to get on international roaming it had to be a Telstra phone. Here we were in the Gobi Desert, with just about every Chinaman you saw with a mobile phone to his ear and mine wouldn't work. Eventually we got good advice and got the phone working. And when I rang home Sophie (Matthew and Marie's daughter) said immediately, "Grandma, Grandpa's broken his back." Matthew grabbed the phone to allay his mother's fears: "Don't be silly. Dad's just got a sore back from gardening."

It was, in fact, a crush fracture of the spine. Despite having received Margaret's strict instruction not to attempt to move wood cut up from a fallen tree in the garden, Don rolled up his sleeves and was no sooner starting the job when it was all over for him for some weeks. His accident happened while he was trying to clear the wood during the height of a storm and fell backwards over a fallen log. 'I crawled inside to bed, where a neighbour found me when he came to visit. He went home and brought me back a bowl of pasta and a glass of wine. It became a daily ritual.'

Don refused to go to hospital because he knew staff there would inform Margaret and he did not want to cut short her holiday. So for the next couple of weeks his neighbour brought him meals, Matthew and Marie called upon him on a daily basis, and family and friends were sworn to secrecy.

Three weeks later Beard asked his neurosurgical friend, Donald Simpson, if he could fly to Sydney to meet Margaret when she flew into Australia. Dr Simpson agreed, with the proviso: 'As long as you do not pick up anything heavier than a bus ticket.' Margaret realised the full extent of Don's injury when he turned up in a wheelchair to greet her return to Australia.

I asked Matthew about his father. What was it like to be the son of a famous surgeon, a man of great passion and standing in the community? 'Dad had three great passions in life and in no particular order – cricket, surgery and the army,' Matthew said. 'You may not be able to compare from today to then because it was a different generation, but he was, I think, fortunate to be able to pursue three passions, not just one.

'My brother and I were no different to other youngsters growing up with a "driven" father. In those days most mums didn't work, so essentially our household was a single-parent household.'

Don Beard had a very full-on commitment with his three passions, plus ensuring the stability and sustainability of his family and home life. Matthew reckons his parents must have possessed great time-management skills. If he wasn't at work, playing cricket, attending a meeting, at a CMF army camp, out attending to a medical emergency or looking after cricketers, he was at home.

'Even if Dad had a long day at work he'd often have a quick meal then leave to attend a journal club with his colleagues, reviewing developments in the medical and surgical literature. He did have a rule that wherever possible we ate together as a family, including hosting an American field scholar for a year and when we were young we used to go out as a family to a restaurant at least once a week. I think it was to improve our interest in all food. We were doing this in the 1970s when there were only a handful of licensed restaurants in Adelaide. Some were good, but some were ordinary. But it was always a lot of fun. I think people need to realise that if you inject that much interest into three major facets of your life there is a limit to the number of hours in the day. How he fitted all that he did into any one day I'll never know. But I don't think Dad neglected the family at all. We always had meals together and we always went on holiday together.'

However, Matthew and Alastair learnt to break from study the instant they heard the sound of the whistle, which Matthew discovered years later was once owned by his grandfather, Alexander Dunn, who, in World War I as Captain Dunn, blew the whistle to herald a charge 'a tot of rum and over the top' on the muddy and bloodied fields of the Western Front. According to Matthew and Alastair that same whistle was used by their father as an instrument of order to his two boys. He'd blow the whistle to signal time for dinner or the call to study.

Matthew explains: 'My brother and I, like most teenage boys, were often reluctant to apply ourselves as much as we should have with our studies. We'd much rather be outside on the tennis court playing cricket or tennis. Dad, who I know came from a fairly austere background, probably got where he was through drive and determination and hard work. He was pretty keen for us to do well and part of it involved that we get down to homework before dinner every night. When dinner was ready and sitting on the table we'd hear a whistle and we were allowed to leave our desks and have dinner. And when the meal ended the proviso that we didn't have to do the dishes was that we return to our desk and continue with our studies.

'The whistle was quite shrill and it wasn't until years later when I heard a similar sounding whistle on a TV documentary about World War I that I discovered that it belonged to my grandfather. He received a Military Cross for valour, which he never mentioned to me or other members of the family. Later, among his papers, they discovered a diary he kept during the war.'

Years later, in 2007, the diary proved invaluable for Donald and Margaret Beard as they joined an Australian War Memorial battlefield tour group, which spent three fascinating weeks retracing Lt Alexander Dunn's footsteps on the Western Front.

'The diary reflected an enormous cynicism he had for the bastard of a life on the battlefield and also his contempt for many of the senior English officers he encountered. It's interesting that Dad is almost an Anglophile, whereas Alexander Dunn, who served under the English, had a very different view.

'Grandfather died in the 1970s quite a sad man. I remember saying to Mum, for someone who had such an interesting life, after military service he had such a dark view on things. Grandfather had never recovered from the death of his son, Bill, who died when his Lancaster bomber was shot down over Berlin. Mum said Bill's death affected her father more than any other tragedy in his life.'

Matthew and Alastair knew that their father was a little tough on them, but they also recognise that in their growing years society was very different. There wasn't the same freedom given children in those days and that applied to most households. 'Neither Alastair nor I would have wished to have been brought up any differently,' Matthew said.

Alastair believes the boys heard so much about medicine and surgery over dinner every night that it reached saturation point. 'When Matthew and I were youngsters we used to accompany Dad on his ward rounds on Sunday mornings,' said Alastair, who never wished to pursue a career in medicine.

'Sure I wanted to do something for myself, but if I really wanted to be a doctor I could always have studied and practised interstate if the motivation for such a move was to get out from under his shadow. As a young boy I really enjoyed languages and other cultures. More than anything I wanted to be a diplomat. Hospitals were full of sick and dying people and a doctor had to deal with everyone else's problems all the time – I'm not sure I was cut out for that sort of career.'

So Alastair followed a different career pathway: economics, finance and rowing. He believes his father's tremendous work ethic has rubbed off on him, but it 'has taken a long time to have a positive affect'.

'I do have a legacy of having trouble enjoying life,' he said. 'When we grew up everything was done for duty or obligation or improvement. Nothing was ever done purely for fun. My wife has corrected me a lot in this area.

'Now I respect Dad's work ethic much more and if I resisted it a bit in my youth I very much try to impart it (or at least support it) in my children. I think the trick is not to tell them what they should be doing. When you see the children really working hard and enjoying a particular project then really encourage and support their endeavours. But I think it best to support them from the shadows, or at least in the background.'

Alastair and Matthew both loved the interaction with international cricketers at home and at the ground. 'I remember the dinners at home where you'd rub shoulders with some of the great names of cricket,' said Alastair. 'Once I observed a verbal sparring match between Sir Donald Bradman and Dennis Lillee. Another time Sir Donald and India's Sunil Gavaskar had an animated discussion about facing hostile fast bowlers.'

Once Alastair was at his father's South Terrace rooms when the doctor had to make a hurried exit. 'Alastair, you're in charge while I'm away. I am expecting two gentlemen – Greg Chappell and Rodney Marsh – any minute now. They are coming for a physical checkup before the coming tour overseas. Look after them until I get back!'

'The captain (Chappell) and vice-captain (Marsh) of the Australian Cricket team arrived in the room long before Dad reappeared. In that time Rod Marsh had invited me to train with the team the next day at Adelaide Oval.

'There was the experience of walking down the stairs from the dressing-room and walking to the nets under the gaze of 5000 cricket fans and the glare of TV cameras. Written all over the people's faces was: Who is that young guy? I bowled quite well, nearly had John Dyson caught and bowled. What a day.'

Another time Alastair became the proud owner of an Australian one-day international shirt, presented to him at the Beard family home by its original owner, Australian fast bowler Lennie Pascoe. The Beard boys got to know many of the cricketers and met some of the game's superstars including West Indian legends Wes Hall and Viv Richards.

Other famous people spent time at the Beard family home. During the US presidency of Ronald Reagan, actor Fess Parker, who won fame for his portrayal of Davy Crockett and Daniel Boone in films and TV mini-series, came to dinner. The pair had met briefly in Vietnam in 1968.

'Fess Parker was in Adelaide as an envoy for President Reagan,' Alastair said. 'He was at our place for only about an hour, speaking mainly about golf and the skins tournament then being staged on the Gold Coast. Despite his short visit our house was fully "cased" by CIA operatives hiding behind trees in the garden.'

Alastair found that while his father's help was always well-intentioned, it was not always well-received. 'Dad helped so much that he would invariably take over,' Alastair said. 'At times his help was just too much and that taught you nothing but apathy. That sounds ungrateful but there is a difference between help when supporting you in the areas you sought to improve and help as "in doing it for you".

'One day we had a school excursion to see Marcel Marceau, internationally acclaimed French actor and mime. For homework we had to write a short piece on the experience. Our essays were to be submitted to the *Advertiser* as part of a competition. I struggled with it – until I reached the age of 30 I hated any form of writing. Dad came into my room and said, "C'mon, get cracking and finish it. How about you say this?"

'His line from my essay ended up being published in the *Advertiser* the next week. It's funny because they were not my words but they were attributed to me.' The line? 'I wish I could speak as well in my own words (i.e. speak as well as Marcel Marceau).'

'Things like this probably made me avoid asking him for help in later years. Together Mum and Dad almost killed you with kindness. If you ask them to help out with your activity, your club or your expedition they would end up helping you so much that the project was no longer yours.'

One New Year's Eve when the Beard family was on their annual Christmas holiday break at Robe, a delightful South Australian beach resort some 340 kilometres south-east of Adelaide, Don took it upon himself to construct a bonfire on popular Grieves Beach. He had discovered where Alastair, then 15, and his friends would see the New Year in while strolling along the sand. 'Dad told me about the bonfire he had set just as I left to go out,' Alastair said, 'and I immediately decided not to go to Grieves Beach that night. I did not want him controlling my special night (even from afar).'

Alastair said that he and his friends had an 'okay time' but confessed they could have done with a base for the evening and the fire would have been great. Next day Alastair ventured down to Grieves Beach and there was the bonfire his dad had erected. It had timber and driftwood stacked a metre high, with kindling and paper underneath – all ready to go.

'When I saw the bonfire and realised the effort he had put in I felt sad and ashamed that I had not taken up his offer because he really had gone to a lot of trouble and the bonfire would have provided a perfect setting for us.'

Alastair and Matthew enjoyed attending the Anzac Day march. 'I am very proud of Dad's military service,' said Alastair, 'and I enjoyed the march and times like this because it was his moment and I could just be proud of him. I remain a fervent monarchist and supporter of our armed forces. I try to get to an Anzac Day march wherever I am each year and have been to the dawn service in Melbourne. I sell poppies and Anzac Day badges each year through my club, Toorak Services Club in Melbourne, and I give a hard time to any of our members who fail to help out. Dad, of course, has continued a long association with his beloved 3rd RAR and the annual Kapyong Day ceremony held on 24 April. He was so proud the day Jennifer and I announced our engagement under the bell in the officers' mess one Kapyong Day at Holsworthy.'

Alastair and Matthew discovered that their father saw an opportunity of bettering one's self in almost every activity. 'Dad wasn't always away from home, but when he was there he was generally working. Of a Saturday afternoon he would drive his car into the driveway where it was sunny. And there he was sitting in his car in the sun, dictating letters to people.

'He hated any form of idleness, even sleeping in was a no-no. Gluttony in any form he detested and while Dad enjoyed a drink and had a great party trick where he could drink four glasses of beer at once, I never saw him drunk. He was always clean-shaven and immaculately dressed. He might have had his controlling ways, but I know he always had the good of the family in mind when he set out to help you. I love him and am very proud of him.'

Whenever Don and Margaret were overseas at a conference, they would record highlights of their trip and send the tapes homes for the boys to listen to while they were in boarding school. 'It was like a postcard and slide show rolled into one.'

In the last year of high school, Alastair dropped cricket, considering himself a cricketer 'lacking skill and any form of confidence', and rowed in the second eight that lost by half a canvas – about one metre – at the Head of the River regatta.

'I joined the Adelaide University Boat Club and in 1984 went to my first intervarsity meet in Tasmania and never looked back,' Alastair recalled. 'Camaraderie, lots of hard work, early mornings and late nights went with the territory and sometimes there was the elation of victory. I was involved in some good wins – Intervarsity Coxed Fours (Adelaide University Boat Club) in 1986 and 1989 and the SA State Championship in 1988. As rowers we ended up getting very fit, tanned, looking and feeling good about ourselves.

'There was a good feeling within the group and we had lots of fun. I got to train and hang out with like-minded people, many of whom were out to have fun. Pleasure seeking was a new thing to me and sometimes I felt guilty about having such a good time. I wasn't used to it.'

Alastair and Matthew had long realised that their mother held the household together. 'I always thought our life was a bit like playing both parts in the TV series *Upstairs Downstairs*,' Alastair said. 'We had the grandest parties with the grandest guests and the finest silver, while at the same time we were in the kitchen doing all that work as well. Mum would be slaving over the stove while my brother and I would be dressed up serving food, pouring wine and clearing plates.'

Alastair is able to look past the obvious and understand how his mother's strength and support enabled his father to achieve so much over so many fields of endeavour for so long. 'Mum could have fought and stood her ground more, but then all she did for him in supporting his career and running the family home allowed him to go from success to success. I believe Dad's mother used to do a lot for him when he was growing up and perhaps so too did the army. Mum's life was tied to Dad's so the better he did, the better it was for her and their family as a whole.

'Dad relies on Mum just as much now, but in a different way because as he is slowing down he needs someone to care for him. Mum is becoming the stronger half of the relationship and does not put up with his carry-on nowadays as she once might have done.'

Don is proud of the manner in which both Matthew and Alastair worked hard to succeed in their studies. 'Matthew and Alastair matriculated well and gained entry to university, graduating in science and physiotherapy and economics. They are great boys and I am very proud of them and I love them both and their children.'

Alastair and Jennifer's children have also succeeded. Phoebe matriculated well and is doing fine arts at Melbourne University. At Merton Hall she was Captain of Swimming and rowed in the Head of the River. She has worked and saved and recently accompanied a small group from the university to Bolivia.

Julian did well at Scotch College, Melbourne in his studies and the school theatre. At sport he played in the school football XVIII and in cricket first eleven. He, too, matriculated well and was accepted by Monash University. His cricket ability has been rewarded by being appointed Cricket Coach.

Matthew and Marie, a theatre nurse, have always been used to leading busy lives. There is respite during the day, for from 7.30 am their disabled son James is taken by bus to a special school near Port Adelaide. There he takes part in all manner of activities to help stimulate the mind and physical movement. James loves company. The family can tell his mood by the way he smiles. When a family member goes into a room to see him they call to him and he always looks at them. Music tends to soothe him and Margaret has discovered that James likes classical music best of all. 'We play soft, gentle music for him at night.'

Matthew and Marie waited two years after James' birth before they dared contemplate having another child. After all the tests had been carried out they decided to try again. Their second born, Sophie, arrived in 2001 with a hole in the heart. Happily the condition corrected itself and Sophie is very much a healthy, happy girl.

'She is great at school and at sport,' the doctor said proudly. At School Speech Day in December 2013 she won the prize for the best achiever in both academic and sporting life. Recently she came second in the SA Swimming Championship backstroke. 'She spends time with us at home when her parents are at work. She has a great imagination and builds things in the garden and has picnics with herself and is sorry James cannot play with her, but she does spend a lot of time looking after him and his dog, Coco.'

Penny Smith recently asked Matthew: 'What would you have done without the help of your parents?'

'We couldn't have done it,' Matthew said matter-of-factly.

Despite the cards they've been dealt, Matthew and Marie Beard press on ensuring all their love and the best and most comfortable life for their two children. And Matthew contends that without his mother's love, understanding and sage advice, his father could never have been the amazing success he most certainly has been. Margaret and Donald give their children and their grandchildren all the love and support in the world. And it all stemmed from their relationship of love and caring.

Matthew fondly recalls being taken by the family to see the famous Israeli Philharmonic Orchestra. 'Part-way through an after-concert party, the conductor Zubin Mehta, Indian Parsi Music Director for Life of the Israel Philharmonic Orchestra, arrived. Immediately a crowd gathered around him, but after a short greeting he came over to Dad and said, "Hi, Doc. Let's talk about the cricket."

Cricket had always been a topic of conversation in the Beard household. Once Matthew played for old scholars alongside his father. 'Dad was then in his late 50s and we opened the bowling. The scorer yelled, "Who's bowling?"

'"Beard," came the reply.

'"He's already bowled," the scorer yelled indignantly.

'"It's okay, that's his son up the other end."'

In the early days of their marriage, it was not always smooth sailing. 'When we first married Don was quite sick,' Margaret said. 'He had colitis, but I really don't think he ate well. He had the wrong diet. The first time I fed him I cooked him roast pork and he was violently ill. It's a wonder he came back again. His mother was a good plain Australian cook, lots of roast dinners, lots of dripping. I think it wasn't good for him. There was no great variety in his diet. His mother could never understand the way we ate.'

Margaret is a great cook. Her cooking embraces recipes from throughout the world and the Beards enjoy seven different, nourishing evening meals every week. Don regards those evening meals as 'always exciting and enjoyable', using vegetables and salads from their own garden. Matthew and Marie and their children come to the family home for dinner on Friday nights.

'Don loves dressing up. He once dressed as Willie Nelson and when we arrived at the St Andrew's Hospital Christmas party, the people on the door refused to believe that the man dressed as the famous country-and-western singer who turned up sitting astride a Harley-Davidson motorbike was in fact Dr Donald Beard. He was denied entry to the party.

'Don and I would go to see the Adelaide Symphony Orchestra, but we'd creep in after the performance had started and we'd be there five minutes and Don would be fast asleep. After a long day of surgery he was exhausted.' Anyone visiting the Beard family home in Norwood on any given day will hear the sound of classical music. It's in the blood.

Margaret has always loved Don's kindness and agreeable nature. 'Whenever we have an argument, it's soon over. He never broods or holds a grudge. He's not even fond of my moving furniture about a room. I think Don would be perfectly happy if we lived in a tent.'

Don's undying love for Margaret is apparent. 'Each day when I wake I look at my Margaret and thank God for my good fortune.'

Nine

Vietnam: The Diggers' Doctor

The man's injuries were the worst I'd seen. The mine had exploded behind him and blown off the backs of both his legs from the feet to the buttocks.

Donald Beard

The Vietnam veterans marched down King William Street, saluted the South Australian Governor and continued on towards St Peter's Cathedral. Teenager Matthew Beard stood proudly beside his father and mother and his younger brother, Alastair.

'Alastair and I always attended the annual Anzac Day march with Mum to watch Dad,' Matthew recalled. 'He alternated between marching one year in the Korean contingent, next year with his Vietnam War colleagues.'

And on this particular day, Colonel Donald Beard, straight-backed like a Grenadier Guardsman, was resplendent as usual in his blazer, hat, and mandatory rose attached above his line of medals. He marched with the Korean contingent and after his march joined Margaret and the boys in the crowd to cheer on his old comrades.

'As the Vietnam veterans approached I noted that some were immaculately dressed, others wore bandanas over their unkempt hair and beards and their clothes, often old army jackets, were festooned in all manner of badges,' Matthew continued. 'But something amazing happened. They saw Dad, standing tall in the crowd with us. There he was in his blazer and Panama hat, and the column of veterans suddenly came to attention. An officer at the front of the marchers bellowed: "Eyes right; it's the Doc!" They all saluted. Most of the people in the crowd didn't realise the significance of the soldiers' show of respect for my father, but the Vietnam veterans gave Dad a far more impressive display than they gave the Governor and it told me something special about the experiences they shared; something we who never served in that war would understand.'

Those at home who had worked with Dr Beard knew his capabilities and were confident that he would give of himself totally, caring for the soldiers on the front line. A day or so before Don Beard flew to Vietnam, he received a letter from his old friend and mentor Dr Russell Barbour:

J. Russell BARBOUR, MS, FRCS
30 North Terrace
Adelaide 5000   27.2.'68

Dear Don,
Eve of departure and Margaret won't be feeling very exhilarated. However, I wish you all the best and know that Central Command have a top Rep.
   This, of course, goes for Australia as a whole as we own it!
   I have much faith in the doctrine that some can stick their neck out and some can't. Your neck is already in the invulnerable class. Perhaps you could console your wife with my opinion, for what it is worth, that you will be a top class rep. and also have stuck your neck out so often it must be invulnerable.

Best wishes,
Russell Barbour

He certainly stuck his neck out during the Battle of Kapyong, running the gauntlet of withering Chinese soldier gunfire while inside a Sherman tank hurtling up and down the Kapyong Valley. Colonel Russell Barbour knew Don would never shirk a challenge on the battlefield and was totally committed to the care of the wounded soldiers. And as I prepared for the first of my four Test cricket tours of England, I learnt the SACA medical officer, Dr Beard, had gone back to war.

The Vietnam War had reached a critical stage. Thousands of Americans were fighting in that war-ravaged country and, in 1968, the Australians had a military force of 8500 men. When the first battalion went to Vietnam they brought with them just one medical officer and all the Australian casualties were evacuated to US hospitals. With the build-up of the Australian force a field ambulance was sent with the additional soldiers. However, because of the nature of the war and the insecure roads, evacuation of the injured was carried out almost exclusively by helicopter. A medical evacuation in Vietnam was called a 'dustoff'. In Vietnam, 9 Squadron RAAF operated the highly versatile Iroquois UH-1D helicopter, universally known as a 'Huey', to transport troops and equipment, provide fire support for ground troops and, most importantly for Colonel Beard and his team, evacuate the wounded from the battlefield and fly them directly to the hospital in Vung Tau.

The treatment role for a Field Ambulance was to assess the sick and wounded, plus any emergency care before evacuation to a surgical hospital, a casualty clearing station, or the US-run Mobile Army Surgical Hospital (MASH). Surgery was rarely performed at the Field Ambulance and until 1967 the unit in Vietnam did not carry a surgeon or anaesthetist. At the time Dr Beard was considering a role in Vietnam, the Australian Army was at its wit's end trying to find replacement surgeons to serve in the war. Beard once again volunteered to serve in a war zone. He wrote a daily log of his Vietnam experience:

> No surgeon could be induced to volunteer – a very sad reflection on young Australian surgeons, both in an out of the CMF (Citizen Military Forces). For a young man it is an ideal chance to contribute to the Australian effort, but even more important to the 8500 young Australians in Vietnam. I fear that the rat race of consultant surgery makes young fellows frightened to take their foot off the ladder. The first hint of my being needed came out on the Deputy Director of Medical Services (DDMS) exercise in November, 1967, when, at lunch on the Sunday, the DGMS's representative, Lieutenant Colonel Ray Grant, called several of us aside and told us of the problem of giving proper medical and surgical care for the Australian force in Vietnam and the intention was to enlist them from the CMF (reserve force), with the only alternative being handing over care of Australian casualties to the Americans, which good though it is, is not like being cared by our own people.
>
> Lt Col. Grant said he had approached Central Command in South Australia on behalf of the DGMS. He added that Major General Colin Gurner, who had suggested that surgeon Colonel Don Beard and the physician Colonel Tom Beare, who had trained as a paediatrician and studied tropical medicine, would be 'ideally suited to his needs'.
>
> I offered my services immediately, as did Tom Beare, however, on the way home that afternoon I thought what this meant and how much I would miss my family and how they would get on without me.

He would need to get leave from Queen Elizabeth Hospital and again call upon surgeon, Dr Dick Dunstan (ex RAN), to cover his absence at his private rooms, undergo myriad medical tests, organise insurance, taxation, wills, power of attorney – in fact cover all possible eventualities at home. After a few days keeping his thoughts to himself, Don told Margaret and she said immediately, 'Well, Don, you are in the CMF and you must help where you are needed.' During the frenetic weeks leading to his departure, friends organised send-offs and parties, even a 'buck's night' at the Sturt Cricket Club. The Army sprang a surprise, their departure brought forward by 24 hours, and the Beards drove to the airport. Initially their car wouldn't start, but a good cranking by Don and perfect acceleration by Margaret got the vehicle underway. A host of friends and family were there to see Beard leave Adelaide, including his mother and Margaret's dad, Alexander Dunn.

> There was my darling Margaret and Alastair and Matthew holding his model DC9 aeroplane. It was very difficult and sad to say goodbye, but also a relief that all the preparation was over.

Don and Tom travelled together. They were in for a hectic few days of reading documents and medical reports and orientation. First stop was Melbourne and straight to the School of Army Health at Healesville for a day at the rifle range, to become firearms proficient.

> We were met by the CO, Lt Col. Coumbe who had 'laid on' an extensive program of shooting with all weapons. We started off with a 9 mm pistol, shooting from three basic positions – hip, standing, lying and aiming with the sights at a target of a man's figure at 25 yards. Tom's accuracy was better than mine, but we both passed after 50 rounds each. Then on to the F1 sub-machine gun at 25 yards and 50 yards. Finally we fired the SLR [self loading rifle] at 200 yards, standing, sitting and lying. By the time we had finished we were hot and tired and dusty. We had ringing ears, but were pronounced 'efficient in the weapons', a certificate of such being necessary before we could be sent to Vietnam.

Colonel Beard was fully briefed by Colonel Douglas (Doug) Leslie, consultant surgeon to Australian HQ, on the extent and increasing volume of wounded soldiers on the battlefield. He was in no doubt that he and his team were about to face a great challenge in the war zone. For their last night in Australia, Don and Tom booked into the Chevron Hotel in King's Cross. They had some time off and spent it wisely on a Sydney Harbour cruise, a few hours at Taronga Park Zoo and a night at a sleazy restaurant where they found to their surprise that it was a venue for a variety of strippers, who, Don reckoned, were 'either under-built or over-built, so not very attractive'. The hours trying to rest in the hotel before they left for Sydney's Mascot Airport proved a testing time.

> My mind went back 18 years to a not dissimilar occasion on the night before leaving for Korea when the war situation was just as bad and there was great uncertainty. But on that night in December 1950, my departure was

accompanied by a night of parties. I was 25 and fit and had no responsibilities and it seemed like a grand adventure, even if a dangerous one. This time there were no parties. I didn't feel like them anyway and I was not a little afraid, both for myself and for everyone at home. I was frightened of losing what meant so much at home and I felt rather lost without Margaret and I didn't want to lose Matthew or Alastair. Everything seemed magnificent in the darkness with the muffled sounds of King's Cross traffic below. I could hear Tom tossing and turning and I sensed that he too was thinking and wondering. It was a most peculiar sensation of unreality and uncertainty with one hand on safe conditions in Australia with everyone going about their lives and meeting their hour by hour problems. What was going to happen to us in Vietnam? How were we going to cope with the work and the climatic conditions, let alone the war itself?

The two men had requested a wake-up call and a bottle of champagne, but hotel staff forgot and they did not receive either the telephone call or the bubbly. In the rush to get to the airport, Beard left behind his large bottle of bismuth and opium, used to relieve his colitis. He ordered more at the pharmacy, but suddenly they were called aboard and he did not have time to collect the mixture.

Their hurried departure was due to uncertainty in Vietnam. Saigon was still under attack and the airport was coming under repeated heavy fire. This meant Qantas would make available to the army a charter plane to take the 186-strong complement of servicemen to Butterworth air base in Malaysia, after fuel stops in Darwin and Singapore. At Changi Airport in Singapore servicemen wore their uniform slacks, but changed to civilian shirts and tops to appease the 'neutral' Singapore Government, which wanted no part in the Vietnam War and did not want its nation to be seen as a staging camp for the enemies of the North Vietnamese regime. En route there were a couple of unscheduled stops. Qantas was awaiting clearance to land in the war zone as Saigon Airport was under fire. Eventually the aircraft was given permission to land. As the aircraft began its final approach Don noticed a distinct change of mood in the cabin of the aircraft. All eyes were trained on the territory below, scanning the streets and houses for signs of activity. Saigon appeared peaceful, the streets crammed with vehicles; there were no obvious signs of fighting apart from the occasional bombed-out building, patched-up mortar holes on the roads and a few wrecked planes.

Saigon: The airfield was a hive of activity with row upon row of planes parked alongside the runway – fighters, bombers, transports, spotters, helicopters and a few civilian planes like our own Qantas. Everything seemed mixed up with planes taking off, landing, taxiing into parking bays, refuelling, loading and unloading; the control tower must have been a frantic area. We were taken off our plane and got into a bus with a truck following and our gear piled high in the back. We drove past the air terminal to the other end of the strip, past a group of Australians waiting to board a plane about to fly home. Their shouts of 'you'll be sorry' and 'why come here?' didn't help our mood. Tom and I managed to identify our gear, except our rifles, which we never saw again. Losing one's personal weapon was a serious crime in the army. We clambered aboard a Hercules bound for Vung Tau.

'The shouts from the soldiers when we arrived echoed those from the Diggers of World War II. In 1942 when budding cartoonist Paul Rigby marched along Collins Street, Melbourne, towards Flinders Street Railway Station en route to the Middle East, men in uniform home on leave and holding their pints emerged from pubs along the route yelling, 'You'll be sorry you enlisted … you'll be sorry.'

Colonel Donald Beard arrived in Vietnam at a time when morale among the soldiers and medical staff at Vung Tau Field Ambulance in South Vietnam was at its saddest and lowest ebb. There in the wake of the horrific Tet Offensive he found the 8th Field Ambulance stretched to the limit. The Tet Offensive was a brilliant tactical strategy initiated by the North Vietnamese General Vo Nguyen Giap, who in January 1968 had staged a bold offensive on two fronts. The first was an attack on the US Marines' firebase at Khe Sanh. Simultaneously the regular North Vietnamese Army and the Viet Cong, involving more than 70,000 troops, staged coordinated attacks on South Vietnam's major cities and provincial capitals. This would present the Americans with a military dilemma. If they opted to defend Khe Sanh, they would be stretched to the limit when battles erupted all over the South. Giap had set the campaign's minimum and maximum objectives. At the very least, the Tet outbreak would force the halting of the aerial bombardment of North Vietnam and force the Americans into negotiations. But there was a chance the offensive could drive the Americans out of Vietnam altogether, opening up the path to liberation and unification.

There was fierce street fighting in Saigon where landmarks like the US Embassy and Presidential Palace were stormed. In the town of Hue 113,000 of the 145,000 inhabitants were left homeless. It was at this time that South Vietnam President Thieu told the allies that the systematic defoliation (the chemical spraying of vegetation that became known infamously as 'Agent

Captain Don Beard back from war in Korea.

Donald Beard at the age of three.

Donald's mother Alison (née Wright).

Medical studies in Adelaide.

Dr Roland Beard MC: Donald's uncle and inspiration.

The University CC opening bowler is seated front row, far left.

Adelaide Technical High School 1940 CC Eleven. Donald front row, far left.

Pitcher for the South Australian Baseball team, 1941, Don Beard stands tall, back row.

Captain Beard at the controls of a Wirraway, Korea, 1950.

Before the battle: a blanket, a beer and a book.

Wearing the jacket given him by a US soldier, Captain Beard braves the cold with Padre Joe Phillips and an Indian stretcher-bearer.

Captain Beard registers Korean patients at the 3rd RAR.

The Diggers dig into the slopes of the Kapyong Valley.

Preparing the 'Barbasol' magic frostbite cure.

PM Robert Menzies visits troops in Korea, 1951.

Captain Beard (at back) talks with captured North Korean troops with frostbite.

Captain Beard with members of the 60th Indian Field Ambulance, March 1951.

Major Donald Beard, Kure Military Hospital, 1951.

Captain Don Beard with good friends Hugh Douglas and Brian Cornish, Kure, Japan.

Colonel Beard in Vietnam, 1968.

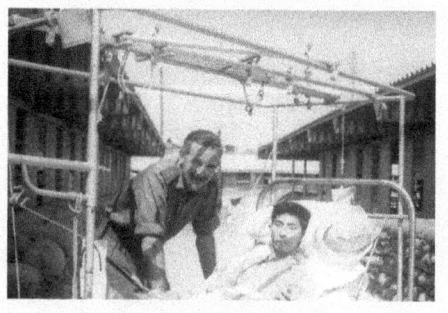

Colonel Don Beard with an injured Viet Cong soldier.

Colonel Donald Beard, 1st Australian Field Hospital, Vung Tau, Vietnam.

Don rests with medical assistants at 1st Australian Field Hospital, Vung Tau, Vietnam 1968, after a long day's work.

Two colonels in Vietnam: Tom Beare (left) and Don Beard, about to take a dip in the South China Sea.

Donald and Margaret meet the Indian Prime Minister Mrs Gandhi (Matthew stands tall at the back).

The two men who saved Doug Ring. Don Beard with journalist Des Colquhoun. (Richie Benaud is on the right).

Donald Bradman and Dr Beard meet the Indian cricketers at Adelaide Airport.

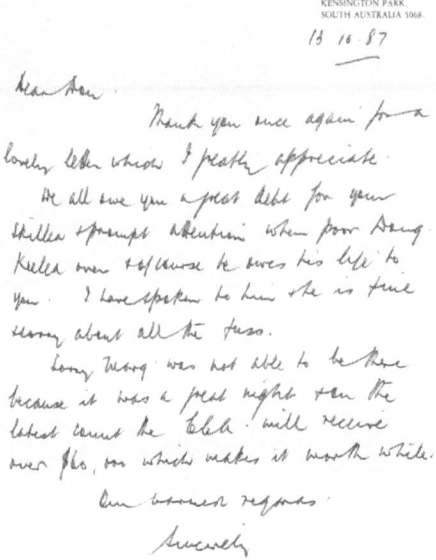

A letter from Sir Donald Bradman.

Don Beard is flanked by Indian batting legend Sunil Gavaskar and Don Bradman.

Bradman gives West Indian Richie Richardson some batting tips.

Dr Beard with Alan Jones at the launch of The Bradman Albums.

Dr Beard with West Indian cricketer Viv Richards.

Dr Beard with West Indian fast bowler Malcolm Marshall.

Dr Beard with Dennis Lillee.
Sturt cricket follower Michael Woolley looks on.

Don Beard with US actor Fess Parker.

Dr Beard unveils a portrait of his mentor
Sir Gordon Gordon-Taylor, Adelaide, 1960.

Australian fast bowler Jeff Thomson and wife Cheryl in the Beard family backyard.

England spinner Derek Underwood with fast bowler Don Beard.

Donald and Margaret Beard ... on their wedding day in 1962.

Don Beard as King Duncan, performing in the opera Macbeth.

Don Beard as Agamemnon in Strauss's opera Elektra.

The Willie Nelson disguise was so good Don wasn't allowed into the party.

A chance meeting in the SACA members' toilet: From left: Basil Sellers, Keith Miller and Don Beard.

Don Beard shakes hands with Group Captain Leonard Cheshire, leader of the legendary WWII RAF Squadron 617, the Dambusters.

Les Favell's testimonial match. From left: Donald Beard, Les Favell, Donald Bradman.

Harold Larwood's sympathy for Rick McCosker (with a broken jaw!) was limited. He opined to Dr Beard: ''E's got a bat, 'asn't 'e?'.

A proud moment for Donald's mother after he received an award at Keswick Army Barracks.

Don Beard at home with his two sons, Matthew (left) and Alastair.

Donald and Margaret Beard.

Not so long ago ... Donald and Margaret Beard run the City–Bay.

Don shares a drink with Yalumba Winery legend Wyndham Hill-Smith.

Don Beard with the SA Premier Dean Brown.

Dr Donald Beard at the time of his retirement from Modbury Hospital.

Orange') of South Vietnam was counter-productive because of the adverse affect it was having on the health of the general population.

Within minutes of landing at Vung Tau, Don and Tom were greeted by the acting CO of 8th Field Ambulance, Major Mick Boyle. Don noticed the US 36th Evacuation Hospital standing on the edge of the airstrip and thought it an odd place to put a hospital, although it 'was convenient in many ways'.

> Everything seemed peaceful except for the howl of planes and helicopters overhead. We came to 1 ALSG – Australian Logistic Support group – with HQ, service corps, engineers and workshops and, in the centre, 8th Field Ambulance.

Don and Tom were taken to their accommodation at Vung Tau – a long, low wood and iron hut, similar to the mess, subdivided by partitions into cubicles. The two newcomers thought it looked comfortable enough and it proved so. A long, narrow cot was Don's bed and in the corner was a solid table and chairs and a steel locker, all better facilities than he had envisioned. Having packed away his belongings Don discovered that his rifle was missing. Tom Beare, too, had mislaid his rifle. In the haste of getting off the tarmac at Saigon, both men's rifles, regular issue 7.62 mm SLRs, had disappeared. The army took a dim view of service personnel who lost their weapons and there was an inquiry. Don said an officer brushed off the incident with a brusque 'What can you expect from the medical corps'.

They enjoyed a 'bucket shower', dinner, a brief meeting then into bed. At 0715 hours on 5 March 1968 the work began. After breakfast Colonel Beard was taken on a round of surgical patients by Major Marshall Barr, anaesthetist and resuscitation officer. Don had heard good reports about Barr from many sources including Brian Cornish, who spoke highly of him. A total of 153 operations had been performed in the month before Don arrived.

> It took us a day to get around the unit and also to visit the rest and convalescent centre in Vung Tau, which was situated in a converted French villa. The R & C centre catered for troops on leave from the task force and about 30 patients from the 8th Field Ambulance waiting for shrapnel and gun shot wounds to heal sufficiently for them to return to their units or, if they are too bad, to be evacuated to Australia.

That afternoon Don began operating. He followed 'normal procedure' for managing war wounds. First the surgeon excises all tissue damaged by the blast, bullet or shell fragment. The wound is left open and a pressure bandage is applied over which is placed a plaster cast. About five days later – infection having been controlled by large doses of penicillin – the patient is re-anaethetised and the wound inspected. There may be a need to remove further dead tissue, but if it is found to be clean it may be closed, either by suture or skin graft. He found much of his time in the theatre performing exploratory operations on soldiers suffering a range of conditions, from abdominal wounds to chest and brain injuries. By 1740 hours Colonel Beard felt he had done well. He had dinner at 1900 hours and was looking forward to a cold beer when a 'dustoff' arrived with a wounded Viet Cong prisoner aboard. He had been shot through the thigh and had a compound fracture of the femur.

> There was a huge gaping hole where the bullet had come out. The entrance wound is a small puncture wound, but as the bullet tears through the tissues, its energy is dissipated sideways and this is what tears the muscles and other soft tissues. If it hits the bone, then all the fragments do their damage, so the exit wound gapes widely. The greater the velocity of the bullet, the greater the force to be dissipated and therefore the greater the damage. Unless all the dead and bruised bone is removed and if infection occurs in the deep pockets of limbs, life may be lost. It was an ironical twist of fate to come so far to help the Australian boys and my first casualty was a Viet Cong.

Instinctively Colonel Beard came to the aid of an injured man, and he made it perfectly clear that his team would treat all of the injured equally – friend or foe. It was a timely lesson for many of the medical team who had become desensitised to the trauma of conflict. His anaesthetist, Major Marshall Barr, later admitted that he had begun to slide 'towards brutishness' in a medical ward which he said had become 'dehumanised' by the war.

A veteran of spending time as a medical officer with the occupying forces in Japan and later running the surgical wing, Colonel Beard swiftly restored order and calm to the 1st Australian Field Hospital at Vung Tau. He saw that the situation was hurtling towards the abyss and he quickly restored humanity to a hospital in danger of losing its way. The number of wounded was almost overwhelming and Beard and his team ended the day exhausted, happy to have saved every one of the badly injured and saddened by the severe disability in young men, whose courage and resolve they would eternally admire.

While General Giap gloated over his shock tactics of the Tet Offensive thrusting a spear deep into the political heart of the United States and its allies, Colonel Beard and his medical team were under great pressure at Vung Tau Base. Don quickly came to dread the sound of the choppers as they flew in never-ending sorties to return the injured to base. On the third day of his arrival at Vung Tau, Colonel Beard and his team operated on two New Zealand soldiers who had stood on a mine. One soldier had his leg blown off and the other leg had to be amputated.

The other boy had suffered extensive shrapnel wounds to his stomach, of which more than half a metre of lacerated bowel needed to be removed. The Beard medical team were amazed that either youngster survived. But worse was to come.

The team often worked through the day and night. A decent night's sleep was a rarity, but Colonel Beard often found time to slip away after the long hours of surgery to have a cold beer with officers at the Peter Badcoe Club, a bar named in honour of Major Peter Badcoe, VC, a fellow pupil of Don's at Adelaide Technical High School. Young, tall and angular with 'hollow legs', Don was said to have been able to down a beer faster than the 1950 Melbourne Cup winner Comic Court could gallop a dozen yards. No doubt he taught the men all about a 'boat race', the beer game he championed all those years ago as a student at Adelaide University. During a visit to Woodside Army Barracks in 1965, Colonel Beard found himself in a 'boat race' and among his teammates were Federal Minister of the Army, Malcolm Fraser, the SA Police Commissioner Harold Salisbury, the commander of Keswick Army Barracks, and the CO of 3rd RAR stationed at Woodside, training for a tour of Vietnam. Each team had a crew of eight, plus a cox. They sat on the floor, legs entwined, facing their opponents, each man with a pint of 'black velvet' (champagne and stout) beside him. 'The race starts with the strokes downing their pints, replacing the empty glass until the team that downs the pints first, without spilling a drop, claims victory.'

After the downing of the pints and winning the boat race, unlike the police commissioner, the CO of Keswick Barracks and Malcolm Fraser, who had their own driver, Don had to drive himself the 60 kilometres home to Adelaide. 'Harold Salisbury had the solution. We drove in convoy, Salisbury in front, me in the middle and the Keswick commander at the rear, and I was escorted home safely,' he said.

On the fourth day of his arrival at the base in Vietnam, Colonel Beard came to the side of a critically wounded New Zealander who had trodden on a mine in the Long Binh hills. Don recalled: 'I thought he was dead, both of his legs were blown to pieces. He had stopped bleeding because he had virtually no blood left in his body.' Colonel Beard could not detect a pulse or any blood pressure, but the man was breathing 'with an occasional gasp'. Private Roger Haenga was given some five pints of blood within a 20-minute period. Colonel Beard then felt a pulse for the first time. When the dressings were removed his wounds even shocked the doctor who had seen horrific injuries, both in the theatre of war and road accident victims. 'The man's injuries were dreadful. The mine had exploded behind him and blown off the backs of both legs from the feet to the buttocks. Both of his legs were badly broken and three inches of sciatic nerve had been shot away in one leg. Although it was an agonising decision to have to make as he looked at the 21-year-old boy on the table, Colonel Beard had no option but to amputate. He cut through the site of the fracture in the lower femur and was able to close the stump with a flap of skin from the undamaged shin. He then had to cut away the dead skin. 'It bled furiously and we had to pump blood in as fast as we could,' he said.

During the long operation there were occasions when the medical team thought they had lost the soldier. After six-hours and a 30-pint blood transfusion, the young Maori soldier was still alive. Colonel Beard and his team were exhausted and the theatre was in disarray, the floor, tables and stretchers a messy mix of blood, plaster, dead tissue, transfusion packs and blood-soaked linen. As the young man slept, the medical team grabbed some much-earned sleep. At 3 am a medical orderly shone a torch in the patient's face. He quickly alerted the doctors. Private Haenga's wounds were bleeding profusely and his pulse was 'fading fast'. Doctor Beard and his team were back at the young man's side.

'My heart sank,' he said, 'but we were back to do the best we could for the youngster. I cut off the plasters and one by one clipped and tied off hundreds of small bleeding points.' Such vessels would normally stop bleeding of their own accord, but the patient had precious little of his own blood to clot.

Eventually the medical team got on top of the crisis and most of the bleeding stopped. The team had done its best. Private Haenga awoke at 8 am. He had undergone 13 hours of surgery, more than nine hours of them under anaesthetic. There was a happy ending. The young man, after a major skin graft, was repatriated home to New Zealand where he was reunited with his fiancée. Dr Beard was elated about the outcome, 'between us (the medical team) we won the fight'. In November 2012 the Doc again met up with Roger Haenga, who travelled from NZ to see him for counselling on post traumatic stress, a condition he had developed long after his experience in Vietnam.

Dr Beard and his team dealt with many victims of mine blasts. One day, Colonel Beard, clad only in his swimming trunks and thongs, rushed to the hospital tent to operate on five M16 mine blast victims. Two youngsters lay side by side almost unaware of the seriousness of their injuries as they chatted in a morphine-induced high.

'How y' goin', mate?' asked one soldier. 'How's the leg? Did you feel the mine click when you put your foot on it?'

'No,' he replied, 'but I felt a helluva bang when it went off. This is a great way to get home. Now we'll be back in time to see the start of the football …'

Colonel Beard recalled that the youngsters showed only gratitude and a fierce determination to overcome their disabilities. The youngster who had lost his leg said to the doctor, 'Do you have to notify Australia? My mum will only worry.'

He was eternally impressed by the raw courage of the Diggers. One day two soldiers were brought in – one a 20-year-old national serviceman, the other a 25-year-old regular army corporal. As they lay in triage, the national serviceman looked up at him, the only surgeon there at the time, and said, 'Sir, who are you going to operate on first? Take my corporal – you might be able to save his legs.' The national serviceman had already lost one leg. It was lying on a stretcher nearby. His other leg was virtually blown off.

'That young man proved to me how the national servicemen and the regular army Diggers got along. They worked together.'

The surgeon repaired the corporal's leg, but the other soldier – Victorian potato farmer John Richardson – lost his right leg and his left foot. Almost 40 years to the day he operated on that young man, Dr Beard was sitting in his office, a small room at the back of his home in Norwood, and looking out the window he instantly recognised the man walking up his driveway. He couldn't then recall the man's name, but he knew the face and he remembered how he worked so hard to save the young soldier's legs all those years ago in Vietnam. John Richardson had learnt to use his artificial legs. He had to quit potato farming and found success working in insurance, and after his release from hospital never missed a day's work. He was married with a son. His wife walked by his side. They sat in the doctor's leafy back garden and chatted over tea.

'I can't really explain my emotions when I set eyes on John, but it was extraordinary. You know he just turned up to thank me for saving his life. And when I spoke of how he asked me to "take my corporal" his wife wept. She had never heard that part of the story before.'

Throughout March the volume of injuries deluged Colonel Beard and his medical team. One day two Viet Cong patients – a boy and girl – were admitted. He learnt that the boy was a teenage soldier, an only child, who had just discovered that both his parents had been killed. The girl was also a Viet Cong soldier. In her attempt to surrender, a comrade shot her through the arm. She had married in January, but her husband was killed at Ba Ria during the Tet Offensive a few weeks later. She was pregnant. Doc Beard treated the pair and hoped that they might fall in love, but 'they left the hospital frightened and bewildered, afraid of what the future might hold for them'.

The medical team was always alert whenever they heard news, via a helicopter pilot's radio message, that heavy casualties were on their way. The pilot would say how many patients he was bringing in and the estimated time of arrival, but the medical team never knew the real extent of the soldiers' injuries. A waiting party met the chopper and the casualties were taken to one of six emergency triage areas, all of which were self-contained and each had its own medical team. The surgeon was not attached to an emergency team, so the Doc rushed about, assessing who was going to be the first patient into the operating theatre.

To an outsider it may have seemed chaotic but these people knew their business and treatment had to come mighty fast. An orderly would take details off the patient's dog tag, while another would cut off his battle garments and yet another would put in a drip. Each operating room contained two operating tables and there seemed an endless supply of badly wounded men being flown into base.

After Colonel Beard got to Vietnam in 1968 the First Field Ambulance's name was changed to the 1st Australian Field Hospital at Vung Tau. The medical team continued to be always on the go, for dustoffs seemed to arrive continuously. Whatever the time of day or night or however tired he was during his tour in Vietnam, Don wrote at least two pages of his A4-sized diary. Every day's diary entry was carbon-paper copied and posted to Margaret, back in Adelaide.

> Day 56 – April 28th: I was duty MO for the hospital today – on Sundays this means covering the whole hospital and the RAP unless there are dustoffs and the whole team is on. Normally in a hospital I wouldn't do duty MO, but as we have only five MOs for the whole hospital, everyone has to do his share. On Sundays this is quite arduous but it only happens every fifth week.
>
> Unfortunately I had some operating to do in the morning and I couldn't

go to church parade and by the time I'd finished operating, sick parade and ward round it was lunchtime. We had a concert party from Western Australia visiting the hospital at lunchtime and they put on a very good show in the wards. Afterwards they joined us for lunch, which we combined with the sergeants' mess. Then in the afternoon everyone went swimming, while I stayed behind to look after the hospital. I must say I was most envious.

The hospital was almost full and I was worried about beds if we had a big dustoff, so I arranged for transfer of 10 patients to the convalescent centre.

I was just getting down to do some writing when I got a message about a boy coming by ambulance from Vung Tau. It was the reverse of the normal road accident in which an army truck hits a Vietnamese swaying over the road on a bicycle or motor scooter. In this case two soldiers were walking along the edge of the road (there are few footpaths) and one was hit from behind by a Vietnamese riding a motorbike and suffered severe head injuries. He was still unconscious when he arrived and had obviously received a heavy knock.

I sewed up his scalp and luckily he gradually came good, although he was very irritable. So the Vietnamese are not the only road victims! I had a few more minor problems until 1700 when the beach party returned and then it was really on. I got one dustoff warning but this was soon followed by another and later another warning. The next seven hours until midnight were confused and hectic, with case after case. I spent most of the time in the theatre operating while the others were outside admitting and resuscitating. It is only yesterday since it happened but I can't remember the sequence of events nor all of the injuries. The worst of them was Private Maguire from C Company 1st RAR. He told me that he'd been the leading scout of a patrol that was going to set up a night ambush in the area where the boys had been hit yesterday. But on their way up they were ambushed themselves – or at least they picked off Private Maguire.

He said he was spun around by the first bullet, which hit him in the hip, and he couldn't turn to fire back. He then remembers lying on the ground while automatic weapon fire hit the dirt all around him. But he said the 'VC' was a terrible shot because it took a long burst of fire before he was hit again in the arm and he was sure he'd be alright. But he got one more hit in the thigh, which fractured the femur – then the rest of the patrol fought off the VC and called in a chopper. Can you imagine lying on the ground being shot at?

On 13 May 1968, the Battle of Fire Support Bases (FSB) Coral and Balmoral began. The enemy overran a platoon of 1st RAR and captured one of 102nd

Field Battery's gun pits. The base was cleared with the help of helicopter gunships, but there was a second ferocious attack two days later resulting in 15 Australians being killed and 56 wounded. Enemy losses exceeded 100 dead.

Many of the allied soldiers suffered horrible wounds. Colonel Beard noted in his diary that Private Forbes was moving along the perimeter defence of fire support when the VC attacked in great numbers.

The Australian mortars were landing just in front of the allied position. Inevitably a mortar hit fell short and Private Forbes, the only casualty, received wounds to the leg and arms. Sergeant Douglas was in a pit when a rocket burst in a box of grenades. It caught fire and Sgt Douglas picked it up to throw it out. It exploded as he was about to scramble back to the pit. He fell with shrapnel in his legs, chest and arms and then he caught a VC machine-gun blast to the stomach. He survived.

> Gunner Hundt was out on patrol at 0330 on 13 May 1968 when the section was ambushed and he received a burst of machine-gun fire in his belly. He said he felt as if he had been kicked; he didn't have a lot of pain but he felt terribly weak in the legs. He had fallen into a drain and as he looked up at the stars he said his thoughts went straight to home to the girl he was going to marry when he completed his National Service. He said he was more worried about her than himself. The section went on fighting off the VC, but the sergeant fell back to Hundt in the drain and with his help he half crawled and was half dragged back into fire support base where they had to wait nearly four hours before a 'dustoff' could pick him up. All the time he could feel himself getting weaker and weaker and he just wanted to quietly go to sleep. But the sergeant stayed with him and talked him into staying alive and held him tightly in his arms for hour after hour, each one seeming interminable to them both. At last the chopper came in and he knew he was going to be alright. His small and large bowel had been perforated 11 times and also his bladder.

There was no doubt Gunner Hundt survived because of the actions of his sergeant. He lost consciousness and it was obvious he was bleeding internally. His sergeant held him to his chest and made him breathe and every time the soldier started to drift off the sergeant gave him another big hug.

> It was a wonderful example of a sergeant and his injured soldier. I operated on him and opened his chest and found that the lung had been damaged. It was bleeding and I had to cut out part of the lung because it was damaged beyond repair and I then explored down through the chest and my finger

kept going and I realised that it had gone through the diaphragm and when I took it out there were lumps of spleen. He was bleeding mainly from that area. Then I had to open his abdomen and remove his spleen.

Afterwards Gunner Hundt told Don about his ordeal during the night in the jungle when the sergeant continually shouted at him, 'Don't die, you're not going to die.'

During the Vietnam War there were many unusual incidents, like what happened in May 1968 when Sergeant Credlin's platoon flushed a number of Viet Cong fighters out of a tunnel. Among them were the head of a VC assassination squad and a fighter in possession of important intelligence documents. As Sgt Credlin and his men were leading their prisoners down a track they heard a thundering roar behind them and before they had time to jump clear a raging water buffalo charged through the platoon, tossing Sgt Credlin in the air, leaving him with nasty lacerations, and allowing the Viet Cong prisoners to escape into the jungle.

Around the time Don arrived in Vietnam, 5 Platoon B Company 2nd RAR was investigating the ruins of a temple in the Long Hai Hills. A sapper triggered a booby trap, killing himself and wounding 13 other soldiers. The Viet Cong were masters in setting traps and during the night they'd dig up land mines set by the Australians, re-set them and plant them in areas of danger to the allies. Colonel Beard went to the Long Hai Hills on a few occasions and said it was imperative that you stuck to the 'safe' paths, which were often shown by a string of toilet paper. Australian anti-mine policy, established in 1965 by 1st RAR's commander Lt Col. Lou Blumfield stated 'go slowly and carefully; avoid tracks and avoid returning along the same route'.

The Viet Cong's ingenuity in the field was ever apparent. In 1966 American intelligence staff estimated that the VC recovered 27,000 tons of unexploded ordnance, much of which they re-used that same year, a year in which 1000 US servicemen died from VC booby traps. The Long Hai Hills proved a haven for the Viet Cong. They usually had more than 1000 men hidden underground in a catacomb of tunnels, equipped with an amazing cache of ammunition, equipment and medical aid facilities. The tunnels were also littered by booby traps. And despite frequent air strikes by the giant US B52 bombers and attacks by Australian ground troops, the Viet Cong always seemed to know when an attack was on: they dispersed and returned to fight another day.

When Australian troops were first deployed in Vietnam their weapon of choice was the Owen submachine gun, highly regarded in World War II for its toughness, ease of operation and dependability. Its simple interior design meant that it rarely jammed, however, its effective range was only 100 metres. After 1965 the weapon of choice was the American M16. The Viet Cong's weapon of choice was the Kalashnikov AK-47, one of the most successful weapons ever produced. It remains in use in many armies, especially in the Third World. The Viet Cong used the AK-47 and its Chinese copy – the Chicom Type 56. As with the American M16, the AK-47 has a range of 300 metres. Colonel Beard discovered that the greater velocity of bullets fired from these weapons created huge damage to a soldier's body.

Don wrote in his diary of 18 May 1968 – his 76th day in Vietnam – of the operation list for that morning.

Name	Unit	Age	Operation
Private Prest	1 RAR	25	DPC (Delayed primary closure) mortar wounds – legs
Corporal Griffiths	1 RAR	19	DPC rocket wounds – legs
L/Corporal McCartney	1 RAR	23	Exploration both elbow joints
Private Hobley	1 RAR	21	DPC – right thigh
Private Hands	1 RAR	21	DPC – right shoulder and chest
Private Mead	1 RAR	21	DPC – both arms, both legs
Private Fairweather	1 RAR	23	DPC – left leg
Private Fulton	1 RAR	19	DPC – chest, back, abdomen

It is a formidable list from one unit in one morning and there are many more to come. They are only boys, but in many ways are now men full of responsibility. Most of them have only been in Vietnam for a month. Three of them will return to Australia, as it will be more than 30 days before they are fit for full duty. The 19, 23 and 25 year olds are Regulars and the 21 year olds are National Servicemen, not that there is any distinction.

During the Korean War, Lt Digger James had been on the battlefront for a couple of weeks when his platoon was ambushed and he jumped into a ditch straight on top of a mine. He lost one leg and part of the other, but stayed where he was to give his mates covering fire for their retreat. They returned later with a stretcher to evacuate him. His courage under fire earned him the Military Cross.

'It was such a short time since he had left Duntroon Military College and his fiancée, who farewelled a fit young man from the Australian airport,' Don said. Now Digger was disabled and he lamented what he might do for a career. He volunteered for the army, but as Don, who had him under his wing, pointed out, 'What army would want a no-legged recruit?' But Digger convinced the army that he could do recruit examinations in Australia and he got his chance to prove his worth in Vietnam when there was a terrible shortage of medical officers.

'Digger convinced the army that he could work at the field ambulance, but he said he was having trouble climbing the sandhill up from the treatment section to his tent and would be better on the hard ground at Nui Dat – Task Force HQ. There he did his best work – receiving casualties from the battalions and preparing them for evacuation to me for surgery. I would receive them well treated and well documented.

'I kept sending complimentary reports about him to Australia. At one stage he accompanied a casualty to me and I asked him to stay the night in my hut. While he was asleep I cleaned his boots (and legs) and leant them against the side of the hut. Next morning he searched for his legs under his stretcher – but there were none; he had to crawl on hands and knees to recover them.'

Don always followed Digger's career with great interest and noted that after his return to Australia where he received several appointments and promotions he finally became Major General James, the Director General of Medical Services.

'I was still a colonel. Digger continued his good work, including supporting the Medical Corps against a barrage of generals because of his days as an infantry officer in Korea. He also became President of the RSL and led the Anzac Day march in Canberra. What a soldier and always a friend!' Major General W.B. James, AC, MC, lives in Queensland, and is still active in leading the Anzac Day march in Brisbane. He wrote the foreword for this book.

In 2009, Warrant Officer Bob Thompson told of his time in Vietnam and his introduction to Colonel Donald Beard. 'It was early May 1968, or thereabouts. I was busy inspecting the weapons of 3rd RAR when a driver from 1 Task Force HQ told me I was wanted immediately at the hospital at Vung Tau and a chopper was waiting to take me there.

'We drove over the dustoff pad where I joined two soldiers. The Huey was already winding up as we arrived and we hopped aboard. An orderly met us at the hospital pads and escorted us into casualty. He asked us to show him our dog tags. The penny dropped. We were to give blood. He told us that there was an operation in progress and blood was required straight away to save a soldier's leg.

'About half an hour later a doctor appeared in hat and gown with blood splattered down the front. He introduced himself as Donald Beard and explained that to save the soldier's leg he had to have more blood and to achieve this we would be woozy and would have to lie on our backs and have our legs tied up to the rail in the passageway.

'Soon there was six of us, all with A2 blood, lying in the passageway drinking as much as we could. It looked like a live butcher's shop, with us strung up by the feet. Eventually Colonel Beard reappeared and one of the blokes asked if he needed more blood, to which he said no, but he said our giving of blood had saved the soldier's leg.'

A week later he sent word to WO Thompson confirming the man's leg had been saved and that he had been invited to lunch at the R&R centre at Vung Tau on the Sunday. WO Thompson could not make the lunch, however, he did learn that Colonel Beard often hosted lunch for the men who gave blood and usually paid for it himself.

Don devoted more than three months in the hell that was Vietnam in 1968, from March to June. It was tough going for even those doctors with experience working in war zones. He was not able to devote more time in Vietnam because his surgical practice had almost disappeared and had to be rebuilt. Four days before he was due to leave Vietnam and return home, he wrote to his beloved Margaret.

Australian Military Forces
Saturday 1/6/68

My darling,

I don't know where I am – the casualties are coming in so quickly. I don't know where to put them and when I am going to deal with them. I don't think I've been so busy since I've been here. And on top of everything I just heard that I have to leave on Tuesday – and I'll be operating until Monday night even if I don't get any more. I don't know where it's going to end, nor how I'm going to cope. I only hope I don't make any mistakes. I've nearly had it!

I love you
Don

Two days later – Day 92 – another diary note:

> A busy morning of operating, organising the Medivac and trying to begin to clean up the wards and documentation for the changeover. And just when the Medivac had gone and I thought I could get some of my Army report done some more casualties arrived including Dick Lippett, RMO 3rd RAR, who had about 20 grenade wounds, mostly in his legs and mostly superficial, but also the blast had damaged his eardrum, so he will have to be Medivac'd to Australia. He'd done his share!

A few days later Colonel Beard was standing on the Vung Tau airstrip waiting to board the giant Hercules aircraft that would take him home. He stood in the sun as he watched the outgoing cargo of all manner of mechanical equipment being transported to Australia: crates of gear, engines, mailbags, and then eight sealed aluminium trunks containing the bodies of the men who had been killed that week.

> I had known two of them – warrant officers who had been in training teams at Da Nang, attached to Vietnamese units. It was sad seeing the seven foot long boxes being loaded on – not done this time by fork lift, but gently lifted on by hand. And then even sadder were the last boxes loaded – labelled simply: 'Declared effects of …'
>
> It made me feel in a way that I didn't deserve to be going home with them – they had given their lives and I had given only three months, I thought of the different receptions for our respective homecomings – the two warrant officers were in their late thirties and no doubt had teenage families who would need them. And the other boys were 21-year-olds – with parents and girlfriends and perhaps young wives who had only a couple of days ago received the news of their death. I believe it would be preferable for a soldier killed in action to be 'buried in action' in a war cemetery. There would be a finality about this and it would save a lot of further distress reactivated by a military funeral a week later at home.

The Hercules flew to Butterworth base in Malaysia where Don had two unscheduled days at the RAAF mess before the plane flew on to Australia. There was a stopover in Darwin then a flight to Sydney. All eyes were searching out of the windows, but Colonel Beard's thoughts turned to Vung Tau, and how they were coping at 1st Australian Field Hospital.

They landed at Richmond Air Base and a young gunner lieutenant informed Colonel Beard that a staff car was on its way to take him to Mascot for the 1800 plane to Adelaide. After 40 minutes it was obvious the staff car was not going to arrive, so Don hitched a ride on the only available transport heading for Sydney – an army truck, which was carrying all the coffins of the men killed in Vietnam. Never so grateful for his rank, he hopped into the cabin next to the driver while the others got in the back of the truck and had to sit in the dark on top of the coffins. After a flurry of phone calls, Margaret got confirmation that Don was arriving that night.

> I had gone away thinking that I was making a sacrifice and a contribution. I returned feeling very humble and privileged to have played a part in the care of the magnificent young Australian soldiers and to be a member of a unit whose standard was so high that I had to struggle to live up to it. It will be a period of my life that will remain indelible!

Don Beard is inextricably linked to many surgeons, officers and soldiers who worked and fought in the Vietnam War. One of his closest friends is Colonel Peter Byrne, whom he first met when Don was a surgical tutor at the Royal Adelaide Hospital.

'It was late 1962. I was a third year medical student,' Colonel Byrne recalled. 'Then Don went to the Queen Elizabeth Hospital as a consultant surgeon for some years. Later, in the early 1970s, he moved to Modbury Hospital, where, as head of surgery, he established the surgical services. I worked for him for 18 months. He was a superb boss, tough but fair and a stickler for detail. He taught me a lot. Mainly, he taught me attention to fine detail, compassion concerning patients, and communication. He brooked no nonsense. I did one or two silly things. I made some facetious comments about him behind his back not knowing that he could hear and I was quickly brought back under control in a disciplinary manner. Also at that time he was my military boss – the Army's Deputy Director of Medical Services at Keswick Barracks and I was a part-time medical staff officer. Colonel Beard was a very good military boss as well.'

In August 1969, Major Peter Byrne began a 13-month tour of duty in Vietnam. He had returned to Australia from the UK at short notice. Although he had an infantry CMF background, Byrne, as was required with all army personnel, had to be tested for weapons proficiency. He smiled wryly but would not comment when I alerted him to the fact that both Colonel Don Beard and Colonel Tom Beare lost their weapons upon arrival in Saigon in 1968. Major Byrne served as DADMS AustForce Vietnam for six months, half of which as the only Australian or NZ doctor in Saigon.

'To my very good fortune I was co-opted by the Australian Army Training

Team Vietnam while in Saigon. It was a unique unit of 200 specialists charged with training and advising the South Vietnamese Army and working closely with a range of units including the US Army, the CIA and a variety of territorial forces including the Montagnard tribesmen in the central highlands fighting the North Vietnamese and Viet Cong,' he recalled.

There were four Victoria Crosses awarded to Australians in the Vietnam War and all of them were members of the AATTV. Major Peter Badcoe and Warrant Officer Kevin Wheatley were awarded the VC posthumously. The other VCs were awarded to Warrant Officer Ray Simpson and Warrant Officer Keith Payne.

'I acted as medical advisor to AATTV on a part-time basis and was sent up north to 1 Corps on several occasions,' he continued. 'They gave me an ArmaLite rifle and put me into jeeps or helicopters to visit fire support bases. I had to examine warrant officers who had been on operations for extended periods. My job was to help physically and also, on occasions, to assess their mental health.'

In September 1969, Major Byrne was ordered to find and (medically) assess Warrant Officer Keith Payne, VC, in Da Nang. WO Payne had served with Mike Force in 2 Corps mountain areas. It was not unknown for the unwary to be confronted in the bush by an array of intimidating creatures including elephants, tigers, wild pigs, monkeys, bears, buffalo, deer, antelope, even freshwater crocodiles.

The bush teemed with insects, especially mosquitoes, spiders, scorpions and snakes, such as the small but deadly krait and members of the cobra family, including one type that spat or squirted venom at its prey. If a soldier was hit in the face by this venom it could possibly blind him. WO Payne was awarded the VC in May 1969 for saving more than 40 of his men when fighting for the 212th Company 1st Mobile Strike Force, which came under heavy mortar, rocket and machine-gun fire from the North Vietnamese regular army. WO Payne was leading the Montagnards and they panicked under fire, so he took on dozens of the enemy by charging at them, all the while firing his rifle and throwing grenades. Later he rescued more than 40 who had been trapped behind enemy lines. He was wounded in the hands, upper arm and hip by shrapnel from mortar and rocket fire.

'I had written orders from CO AATTV Lieutenant Colonel Russell Lloyd. Payne was working under considerable difficulty,' Byrne said. 'His behaviour was, according to those at AATTV regional base in Da Nang, out of character. When I met him and showed him my written orders for him to be examined medically in detail, he was not happy. When the diagnosis was made – he was suffering from peptic ulceration – he was, to put it mildly, more than a little cranky, especially when told he was returning at once to Australia for treatment.'

In early 1970 after a short time at 8th Field Ambulance Nui Dat, Peter Byrne was posted to the 1st Australian Field Hospital, Vung Tau, and ultimately served as second in command.

'The injuries from mine detonations was horrendous, ' he said. 'Australian troops laid US-made M16 'Jumping Jack' mines along a road – Route 44 – running south in Phuoc Tuy Province, east of the Long Hai Hills. The South Vietnamese Army did not guard it and at night Viet Cong women would detect the mines with their toes, make them safe and then lift them. The mines would be re-laid as booby traps throughout the province.

'Our infantry soldiers had little time to relax. If they were in Vietnam for a year, they could be in the bush up to nine or 10 months of that time. They lived in the knowledge that at any time they could be killed or severely injured.'

Vietnam had a significant impact on Don Beard and Peter Byrne. They share enormous respect for the Australian soldier and for the best people that the Americans offer in terms of soldiers and doctors.

'The American 45th dustoff company air medical evacuation teams had the utmost trust in the Australians and New Zealanders in the field. They knew that if an Aussie or New Zealand company wanted help then they would make the landing place as safe and secure as humanly possible. They trusted us more than some of their own men. Sometimes they would even collect casualties from non-secure areas.'

Peter Byrne worked with Don as medical officer of the South Australian Cricket Association for 15 years in the 1980s and early 1990s, and stayed on for a total of 19 years. In 1992 Colonel Peter Byrne was made a member of the Military Division of the Order of Australia.

He is only the second South Australian Army medical officer to receive this military honour from Vietnam. The first was Colonel Dr Donald Beard, in 1987.

More than 40 years after Don's Vietnam War experience, Don and Margaret's good friend Penny Smith took them to dinner in Melbourne. The scene: a Vietnamese restaurant in Victoria Street, Richmond.

'We arrived and sat down before a little old man, about Don's age, sidled up to the table with notepad and pen. Don asked the man where he was during the Vietnam War and he said he had been living in Da Nang. "Ah," said Don, "I was there too, at a military hospital. What were you doing during the war?"

'"I was a Viet Cong soldier," the man said proudly.

'Well, Marg and I were horrified. There was a long silence. We sat stunned, I guess guilty that we had placed poor Don in this situation.' Tears welled in Penny's eyes as she continued: 'Yet Don and the man talked at some length. Then something happened that I will never forget. Don stood. He was twice the height of the ex-Viet Cong soldier and the pair of them looked at one another. Their gaze was fixed on the other for what seemed an interminable time. Then to our utter amazement the two men embraced.'

Ten

War's Daily Battle

I am tired and sick of war. Its glory is all moonshine.
                    General Sherman, American War of Independence

Even when the guns fall silent the men in the field are fighting their own personal battles. A soldier in a battle zone has plenty to concern him: the enemy and all the obvious dangers which go hand in hand with combat; the weather, the heat or the cold, the chill wind or a blazing sun. Fear. Every mother who has ever farewelled a son off to war knows all about the obvious dangers, but she rarely gets an insight into war's daily battle to stay fit and clean on the front line.

Weather, of course, was a key component in prosecuting the Korean War. The temperature in winter often fell 40° below freezing. Everything froze, even feet in the men's boots. Any uphill action on an icy slope was a nightmare. In summer the heat was oppressive and the men and machines caused the dust to fly and become a constant menace. Medical supplies were uncertain and inadequate. Supplies came through the US and British commands.

Capt Beard was always with the men. He was in an infantry battalion and the medical officer is an integral part of the battalion. There were times when he moved around the mountains to find the men in their weapon pits: he had arrived to administer inoculations for Japanese encephalitis.

'There were other diseases that appeared on the men. Soldiers would come to me with bruises on their body, fever and urinary symptoms. They were suffering from haemorrhagic fever, a virus infection that had been brought down from the north, brought down by mice. This particular disease came just after the thaw.'

When Don Beard went to war in Korea it was one of the coldest and most severe winters on record. Freezing winds and driving snow added to the discomfort of fighting the North Koreans, backed by 300,000 Chinese soldiers. The ground froze solid, making the simple act of digging in on the slopes of the Kapyong Valley a nightmarish experience. Captain Donald

War's Daily Battle

Beard and his medical team did what they had to do; they adapted, as all soldiers in a war zone must adapt, in order to survive:

'I didn't change my clothes for two months,' he revealed. 'It was too cold to change anyway, but we had no facilities to wash and dry our clothes. There was no static medical facility as we were always on the move. So we had to live, fight and tend the sick and injured in the same clothes, day in, day out. Imagine fighting and working in a frozen war zone for two months without taking a shower or a bath, wearing the same clothes. Thankfully, there was a change of underwear and the absolute necessity of changing socks. The men would either discard their used underwear or place them in a bag, to be washed at the earliest convenience. Frostbite was a constant worry for everyone and it proved as much a threat to the men as an enemy bullet.

'Patrols would go out, particularly at night, to observe Chinese and North Korean troop movements,' he said. 'At times there was conflict and the odd casualty was brought by the stretcher-bearers into the RAP. Everything had iced over, even the snow, so at night you would sleep in a hole that was dug through the ice. You'd place your sleeping bag at the bottom of the hole.

'A medical problem – other than frostbite – that first winter in Korea, was pneumonia. I saw our men coughing blood into the snow and if I saw anyone with that problem he was sent straight to an American MASH with no argument for pneumonia could kill you – or at least ruin you for life if you did not get some penicillin, rest and warmth. I also got a touch of pneumonia and treated myself with antibiotics and eventually went to the MASH, about which the largely accurate book and the TV series were based.

Every day each soldier in the war zone was handed a shoebox-sized parcel of essentials called C Rations. The box comprised two tins of meat and vegetables, opened with a little key used to open a sardine can, a tin of sausages, preserved fruit, crackers (dried biscuits), a tin of sweet biscuits, a pack of 20 Camel or Lucky Strike cigarettes, and the mandatory roll of toilet paper. While on the move on the front line there was rarely a dug latrine, so the men found a quiet place in the snow. Dr Beard believes he contracted colitis by drinking contaminated snow after it had thawed.

'Drinking water was usually gained by heating a tin full of snow or ice with a small Bunsen burner. Jellied petroleum was used as fuel for the burner, although some of the unwary soldiers, especially the French Canadian Battalion, out of sheer ignorance, would tip the heated petroleum jelly into a handkerchief, squeeze the contents in their mouth and consume it. Some of these men went mad from the experience and others went blind. Every three weeks the men looked for their ration of a bottle of beer. It was a major prize for the men fighting in Korea.

'They'd grab their precious bottle and place it in one of the pair of socks they always wore close to their chest of a night to replace the ones they wore during their sleep, socks that would be sodden by morning. By daylight the beer would be sufficiently thawed to drink. A cold beer before breakfast: it was always a happy time.'

Often Captain Beard's RAP was a tent pitched in open ground; its position identified by a Red Cross flag strung to a post or a tree. The wounded were stretchered to him at the RAP, where he would provide more treatment, apply better or firmer dressings, stop bleeding, put splints on arms and legs, and tighten bandages round chest wounds. His job was always to fit them for evacuation. They'd be taken by jeep to the 60th Indian Field Ambulance. In Korea some of the wounded had to wait up to 12 hours before surgery. Most of the soldiers would not have washed or changed their clothes for weeks, so hygiene would have played a bigger, perhaps more critical part than in another theatre of war where the men had access to regular showers and a change of clothing. Soldiers often wore pyjamas under their battle gear, scarves and balaclavas, but they found they sweated profusely while trudging up snow-covered slopes. To add to their discomfort, the sweat froze under their clothing.

The people at home were sick of their men going off to foreign lands to fight. Korea was very much the 'forgotten war'. There was a vastly different set of circumstances for soldiers fighting in the Vietnam War. In Vung Tau there was a static field hospital and the soldiers' clothes were sent to a local Vietnamese laundry. When the men went on patrol in the jungle they carried a change of clothes and a ground sheet. All of their soiled underwear was placed in a bag and when they returned to base it was sent to the laundry. They slept on a ground sheet in the open, but always under a mosquito net.

In Korea the men couldn't wash or change their clothes because of the extreme cold, but in the sweltering heat of the jungle, soldiers could find some water in which to wash; a still pond or a stream. And after a couple of days in the bush they'd be back to the relative safety of base. But there were many other considerations for the men to be wary of in the jungle: the bush was teeming with snakes and a variety of creepy crawlies, plus there was a constant fear of booby traps; the Viet Cong were clever and ingenious in the way they created death traps from bamboo spikes and improvised time bombs and land mines.

War's Daily Battle

Nature sometimes causes fear in the bush. During the uprising in Rhodesian Bush War, cricketer and later Tasmanian politician Brian Davison was on patrol in the bush. He was some 20 metres from his mates when a group of 30 enemy soldiers stopped in a clearing near where he was crouched in the long grass. He kept low and when he looked left he saw the unmistakeable shape of a huge black mamba, one of Africa's deadliest snakes. He had to make a split-second decision. Would he shoot the snake, thus giving away his position and almost certain death, or would he hold his fire in the hope that the deadly reptile would simply slither away?

Black mambas are, by nature, fiercely aggressive and will strike at the slightest movement. Then Davison got a welcome reprieve. He noticed a second black mamba. For the reptiles it was love at first sight and while the snakes mated passionately, Davison kept his head down and waited for the enemy patrol to march away.

The war between Ian Smith's minority white-ruled Rhodesia, Robert Mugabe's Zimbabwe Africa National Union, and Joshua Nkomo's Zimbabwe Africa Peoples Union raged from 1964 to 1979. A few years after the Rhodesian War ended, Dr Beard saw Davison in another light. 'Brian (Davison) was playing for Tasmania on the Adelaide Oval and was hit on the head, suffering severe concussion,' he recalled. 'I admitted him to Wakefield Memorial Hospital where a scan revealed a fractured skull. I sought the aid of a neurosurgeon, but by the time the specialist arrived an hour later, Davison was not in his bed and nowhere to be found. He had called a taxi and returned to continue his innings and he saved Tasmania from defeat. A tough man, Brian Davison.'

In Vietnam, operations were done almost immediately; a strategy which saved many hundreds of lives. In fact, during the period Colonel Beard served in Vietnam, if a casualty arrived at his field hospital alive he survived.

Colonel Beard's daily battle in the war included making decisions on those who needed treatment immediately and those whose injuries were such that they could be treated later. 'The uncircumcised in the field were at risk,' he said, 'because in the bush there was no chance to take a shower and hygiene became a major concern.'

Each morning in Vietnam he rose at 6.30. After a shower under the canvas bag full of hot water, he would dress, then sit on a stool overlooking the South China Sea to gather his thoughts, a mental boost to the inevitable trials of the working day. 'They (the boys) used to bring me a brew, which comprised some tea, some coffee and something else.'

Where time permitted Don Beard and Tom Beare enjoyed a run along the beach then a swim in the South China Sea in their lunchtime break, but often they had ominous company in the surf. 'Sea snakes liked to swim alongside us,' Don laughed. 'They were probably deadly, but they didn't seem so to us, although it was a little unnerving when one brushed up against your body in the water.'

Having served on the battlefields of Korea and Vietnam, he has seen amazing advances in the care of the wounded soldier. In Korea it often took hours for a wounded man to be stretchered back to safety because of the weather and terrain. Helicopters were used in Korea, but sparingly and they were not the advanced machines they were by the time of the Vietnam War. He can remember just one of his casualties in Korea being evacuated by chopper. 'Today battles can be conducted from long distances. Casualties will be retrieved on the battlefield by robots and surgeons will be able to conduct operations at a safe place often miles behind the front line,' he observes.

'Helicopters can deliver casualties from the point of where they were wounded to the surgeon in less than half an hour – a far cry from the 12-hour carry through the snow in Korea in which I took part in 1951. Limbs can be salvaged by arterial grafts instead of needing amputation.'

Australians have been involved in many wars and they have provided our surgeons with a wealth of experience in caring for the wounded. Dr Beard predicts that technology will play an increasingly greater role in the transport and care of wounded soldiers on the battlefield. 'While the army will in future increasingly utilise robots in retrieving wounded on the battlefield and in undertaking surgical procedures, there will be a constant need for surgeons. Their numbers may be reduced slightly, but not significantly as a surgeon will always be needed to guide the surgical instruments.' As a general surgeon he could attend to any emergency. However, he is wary of today's 'over specialisation'.

'Once a surgeon could look after any injury, whereas today some specialists can only operate within their own field. There are surgeons brilliant in their field of specialisation, better than the old surgeons, but their expertise is limited. But one thing never changes. The basis for good military surgery remains with the medical officer who is devoted to the patient.' Remember the sergeant in Vietnam, who tightly held his wounded comrade, whose chest was riddled with bullets? 'Every time he collapsed, the sergeant shook him and held him tighter and wouldn't let him die.'

Dr Don Beard's involvement in Korea and Vietnam has brought him before the public on television and radio many times. With dwindling numbers, especially those who fought in Korea, he has become a spokesman for the veterans. Ever articulate, he always speaks with authority. The study of ancient history, wars gone by and the way the wounded on the battlefield have been cared for by medical personnel over time has provided him with a wealth of knowledge and a large slice of credibility.

Eleven

'The Don Bradman I knew'

I had many detractors in the 1934 touring party, a coterie led by (Alan) Kippax (who for a variety of reasons hated my guts and made it clear).
Letter from Don Bradman to Dr Donald Beard, 10 February 1986

A few months after Major Donald Beard began work as a medical officer with the British Occupation Force in Kure, Japan, that splendid English wordsmith R.C. Robertson-Glasgow's glowing tribute to Don Bradman appeared in the 1949 edition of *Wisden Cricketers' Almanack*.

With these memorable lines, Robertson-Glasgow used his pen like a literary version of the incomparable Bradman wielding the willow:

> Don Bradman will bat no more against England, and two contrary feelings dispute within us: relief, that our bowlers will no longer be oppressed by this phenomenon; regret, that a miracle has been removed from among us. So must ancient Italy have felt when she heard of the death of Hannibal.
> R.C. Robertson-Glasgow, *Wisden Cricketers' Almanack*

Great deeds evoke great words. And the deeds of great men influence others in many walks of life. Don Beard and Don Bradman got to know one another just after the end of World War II. Bradman was contemplating a return to international cricket and the rangy, University opening bowler Donald Beard was taking wickets in Adelaide grade cricket and intervarsity matches with such frequency that he believed he had an excellent chance to play for South Australia against the visiting England Eleven on Adelaide Oval.

However, to his great sorrow, he missed State selection. There are those who believed the selectors could not pick two fast bowlers with 'wristy' actions. In retrospect the State coach gave Don false hope, although one feels that if Bradman wanted him in the side he would have played. Arthur Richardson's position as State coach was virtually forced upon him when he took on the role in 1946. Money for the Richardson family had become intolerably tight after Arthur lost his life savings due to the criminal mishandling of unsecured creditors' funds by sharebroker Harry Hodgetts, the man who engineered Don Bradman's move from Sydney to Adelaide in 1934. Don Beard knew of Hodgetts' cricket connection and, as fate would have it, he met the disgraced sharebroker in 1948 soon after he was transferred from jail to the Royal Adelaide Hospital where the young house surgeon (intern) Donald Beard worked.

'Hodgetts was terminally ill,' he recalled. 'He had bowel cancer. Unfortunately his cancer was not identified in prison and by the time he was admitted to the RAH his condition was terminal.' Hodgetts died of bowel cancer on 4 October 1949. Beard knew of Hodgetts' leading role in luring Don Bradman from NSW to continue his cricket and business career in Adelaide. South Australia was keen to bolster its Sheffield Shield side's batting strength. Bradman was the main target, although Tasmania's talented right-hand batsman, Jack Badcock, was also seen to be a 'required player'.

Bradman and the NSW team arrived in Adelaide in time for its December match against South Australia, perfect timing for South Australian cricket administrators to strike. On Thursday 14 December 1933, Don Bradman met with four members of the South Australian Cricket Association's finance committee: Harry Hodgetts, Roy Blinman, Bernard Scrimgeour and Roy Middleton. The four outlined their wish for Bradman to move from Sydney to Adelaide.

Over the next few days, while SA set about the thrashing of NSW by 10 wickets, Clarrie Grimmett getting 5/107 in the NSW second innings, an extraordinary meeting of SACA's Ground and Finance Committee was held. The committee resolved 'that this association would be justified to substantially subsidise any remuneration he (Don Bradman) could otherwise obtain'. Scrimgeour suggested the figure should be 'up to £500 per annum', but SACA President Joe Travers disagreed. He believed Bradman should be offered a figure of £750 a year over a period of five years. Travers' motion was carried unanimously.

Hodgetts also won support to bring promising Tasmanian right-handed batsman Jack Badcock to Adelaide. He would be employed at Brown's Furniture Warehouse in Hindley Street at an annual salary of £338, half of which would be subsidised by SACA. After a career-best 325 for SA versus Victoria in Adelaide, Badcock made his Test debut in 1936 and was selected in the 1938 Australian tour of England. But he never managed to take his prolific scoring feats of State matches onto the Test arena. In seven Tests he scored just 160 runs at an average of 14.54.

For SA, Bradman was the biggest fish of them all and Hodgetts effectively hooked him by offering him a place in his sharebroking firm and a guaranteed £700 a year for five years. (SACA committed to paying Bradman an annual subsidy of £750. Even when Bradman was out of Australia he was guaranteed a minimum of £500 p.a.) Given that Australia was in the middle of the Great Depression, where thousands were on the breadline and jobs were tough, sometimes impossible to find, the SACA offer was almost too good to be true. He was guaranteed an annual sum of £1450 from two sources – the SACA's £750 and Harry Hodgetts & Company's £700 – for a minimum term of five years. It was an extraordinary offer given that the great leg-spinner Clarrie Grimmett had scrimped and scraped for years to raise £1775 to build his home in the leafy, near-city suburb of Firle in the summer of 1926–27.

House prices didn't increase during the Depression and Bradman, in the course of less than two years, could have bought and sold Grimmett, who was, by then, one of SA cricket's favourite sons. In Bradman's last match for NSW he hit 128 against Victoria. He then took his place in Bill Woodfull's 1934 Australian team to tour England. After failures at Trent Bridge (29 and 25); Lord's (36 and 13); Manchester (30), Bradman hit back with a brilliant 304 at Leeds; an innings which occupied 430 minutes batting time, and included two sixes and 43 fours. Bradman didn't, by choice, hit many sixes in his career. His simple philosophy was ' if you don't hit the ball in the air, you can't get caught'.

Right at the end of the tour, after the last Test had been played, Bradman fell seriously ill. He had been strangely off-colour throughout the tour, but this time his surgeon was concerned about the great batsman's condition. Before the tour Bradman was searching for a job in NSW. He couldn't land a decent position and a friend approached the NSW Cricket Association secretary, Harold Heydon, on his behalf informing him that Bradman might have to leave NSW and go to another State.

In a letter to Don Beard dated 18 February 1986, Bradman claimed that Heydon's reply was: 'He can't afford to leave NSW. The NSW Cricket Association has made him what he is.'

Such a remark to Bradman at any stage of his life was a veritable red rag to a bull. In an earlier letter to Don Beard, dated 10 February 1986, Bradman tells the story of this time. 'I accepted a contract with Harry Hodgetts which provided that I had to move to Adelaide to take up residency in SA in 1934, before I might have to leave for England, in order that I would be residentially qualified to play for SA on my return. In those days it was it was a three month qualification and if I returned in say October I would not be able to play for SA until the season was about over. Jessie and I agreed to this move with great reluctance because it meant a new home, new life, leaving behind all friends and relations to start in a business of which I was completely ignorant.

'We arrived in Adelaide and temporarily resided with the Hodgetts. We found ourselves in the middle of a bad heatwave. I felt so off-colour that I went to (Dr) "Papa" Hone, at my own expense, told him I did not feel I was well enough to go to England and asked for a complete examination, even though the Board doctors had previously passed me as okay.

'For two weeks I was never without a headache – day or night. I was listless and just felt wretched without being able to pinpoint the cause. Hone passed me as fit to go but ordered that I should not play in Tasmania, Perth or Colombo en route as I was very run down and needed a complete rest on the voyage. Later on I was told that privately (to medical colleagues) he expressed the apprehension that I might have been heading for a brain tumour. Thank God that didn't eventuate.

'Well I went to England under the helpful and friendly guidance of dear old Dr Roly Pope, our honorary medical officer. When we got to Colombo (where the team played without me) Pope asked me if I would go ashore with him. I said, "No, I don't feel up to it." However, he insisted and our first call was the G.O.H. Hotel where he ordered me to have an alcoholic drink – the first of my life. And so I merely survived until England, feeling wretched the whole time. When we selectors sat down to pick the first team v Worcester, I told Woodfull that I didn't feel up to playing and should be left out. He insisted that I should play because otherwise I would be seen to be unwell (as the newspaper scribes were claiming) and this would be a morale booster to England.

'Against my wishes I agreed and busted my boiler for the side in making a double century. When we sat down to pick the side for the second match against Leicester, I then told Woodfull I had drawn on all of my reserves at Worcester but now must have a break. Not only did he refuse my plea – he insisted I play and captain the side so that HE could have a rest. I was outvoted and played, but from then on had a disastrous run of failures, only one century in 19 innings. I just wasn't fit to play. I had many detractors in the 1934 touring party, a coterie led by (Alan) Kippax (who for a variety of reasons hated my guts and made it clear). In the midst of my gloom, shortly before the Fourth Test, a "friend" in the party confided in me that certain team members were gloating over my misfortunes and failures. That goaded me into making a special final attempt to overcome my mental and physical problems. The record shows that from that moment of resolution I made 1144 runs at an average of 163. Fortune came to my aid in that I so badly injured a leg in the Fourth Test that I didn't play another first-class match until the Fifth Test. But when the last match finished I was at the end of the road.'

For the statistically minded, Bradman hit 304 at Leeds, then 244 and 77 in the Fifth Test at The Oval. Despite his poor health Bradman helped Bill Ponsford (266) to score 451 runs in 316 minutes for the second wicket in the Australian first innings.

Bradman continues his story of life after the Fifth Test in his letter to Don Beard of 10 February 1986. 'On returning to London I felt exhausted, nauseated, had constant pain in the stomach region, headaches, little appetite and called the team physician in London, Dr John Robert Lee. He examined me but made no diagnosis. Later he confessed to having gone for a long motor drive into the country just to try and decide what was the matter. On his return he brought along Sir Douglas Shields, the eminent Australian surgeon, who had a hospital in Park Lane. In very little time Shields gave his verdict and I was operated on next day. Dramatic newspaper headlines aroused the nation but I don't think I was ever really in serious danger of dying from appendicitis.

'Shields was astute enough to realise what all the years of torment had done to my constitution, as distinct from the local infection. He kept me in hospital for five weeks then arranged for Jessie and me to take life quietly in England until catching the boat to Australia in January. On returning to Australia I went to stay at my father-in-law's farm in Mittagong for three months to try and build up my strength. I eventually returned to Adelaide on Anzac Day 1935 to start my new job but on Shields' advice I did not go to South Africa. The Board wanted me to go as captain but I declined and that is how (Vic) Richardson got the job. Had I gone he would not have been in the team. That I overcame the mental and physical hurdles was a great triumph for Sir Douglas Shields who will always remain in my eyes a wonderful surgeon and psychologist.

'By carefully following Shields' advice I was enabled to return to the Test arena in 1936/7, albeit at a much lower level of efficiency than pre-1932, but with a physical and mental maturity that enabled me to survive. Meantime I personally thank you for the long and valuable service you have rendered to cricket in an honorary capacity. Such service shines like a beacon light in an age when overpaid players are being spoilt beyond belief.'

At the height of the Bradman health crisis in England some of his teammates and associates were taking a decidedly light-hearted view. Teammate Bill O'Reilly was dining with former Test spinner Arthur Mailey and two leading Fleet Street journalists when Mailey, at his mischievous best, put forward the proposition: 'How would the British press react were Bradman to pass away on the same day as the Prince of Wales, next in line to the throne of England?' After lengthy discussion the four men concluded that the front pages would have to be split down the middle, 'Such,' O'Reilly mused, 'was the fame of Bradman in England in 1934.'

Bradman, of course, survived. A nationwide collection was held throughout Australia to help fund Jessie Bradman's rushed trip from Australia to England to be beside her husband. Legendary Australian aviator Sir Charles Kingsford-Smith had offered to fly Jessie to London, but in the end she embarked from Fremantle on P&O's *Maloja*, arriving three days after Don had been released from hospital. He convalesced in London, Switzerland and on the Riviera before going to his father-in-law's farm at Mittagong.

Jessie and Don finally got to Adelaide where Bradman took up his post at Harry Hodgetts' sharebroking house. Bradman did not play a match in 1934–35 and, of course, he had made himself unavailable to tour South Africa with the Australian team in the summer of 1935–36. Instead he stayed in Adelaide and played Sheffield Shield cricket. In his first match for SA against NSW, Bradman hit 117 against his old State. Badcock scored 150 and SA won by an innings and five runs. Bradman's South Australia won the Sheffield Shield and next summer he was appointed Australian captain for the Ashes series against England. He was enjoying his role as a stockbroker with Harry Hodgetts' firm and his batting was a good as ever.

In the late 1930s Donald Beard knew Bradman from afar, sometimes catching a close-up glimpse when he saw the champion stride to the crease. There was teenager Donald Beard, Haigh's chocolates and chewing gum vendor, at cricket matches played on Adelaide Oval watching Bradman in full flight. A job at the cricket was the only way for Don to get into the ground to watch play. Bradman, the batsman, was always on a mission.

Young Don Beard would study Bradman's walk to the wicket, a journey which began at the top of the George Giffen Stand, that splendid colonial back-drop, now lost to the ages in a major Adelaide Oval facelift, continued down the steps and on to the concrete concourse before he trod with those brilliant, dancing feet onto the green sward basking under a searing summer sun. Glorious Adelaide Oval: 100 in the shade with Bradman 200 in the middle. A few years down the track, as Don Beard was working his way towards gaining a medical degree at the University of Adelaide, the community learnt of a looming cricket crisis via the Saturday *Advertiser* news hoarding which read: 'Hodgetts Gone'.

Harry Hodgetts, a stalwart of cricket and society at the highest level, the man who brought Bradman to Adelaide, was in dire trouble. He had bought a seat on the Adelaide Stock Exchange in 1917. Four years later he established H.W. Hodgetts & Co and he flourished. In the wake of a slump in earnings in the early part of the Depression years, Hodgetts' business improved. Britain abandoned the gold standard in 1931 and that one strategic move helped in Adelaide's share-trading revival. While Bradman struggled with ill-health and poor batting form in the early part of the 1934 tour of England, back in Adelaide Hodgetts' fortunes soared. More than £2 million passed through his books in that year. He was then a top cricket administrator, a member of both SACA and The Australian Cricket Board of Control for International Cricket. It was the year of his greatest financial success and his greatest cricketing administrative coup, signing up Don Bradman. But losses in a number of ventures and failure over speculation in wheat futures hit Hodgetts hard. In 1941 there were more financial concerns. He had underwritten the float of Hotel Darwin Ltd and the deal went bad. It was at this time that he began to borrow clients' money to secure advances. He pawned his Adelaide Club debentures, however bankers' demands on him became increasingly urgent. From 1942 Federal Government wartime control over stock-exchange transactions denied him opportunities to trade out of his financial woes.

On 2 June 1945, Hodgetts advised the Adelaide Stock Exchange that he could not meet his commitments. Examination revealed a deficiency of £82,854 in Hodgetts' estate. Seventeen days later Hodgetts wrote to SACA secretary Bill Jeanes withdrawing his position of association trustee and membership on all committees. In July 1945, an affidavit was filed in the bankruptcy court showing debts of £102,926. Criminal proceedings were about to be taken against Hodgetts. Shocked to the core, Adelaide people were wondering about Don Bradman's role, if any, in all of this business.

Solicitor Guy Fisher and old Test cricketer Arthur Richardson were high-profile victims among the 238 unsecured creditors. Fisher suffered a substantial loss of £34,567, but poor Arthur Richardson lost his entire life savings. He was the South Australian State coach for four seasons, from 1923 to 1927. Richardson played nine Tests, scoring 403 runs at an average of 31 and took

12 wickets at 43.41. His one Test century at Leeds in 1926 was compiled when he was just 14 days shy of his 38th birthday. Because of his tremendous financial losses in the Hodgetts fiasco, Richardson needed a job to subsidise his normal work and he returned to again coach the SA State squad in 1946–49. Other high profile 'victims' of the Hodgetts scandal were retired governor-general Lord Gowrie and Don Bradman himself; eminent Adelaide surgeon Sir Ivan Jose (who had played such an important role in Donald Beard's rise as a surgeon) lost a huge sum, believed to be in the vicinity of £60,000. Hodgetts became so desperate to turn his fortunes around that he misappropriated funds of the Royal Institution for the Blind. In his summing up the judge said Hodgetts succumbed to temptation via a 'disastrous combination of embarrassing difficulties'. He was sentenced to five years' jail.

'His cancer of the bowel had spread by the time he was admitted to Magill Ward,' Dr Beard recalled. Adelaide discovered Hodgetts' deception through the local newspaper. 'I well remember headlines in the Saturday edition of the *Advertiser*: "Hodgetts' Gone". The story told of how Harry Hodgetts had been charged with false pretences and fraudulent conversion.'

The following Monday the *News* ran a story showing the sign on the stockbroker's front window. H.W. Hodgetts & Co had been scrubbed off and replaced by Don Bradman & Co. Harry Hodgetts incarceration shocked the Adelaide Establishment.

Years after the Hodgetts scandal, Bradman confided in Don Beard. Don remembers: 'Now there was a lot of talk about Adelaide whereby people reckoned Bradman knew all about what Hodgetts had been doing, but Bradman spoke to me about it and he said he did not know about anything underhand Hodgetts had been involved in. "I knew Harry was in financial difficulty," Bradman maintained, "but I didn't know he was fiddling the funds from clients. I can say with all sincerity that I did not know. They say I did. I wouldn't have done it. When I took over the business on the Monday, the name had to be changed quickly because we didn't want Hodgetts & Co on the window in big letters."

'There was a bit of talk about how Bradman became boss of the firm. There was so much controversy surrounding the whole business. Knowing Bradman as I did over such a long time I don't think he would ever have done anything untoward. And I must say in my financial dealings with him he was always ethical. In the late 1950s he said to me, "Don, Oil Search Company, New Guinea, it's going to do very well. I would advise you to get a few shares." And I think I only bought £100 worth. Later he told me about

Argo. Bradman was a big mover of Argo and that has been probably the most successful investment company in Australia.

'I remember Sir Donald coming to our home in Marryatville and urging Margaret to remind me to send back his share rights forms straight away.' This was a friend reminding a friend to meet a shares rights deadline, not a sharebroker ensuring that his client met his commitment in time so he could collect a fat commission. 'In those relationships Sir Donald never showed signs of anything other than being completely aboveboard. He was always up-front and ethical.

'But Bradman was something of an enigma. You could never really explain the man. He was a wonderful businessman with a very good stockbroking firm and he looked after so many people. He was never a high-flier, yet he was a fascinating and interesting man to engage in conversation. When he trusted you he opened up. Bradman was very much a one-off. You knew he loved cricket with a passion and he loved batting more than any celebrated cricketer I have ever known.'

One of Don Beard's greatest cricket disappointments was that he never got the chance to bowl to Bradman in a club match. Either Bradman was away playing for SA or Australia, or he was absent on business. As a member of the State squad Don bowled to Bradman in the nets and while he did occasionally get a ball past the Bradman bat, 'I never actually dismissed him. But there was one night when at his request I was moved from where Bradman was batting to the next net. I must admit the wicket was a green top and the light was failing.'

Once he quizzed Bradman about the way he rolled his wrists on the hook stroke. 'He would get up off his chair and demonstrate his footwork, how swiftly he moved his feet – always with his back foot placed well outside the line of off stump and using the full depth of the crease – to get into the best position to hook or pull. The manner in which he rolled his wrists meant that by the time the ball reached him the ball went into the ground.

'"Must be difficult getting your feet in that position, Sir Donald" – I always addressed him as Sir Donald.

'"Oh, you have to be very quick!"'

Don and all those who knew Bradman recognised there were no grey areas with the man.

To Bradman there were only two sides to any debate: there was black and there was white. While he could be abrupt there was never confusion. You knew where you stood. He was committed and very confident: a paradoxical mix of humility and supreme confidence, leaving some with the impression that he boasted about his ability. Don believes Bradman did not boast. 'I think it was pride in what he could do and what he achieved.'

At the launch of the *Bradman Albums* at Adelaide Oval, Bradman mentioned there were only two people in his lifetime of cricket he knew who had taken more wickets than had made runs. One of them was an Englishman; the other was Don Beard. Apart from Bradman who led the 1948 Australian team to England, there were a number of Invincibles in the marquee that evening, including the left-arm fast-medium bowler Ernie Toshack and leg-spinner Doug Ring. Sir Donald had agreed to a launch of the *Bradman Albums* on the condition that the lion's share of proceeds for the evening went to the Crippled Children's Association, a charity Sir Donald and Lady Bradman both supported. Don Beard will never forget what happened that night.

'Early on at the dinner Ernie Toshack rushed up to me and said, "Come quick, Doc, Doug's gone!"

'I ran up to the table and sure enough there's Doug lying on the ground. He had no pulse. I felt his heart; he had no heartbeat. He was unconscious, not breathing. So he'd obviously had a cardiac arrest. I started to give him mouth-to-mouth resuscitation and as I was pumping his heart I said, "Quick I want someone to come here and pump his chest while I'm breathing him."

'A newspaper reporter volunteered (celebrated *Advertiser* columnist Des Colquhoun) and I said, "I want you to give him four to one." (Four pumps of the chest to one breathing.) We kept going. After about 10 or 15 minutes as I was breathing into him I felt the slight resistance. Up until that point there was no resistance at all. I called out, "We've got him, we've got him!" And at that moment Doug brought up the contents of his dinner, because I'd been filling his chest with air, but a lot of it was also going down into the stomach. He vomited straight into my face ... and then all down my dinner suit. Fortunately it was early in the dinner and he'd only had a white wine, he hadn't had any red. He came good; I found a pulse.

'I called out to Johnny Selth (the SACA caterer) to get an ambulance, we had to get Doug to hospital. The table was over towards the edge of the marquee. They brought the ambulance to the back, we lifted the flap and smuggled Doug out and into the ambulance and off to hospital.'

Geoff Jones, senior journalist with the *News* knew a front-page story when he saw one. So there on the front page of the *News* on Tuesday 6 October 1987 appeared Jones' story under the banner: 'Winning Team Helps Doug Beat the Odds – Geoff Jones On The Spot':

Former Australian Test cricketer Doug Ring had odds of 250–1 stacked against his life at Adelaide Oval last night. And he beat them, thanks to a winning, if not unusual team. Mr Ring, 68, had collapsed with cardiac arrest during the gala banquet to launch *The Bradman Albums*. He made a good recovery overnight and today was out of intensive care and resting comfortably in a ward at Royal Adelaide Hospital. But it was a very different story last night when he started to feel ill in the brief interval between the speeches by Australian Rugby Union coach Alan Jones and the Prime Minister, Mr Hawke. And that's when the winning team stepped in. The line-up read: Adelaide surgeon, deputy chairman of the Road Safety Advisory Council and former Sturt fast bowler, Dr Donald Beard; Advertiser columnist Des Colquhoun; Adelaide stockbroker Bill Whiting; sports commentator Ken Cunningham and Adelaide Oval caterer John Selth. Dr Beard agreed to speak to me about the incident only on the condition that I highlight the need to learn mouth-to-mouth resuscitation.

'Doug had lapsed into semi-consciousness and then stopped breathing altogether. I think he stopped breathing for about two minutes. I was conscious of someone standing behind me and I just shouted,

'Whoever you are start pumping his chest.' After it was all over I realised it was Des Colquhoun. Well done, Des. (MC) Ken (Cunningham) did a wonderful job calming everyone down and continuing on with the show. And while all this was going on John Selth had quickly got an ambulance and alerted the hospital.

Were you the only doctor present? 'I think so.'

Would you agree that only one person in 250 knows how to administer mouth-to-mouth? 'That would be about right. It is simple and easy to learn and there are courses readily available.'

Dr Beard was delighted over the team working brilliantly to help save Doug Ring's life. Ring lived another 14 years. Cricket and caring for the injured and the sick were intricately woven into the pattern of an amazing tapestry, which details his life journey. While the doctor fought to save Doug Ring's life, Sir Donald Bradman was sitting at a table at the other side of the marquee and, like most people at the launch, was enjoying the speeches, oblivious to the real-life drama being played out little more than the length of a cricket pitch away.

Once when playing for Sturt at Hawthorn Oval, Don was padded up ready to go into bat as the number eleven, 'the hope of the side', when a cry rang out from the bowling club next door. A man had collapsed on the bowling green. Don, still wearing his batting pads, raced to the man's aid.

He cleared the little fence next to the pavilion and set about reviving the man, who, like Ring, had suffered a cardiac arrest.

'I think it was one of the Walshe brothers, a licensee of the Oriental Hotel. I got to work on him, but I realised as soon as I stopped breathing into him, he stopped. I hadn't got him going 100 per cent, so I went in the ambulance with him to the hospital. I delivered him to the RAH alive, but unfortunately a week later he had another cardiac arrest and that time they couldn't save him. I raced back to Hawthorn Oval and they were just coming off the field and I called out, "I'm back, I'm back!"

'"Too late," they said. "That was the ninth wicket to fall. The game is finished and you've lost."

Don said Bradman would get excited about such things as a chance to win the B grade golf championship at Kooyonga. 'One Sunday morning I called on him and asked about his golf. He replied, "I looked at the *Sunday Mail* to see the results because I won the championship, but I forgot to put in my card, so I lost."' Such was the man who in England had his name in foot-high capitals on the newspaper hoardings, but here he was searching for his name among the results of a B grade golf championship printed in tiny figures in the Sunday newspaper.

He would talk about his accomplishments in squash. In 1938 Bradman won the SA squash championship by beating Don Talbot, a Davis Cup tennis champion. World champion billiards player Walter Lindrum enjoyed many a visit to the Bradman home in Holden Street, Kensington Park, to partake in a glass of sherry with him and then the two sporting men would play a keen game of billiards.

'I once had a meal in London with Joe Davis, the world famous snooker player,' Dr Beard said, 'and Davis confessed that he only took up snooker "because I could never beat Lindrum at billiards".'

As Don got to know Bradman better, they went to one another's homes for dinner. At other times they met up for a small and private gathering of mutual friends. On 30 January 1978, Jeff and Cheryl Thomson arrived at 134 Beulah Road Norwood for dinner with Don and Margaret Beard, Sir Donald and Lady Jessie Bradman and a few Indian Test cricketers, including Sunil Gavaskar, Bishan Bedi and Gundappa Viswanath. To all and sundry The Don looked pretty fit for a man of 70 years. The group was enjoying pre-dinner drinks as they wandered through the splendid Beard family garden where the Doc's two sons, Matthew and Alastair, both tall boys, were having a hit in the nets. The pitch had been laid by renowned curator Les Burdett, lovingly placed in a bed of Adelaide Oval soil.

Matthew Beard laughingly asked The Don, 'Would you like to come over to the nets and have a bat against us, Sir Donald?' All eyes turned to Bradman, who initially declined but then said, 'Yes, I'd love to have a hit.' As Sir Donald moved towards the pitch, Thommo declared: 'If Bradman's batting, Thomson's bowling!' He took the ball from Matthew.

Guests were amazed. Here they were about to witness Don Bradman batting against Jeff Thomson in the Beard family garden. Someone found a bat, a Stuart Surridge special, and The Don strode to the net area, accompanied by Jeff Thomson, who later related what happened.

'The Don said, "Gee, Jeff, I don't know why I'm doing this – I haven't batted for twenty years." He smiled and had a gleam in his eye.'

Thommo was transfixed. 'There was total certainty in the way Bradman carried himself. Instinctively I knew that this was going to be some event. Bradman faced his first ball. The wicket was covered in a thick mat of grass: green and hard. It looked as if it would bounce and seam. It was made for any fast bowler. The Doc liked green tracks and he prepared his home-garden wicket. I didn't realise it at the time but I was about to see one of the greatest events of my cricketing life.'

While neither Matthew nor Alastair Beard was of the quality of an Australian fast bowler, they bowled at a fair pace. 'Here was this little old guy in horn-rimmed glasses facing fast bowlers on a green pitch in an Adelaide backyard on the rest day of a Test match. Thommo and Matthew maintain that Sir Donald held only the bat and wore no pads, gloves or an abdominal protector. 'He was just standing there with a borrowed bat. I couldn't keep my eyes off Bradman. He was beaming. I'm sure those two young fast bowlers were thinking, How good is this? We've got Bradman and Thomson in our back garden net.'

Thomson said he thought that he better not go off on his full run to bowl. In fact he queried whether he would bowl at all because he could envisage the headlines: 'Thommo Kills Bradman in Backyard Test'.

'But bowl I did!'

Thommo said at the sight of the two young fast bowlers Bradman's eyes lit up 'and you could see he was thinking, Who are you two blokes? Do you think you are going to get me out? I've got news for you'.

'He assumed an air of supreme confidence, it was as if Bradman was wearing a suit of armour; he was invincible. That little old guy in glasses was suddenly transformed into Don Bradman, the human thrashing machine. He

'The Don Bradman I knew'

did not play a false shot in twenty minutes of the most amazing batting I've ever seen.'

Thommo said: 'At first I just rolled my arm over, but I soon realised Bradman's strokes and dancing feet were still there so I quickened my pace, but to no avail. At the end of his knock we walked off arm in arm to dinner and Bradman said to me, "You know, Jeff, I enjoyed that knock, but I'll never do it again.' And so I realised that I had been the last bowler ever to bowl against Don Bradman.'

Matthew Beard told how one guest, Bishan Bedi, the Indian left-arm spinner, turned up late and was 'tearing his hair out' over not getting the chance to bowl to Bradman and watching him bat. 'What amazed me was how Bradman kept from slipping over on the green turf, given he was wearing street shoes,' Matthew added.

Another time Don and Margaret prepared for a guest list of 20 people. 'I went next door to borrow some chairs,' he recalled, 'and my next-door neighbour said, "You can have these chairs, Don, but don't let Dennis Lillee sit on one."

'I think Mrs Brumitt didn't like Dennis, or she didn't like the fact that he was so fast and often hit the opposition batsmen.'

That particular party went down a treat, but for the peculiar behaviour of one of the guests, the eccentric Alan Knott, England's brilliant wicket-keeper. 'Knott picked on every course on the menu. "What's in this?" he asked Margaret, who had carefully prepared the meal. "What is this? Did you cook it properly?"

'It was extraordinary stuff and the gathering was made even more uncomfortable when Knott, between courses, got down on the polished floor in the dining room, and proceeded to exercise – push-ups, sit-ups you name it. Eventually Knott had so embarrassed our English guests they left taking Knott with them.

'Dennis Lillee was a great guest, so too Len Pascoe. The day after Len dined with us, Margaret took delivery of a lovely bunch of flowers from the big fast bowler. I think that was the only time she ever received flowers from a cricketer who shared a meal with us.'

While Don says he was blessed by the wonderful dinners and chance to get to know a wide diversity of people, there were times when the odd guest over-stepped the mark. Once Frances Edmonds, author of *Not Another Bloody Tour* and wife of Phil Edmonds, the England left-arm spinner, took exception to Phil talking to one of the guests, the wife of a Supreme Court judge, both good friends of the Beard family. Mrs Edmonds apparently thought her husband was doing a line with the lady. Out of the blue, from across the room, she threw her glass full of champagne at him. Phil ducked in nonchalant fashion, the missile missing his head by inches before shattering against the wall, champagne spilling onto the carpet. He carried on as though his wife's tantrums were an everyday event and she left the house immediately.

Once a visiting surgeon from Edinburgh said to Don, after their subject of conversation turned to the exploits of Don Bradman, 'Oh, Don, if I could just get to see Bradman from a distance, at the end of the street, anywhere, I could go back to the UK and tell my friends that I saw him.' Typically Don Beard went the extra mile for a friend. He arranged for his friend to come to dinner and he sat him right next to Sir Donald.

As the years wore on Don and Sir Donald met frequently and the conversation sometimes turned to health issues. Bradman made what people today might consider an amazing confession. At the age of 18, Don Bradman, the brilliant emerging champion batsman, had six teeth extracted. And he told his friend of his ordeal in part of a letter he wrote him dated 28 February 1986.

> The dentist who started all my trouble was Mick Bardsley, brother of Warren. I went to him for treatment and he said I had pyorrhoea and must lose one of my double back teeth. Always trusting my medical advisors I said okay, take it out. But before I left the chair he had removed six, three on each side. I was then boarding with Frank Cush. I went home but Mrs Cush was out so I lay down with a bowl beside me and when Mrs Cush returned the bowl had so much blood in it that she became alarmed and rang the doctor. He came round and plugged my gums to arrest the bleeding. That was on a Friday evening and the doctor said he didn't think I should play in the grade match due to start the next day. However, I was captain, didn't want to let the side down and disregarded his advice. So I played. Won the toss and sent the opposition in because I felt weak and not up to batting. For the same reason I put myself at first slip, much to the annoyance of the crowd who knew I was the best cover fieldsman and wasn't any good in the slips. You guessed it. I put down two catches in the first 10 minutes. But worse was to follow. We bowled them out by 4.30 pm and we had to bat. I dropped myself down the batting order, hoping our early batsmen would stay in. But they didn't. By ten to six we had lost eight wickets and I could no longer refuse to bat. So I walked out to be roundly hooted by the spectators (the only time I can remember) who knew nothing of the drama being enacted behind the scenes.
>
> By stumps we were still eight wickets down and about 40 runs behind,

with Frank Ward my not out partner. The following Saturday I had recovered. Frank and I put up a record ninth wicket partnership, my share 116 not out, then bowled Marrickville out again and won by an innings. I went from villain to hero.

Interesting that the young Bradman's dentist Mick Bardsley was a right-handed batsman who played 11 first-class matches for NSW, hitting a highest score of 87 and averaging 31. His more famous brother, opening batsman Warren Bardsley, played 41 Test matches, hitting a highest score of 193 not out and finishing with an average of 40.47. Frank Ward was a St George teammate of Bradman's in Sydney and in the 1935/36 season Ward joined Bradman in the South Australian team. Ward, a leg-spinner, was controversially selected ahead of Clarrie Grimmett for Australia's tour of England in 1938. He failed. 'I was upset by Grimmett's exclusion and walked in my sleep to complain to my parents.'

'Don Bradman was a man like no one else,' said Don. 'I think he was great. But he wouldn't have got where he did without the support and love of Lady Bradman. She was a wonderful woman.'

It is said that Lady Bradman's influence convinced their only son John to change his name back from Bradsen to Bradman. There were those who thought it strange that when John Bradman changed his surname by deed poll, he chose a new name so much like the surname he inherited.

'It was a strange thing, to take the name Bradsen. Sort of half a change,' Don said. 'Sir Donald talked a good deal about it. He was disappointed that John changed the name, but he said he completely understood why he had felt the need to do so.' Don Bradman was very much a prisoner of fame and anyone with the name Bradman was going to be under the spotlight, purely by association.

Thanks to Jessie's gentle persuasion, when Sir Donald and Lady Bradman were in the twilight of their lives John relented and changed his name back to Bradman and returned to Adelaide, something that genuinely thrilled Sir Donald. Don said it was a good thing that Bradman was dismissed cheaply in his final Test match, because 'no one is perfect in this world and to have batsman strive to get that average some time in the future is right and proper'.

'I've seen the humble side of Don Bradman. The times I'd go to his home and find he was on the roof cleaning the leaves from the gutters or pruning the roses. And I have also seen the side of him that can be a little cutting. Bradman could be charming or a little blunt. But he also had a very quick wit.

'Once I was bowling at Adelaide Oval and found the ball swinging from the outset. I looked at the ball. Umpire Jack Kierse had thrown me a two-piecer, and those cricket balls swung late and all day. I got a couple of wickets and thought I'd better tell the umpire. Then I got a third wicket and my conscience was starting to get the better of me. I think my Sturt slips fieldsmen John Lill and Ian McLachlan were amazed by the amount of swing I was getting. Finally I went to the umpire and said, "Oh, Jack, would you believe it, this is a two-piece ball."

'Jack smiled, looked at it and threw it back to me, "So it is, Doc."

'Years later I was in the company of Sir Donald and Ian McLachlan at lunch at Adelaide Oval and Ian recounted the story. I said to them that I didn't have any idea it was a two-piece ball until well into my second over. Bradman laughed and said: "Oh, Doc. You would have known it was a two-piece ball the very moment it first swung."

'At the same lunch we got around to talking about swing bowling, and Bradman said he had discussed the swerve of a cricket ball at the Adelaide University. He said, "Once the ball gets to about 96 miles an hour it will no longer swing. The force of propulsion was so great as to ensure that no swing develops."

'Then I said with a smile, "Oh, is that what happened when I stopped swinging the ball?"

'Sir Donald replied in a flash, "Don, I don't think you needed to worry."'

Even in a situation when it might well have been prudent for him to do so, Sir Donald never held back. Such a time befell him in the early 1980s. He was driving his silver Toyota Celica east along Wakefield Street in the city. Sir Donald generally stuck religiously to the speed limit. However, he came to a section of road that very suddenly sloped downwards, and the speed increased. Sir Donald looked at his speed dial and realised he was a few kilometres over the limit. He immediately put his foot on the brake. Too late. A police patrol car had been right on his tail. Bradman was caught. Sir Donald pulled to the kerbside and the police car passed him and parked a few metres in front of his Celica. A policeman got out of the car and walked back towards him.

'Ah, driver do you realise that you were exceeding the speed limit?'

Sir Donald did not reply.

'Licence, please, driver.'

Sir Donald reached into his wallet and produced his driver's licence. When

'The Don Bradman I knew'

the policeman noted the name of the motorist, he said, 'Oh, Sir Donald Bradman ... it is a pleasure to meet you!'

Sir Donald maintained a straight face: 'I can assure you, young man, the pleasure is not mutual.'

A few months later, on 8 January 1981, a small man in a grey suit visited Dr Beard's rooms in South Terrace, Adelaide. 'My secretary, Betty Schubert, came into my room and said, "Oh, a little old man brought you in this book, which he said you might like to read."

'I looked at Betty and said, "That little old man was Sir Donald Bradman."'

Don Beard stood and selected a book from the shelf in his study. He smiled and opened the book, *Barclays World of Cricket: The Great Game from A to Z*. A note was attached to the title page. It was a letter from his friend.

Sir Donald Bradman   2 Holden Street
                                                      Kensington Park, SA 5068
                                                      8.1.81

Dear Don,

You have been a great lover and supporter of cricket and I would like you to have the enclosed book with my compliments.

It is the most comprehensive work ever produced on cricket – a veritable mine of information – and for the rest of your days will I hope bring you much pleasure.

With best wishes
Yours sincerely
(signed) Don Bradman

Don remembers Sir Donald Bradman being 'always polite, and following each dinner at the Beard family home a thank you letter would come to Margaret'. He holds a special place in his heart for Don Bradman, cricket's batting maestro and his long-time friend. Silent testimony of his affection for Sir Donald comes in the form of a bronze sculpture of Don Bradman's famous cover drive adorning Don Beard's home study.

Twelve

Gems and Rough Diamonds

I assure you doctor that I do not need your surgical services, however, come down and have tea with us on the Royal Yacht Britannia.

HM Queen Elizabeth II

Don Beard has made many friends over the years: dozens of gems and rough diamonds. Sir Donald Bradman is high on his list of gems. I cannot list in this book all of those who have come into Don's life, just a good selection.

Reg Saunders was the first full-blood Aboriginal man to become an officer in the Australian Army. Within five months of enlisting in 1942 he joined the 7th Battalion 2nd AIF and gained his sergeant's stripes. The battalion was trapped at the fall of Crete and Reg, along with a few mates, hid in caves and olive groves. They scavenged for food, scrounging wild honey, olives, eggs and milk. Sometimes sympathetic villagers, risking death by the Nazis, supplied Reg and his soldier mates goat meat, but Reg survived mostly on his own for more than 11 months. Underground fighters then rescued him and within months he was back in his old battalion, this time fighting the Japanese in New Guinea.

'Reg Saunders proved to be an outstanding patrol leader in New Guinea at a time when the Australians contested every inch of jungle terrain with the Japanese west of the Wau Valley. He was clearly officer material but the top brass had not then reckoned upon a black man in charge of white troops.

'Eventually he was recommended to attend an Officer Cadet Training Course and in November 1944 Reg Saunders graduated 10th out of a class of 33.'

A battle-hardened soldier, Saunders rose from the ranks in the Second World War and later served in Korea. Reg Saunders' father fought in the First World War, as did his uncle, Reg Rawlings, who was awarded the Military Medal and later killed in action. Following in this military tradition, Reg and his brother Harry enlisted for service in the Second World War; Harry was later killed in New Guinea.

In June 1950, when North Korean communist troops crossed the 38th parallel into South Korea, Reg Saunders was working as a labourer on the Melbourne wharves. The Australian Government promised US General Douglas MacArthur troops and this time the military did not object to recruiting Aboriginal soldiers. Captain Reg Saunders fought in the 3rd RAR at the battles of Kapyong and Maryang San in Korea.

'Reg Saunders was a wonderful human being. He was a great friend to me and my family,' Don Beard recalled. 'He gave me a book entitled *Aboriginal Men of High Degree* by A.P. Elkin along with the notation: "Don, I have given you this book because you have shown more sympathy and understanding that any white man I have known." At one stage my two young sons went to Canberra and Reg looked after them. In his will he asked me to "say a few words at my funeral". I was prevented attending because of the pilots' strike.'

In a letter dated 28 June 1978, Reg wrote to Don, enclosing his beautifully crafted interpretation of Land Rights, which has been reproduced here.

Land Rights

How can you own the sky? Is not the smell of wattle blossoms free for all? The birds of the air live with the wind. The sun is the creation of God and the giver of life. The land bears the ashes of our fathers' fathers. Creation is the essence of our living, sharing is our life-long task.

When all these things are gone we have to die. The Aboriginal standing in the forests sees his brothers, the trees. He hears the talk of the river and he sees his grandfather, the mountain. The wind in his face is a caress of his mother; the earth upon which he stands is eternal. He belongs to this land. The Dingo mother fed his Spirit Forbears with milk from her tits. The Rainbow Serpent made the rivers. The Spirits of the Dreamtime came from the darkness behind the sun to make this land and then they created the Aboriginal from the earth's own creation. They made the sacred places for the councils of the Aboriginal, they gave him wisdom and knowledge. They made him the keeper of the old, the protector of the weak, the teacher of innocents.

The Dreamtime is the beginning; the beginning is eternal and timeless, for when he is born again and again it is always the beginning. Only the wind and the sun and the warm red earth are eternal life. To take the power from the earth is to cause great danger to us the Aboriginal; to invade our sacred places violates the wishes of the Creator Spirits and despoils our Dreaming.

We respect the white mans' Dreaming. We wont invade his scared places. We don't mind his God sharing this land with our God.

We only want our lands to remain timeless, we only want the purity of the air we first breathe to remain pure for our last breath, and when we return from our Dreaming we want to breathe that same pure air again and again.

We the Aboriginals love our land, our country and the water and sky around us. We bore arms alongside white brothers to defend it in two terrible conflicts; we volunteered although we owe no loyalty to the foreign kings. Our loyalties and love lie within the boundaries of our timeless land and are tied to our ancient cultures.

We have lived in this land for many thousands of years, we have obeyed its laws and bent to its will. We have no right to destroy the purity of its blood in the streams because it is our blood. To spit upon and ravage the land is to spit upon our father and our mother. How can we sell or barter that which we do not own? Our sacred Spirit Fathers must sleep in uneasy peace as we the mere children stand in silence. The Aboriginal speaks in many languages and like all people will disagree on many things material. Today when we speak of Land Rights we do so with one voice, because Land Rights is both spiritual and material. It is material because I can put my 'home' there, and spiritual because it is where I shall want to rest my ashes.

I cannot believe that my soul will be lost because my Spiritual Forbears have been dispossessed.

This land bears the ashes of our Fathers.

It bears the will and titles of Spiritual Ancestors.

It is our Peace and Love. It is our Lore.

Djambi

Reg Saunders © 27 June 1978

Sir Donald Dunstan was a career soldier who fought with distinction in WWII, Korea and was commander of the 1st Australian Task Force in Vietnam. Sir Donald became South Australia's 30th governor in 1982. During his nine years in high office Sir Donald asked Dr Beard to be his medical advisor.

'He was a very good soldier and a good friend,' Dr Beard recalled.

Kym Bonython, successful art dealer, racing car and speedboat driver, raceway promoter and owner, businessman, art dealer and entrepreneur, was one of Don Beard's best mates. Bonython jammed so much adventure and achievement into his long life. A WW II fighter pilot, author of six books on modern Australian art, and a farmer, Bonython introduced Australia to singer Chuck Berry and jazz legend Dizzy Gillespie. He brought Dave Brubeck, the Beatles, and along with Thelonius Monk and Gillespie, a whole list of the world's who's who in jazz to this country. Broadcaster John Laws described Bonython as 'the ultimate playboy. He was something that Australians had never seen before. I mean, he had the money, he had charm. He still has charm and good looks. They say you can count your friends on one hand. Well, Kym Bonython takes up three fingers on mine'.

Bonython ran an art gallery in North Adelaide and it was there he discovered Broken Hill-based artist Pro Hart's unique skill and launched Hart into the art world. 'Pro Hart was chairman of St John Ambulance and a wonderful philanthropist,' Don said. 'A true Christian.'

Later Kym opened the Hungry Horse Art Gallery in Sydney, where he premiered the works of Sydney Nolan, Arthur Boyd and Brett Whiteley. While living in Sydney, Kym lived next door to broadcaster Peter Luck, who discovered his neighbour would vacuum his front lawn every evening. 'It was strange,' said Luck, 'but then, Kym was always very neat.'

Don Beard cannot recall the exact time he met Kym Bonython, but he found they shared similar interests. They both served in war zones and Don was a trackside surgeon at various car and motorbike race meetings held at Rowley Park, Kilburn, Mallala and Collingrove Hill Climb.

'It was at the Collingrove Hill Climb one year when a fellow crashed his car and I rushed to his aid, only to find the driver had his leg pinned. His leg was broken. When I reached into the car and felt the leg I asked him if he felt pain. "Can't feel a thing," the man replied.

'Sadly that man was a paraplegic, but he survived.

'Kym ran Rowley Park Raceway. He was a daredevil behind the wheel of a race car and a speedboat. Once a patient of mine fished Kym out of the river, saving him from drowning. Kym had flipped his speedboat and he was dragged under the water. Kym never gambled, yet throughout his life he has always taken risks.'

Rowley Park Speedway entertained race-car fans from 1949 to 1979 and Kym Bonython not only ran and promoted Rowley Park, he was among the drivers who risked death on the track. In those days there were not the safety requirements that are in place today. In the 30 years Rowley Park ran, nine men lost their lives, the first in 1957, the last in 1970. On 29 November 1955

Bonython, an excellent driver of the midget race cars, stood his SA1 on its nose at the Coglin Street end of the track. He survived with hardly a scratch, as did drivers Billy Wigzell and Dave Cooper, who were also involved in the pile-up.

'Kym loved life. He never smoked or touched alcohol, yet you'd think that he did drink, such was the high spirit of his personality,' Don smiled. 'He ran a farm at Mount Pleasant and he imported Jersey bulls that did a lot in the dairy industry. One day the bull was supposed to be shown at the Mt Pleasant Show. Kym was in the paddock with it and it turned on him, got him down and gored him. A patient of mine went in and got Kym out by dragging him under the fence with the bull still roaring and jumping up and down.

'Kym was taken to hospital and the bull went to the show. People came from all over to see the bull that had hit Kym. He had more than 100 stitches in him. He spent days in the Mt Pleasant Hospital and the bull won first prize at the show.'

Kym got his own back on that bull. He recorded the roar of the bull that gored him and the sound of the bull's roar became the sound Kym Bonython's car made when he pressed the car horn. Dr Beard attended Kym's 90th birthday party, held early in 2010.

'Some 2100 people attended. It was a wow of a party. Right up until his death I'd call in and see Kym regularly. Every Christmas he sent a card, which depicted a recent photograph of him on the front and a detailed word picture of his doings during the year. Kym Bonython was a great man and a great friend.'

In January 2009, Kym amazed his friends by announcing in a newspaper article that he supported euthanasia and believed people had the 'right to end their lives in dignity'. He did not realise the complexities of the issue. A few years earlier Kym, already in his 80s, said in a radio interview: 'Waiting on my hall table are the tapes for my funeral. As people walk out of the church, I've got Gerry Mulligan playing "Please don't talk about me when I'm gone".'

Arthur Dickson Wright was born in Dublin in 1897, the third child of a medical student who worked in a bank by day. His father went into practice in Paddington and Dickie became a medical student at St Mary's Hospital. He was still studying medicine when he enlisted in the army, serving as a gunner on the Somme and at Ypres and as a balloonist in the Flying Corps. At the age of 26 he became professor of surgery in Singapore but returned to eventually become senior surgeon at London's St Mary's and the Prince of Wales hospitals. An outstanding surgeon, Dickson Wright was most comfortable in operating on the abdomen, chest, heart and brain. He was a surgeon said to being able to 'cut well and his patients got well'. He was also a brilliant after-dinner speaker. At one debate he had to follow a dull talk by a renowned homoeopathist. Dickson Wright compared homeopathy with the throwing of an aspirin tablet in the Thames at Dagenham and drinking the water at Westminster Bridge.

As mentioned earlier, Don met Dr Dickson Wright in London. 'We became friends because of our shared interest in cricket. Mrs Barrett, owner of a confectionery company and a board member of the British Anti-Cancer Federation with Dr Dickson Wright, kindly introduced me to London society and took me to balls with the Anglo–French and Anglo–American Society and to the FA Cup final at Wembley. She thought I should learn something of London apart from surgery.

'Dickson Wright was a hard examiner for the fellowship of the Royal College of Surgeons but on the final day of my clinical examinations he sidled up to me at lunchtime and whispered in my ear, "Keep it up but don't try to be too clever – you only have to pass" – and pass I did in June 1957.'

Sir Gordon Gordon-Taylor was a wonderful surgical mentor for Don Beard in London. He was also street smart: 'When I was about to return to Australia from London in 1957, Jim Mill and I invited two girls from the college for a farewell thank you dinner. One of the girls was Sir Gordon's secretary, Hazel Argent. At dinner I mentioned I had never been to the Cotswold's. Everyone said I must. Jim Mill offered me his car – a 1938 slip differential Daimler and Hazel offered to be my guide. There was the matter of getting a couple of days off – she told her mother she was staying overnight in London with a friend and rang the college to say she was sick. Next day Sir Gordon rang Hazel's mother to enquire about her health. Her mother told him she was all right and staying in London. I understand Sir Gordon simply smiled.'

Sir Henry Simpson Newland was born in Adelaide on 24 November 1873, eldest son of Simpson Newland. He was educated at St Peter's College, Adelaide, and attended the University of Adelaide where, in 1902, he was awarded the university's first master of surgery degree. In the very year of Henry Newland's final examinations, he and his peers were caught up in the infamous 'Hospital Row' of 1896. His biographer, J. Estcourt Hughes, said in his book *Henry Simpson Newland*: 'This lamentable business started in 1894 as a dispute about a nursing appointment at the (Adelaide) Hospital but, as often happens, a minor conflict developed into a major one.'

The medical superintendent, matron and the 17-member honorary medical staff resigned, a royal commission was appointed and, worse still, the row saw the complete disruption of clinical teaching at the hospital. This was the first break in this important education of medical students since 1887 when the hospital was established. It also meant that the medical students would need to transfer to Melbourne, Sydney or the UK to complete their studies. The Hospital Row dragged on until 1901.

In 1897 Henry sailed to London to further his medical studies and to gain the attention of Sir Arthur Treves, the famed surgeon who years later operated on King Edward VII for acute appendicitis. From 1898 to 1902 Newland undertook postgraduate studies at London Hospital; he was surgical registrar in 1901. He observed paediatric surgery at Great Ormond Street and was senior house surgeon for six months at the Poplar Hospital for Accidents. He visited European capitals to observe leading surgeons, commenting sharply upon some.

Dr Beard greatly admired Newland: 'He got the job as a house surgeon and then in what would lead to a wonderful surgical career he worked in whatever job became available and after several years passed his Fellowship in Surgery. He then went to the US where he worked at the Cleveland Clinic with George Crile who presented him with a beautiful hand-made needle holder, which Newland eventually gave to me. When he returned to Adelaide, he anticipated an immediate appointment at the Royal Adelaide Hospital, the six-year row now over. But medical politics were the same then as they are now and the appointment was not forthcoming and, in fact, he had to take a variety of jobs including radiotherapy.' Ten years passed before he was appointed.

Today, Dr Beard often sifts through old books and magazines written by Sir Henry's father, Simpson Newland, who was a parliamentarian in South Australia and one-time State treasurer. Sir Henry Newland was one of the influential figures who fired Don Beard's enthusiasm for the history of surgery. On 31 May 1985 he found himself standing at the foot of the magnificent Waterloo staircase, an integral feature of Carrick Hill in Adelaide, to deliver a lecture on 'Surgery on the Battlefield: Legs and Waterloo'. His research found that under the guiding hand of the British Surgeon General, Dr James McGregor, the Duke of Wellington had a total of 36 regimental medical officers and 69 assistant surgeons, all of whom were unqualified apprentices with little experience. 'The regimental surgeons worked on the outskirts of the battle in farmhouses to which casualties were taken by friends and volunteers. The types of injuries included heavy, blunt, lacerating or avulsing wounds caused by six, nine or 12-pound round shot. A ball of this size could kill six men in a line. Low velocity lead, musket or pistol balls frequently fragmented on impact. Canisters containing many small round iron missiles were particularly effective against mass infantry. Cutting or piercing injuries, mostly to the upper body, thorax and abdomen, were inflicted by a variety of weapons including sword, lance, bayonet or pike.'

He detailed the types of wounds; the site on the body the injuries were inflicted, and the treatment of the day. Compound skull fractures were, of course, frequent at Waterloo. Dr Beard also spoke of the amputation of limbs and the drainage of abscesses, but he never lost his audience, nor his sense of theatre.

'Towards the end of the battle, Paget, the cavalry commander, was on his horse alongside Wellington when he was hit by a cannonball. He looked down and said, "My leg's been shot off!" Wellington looked down and remarked, "My God, sir, so it has!"

Our Paget (of the many Paget's diseases), was a nephew and was born the day before Waterloo. One hundred and twenty years later Beau Desert, the home of Waterloo Paget, was demolished. The oak panelling and the staircase were brought to Adelaide and formed the basis of Carrick Hill, the home of the well-known South Australian Hayward family.'

Fess Parker played Davy Crockett and Daniel Boone in television and in films. Don Beard met him in Vietnam in 1969 when Parker was on a goodwill tour representing the US President, Richard Nixon. He later represented President Ronald Reagan in Australia for the Coral Sea Memorial. In Adelaide Fess dined with Donald and Margaret Beard at their home.

'As he left our place he said, "You must come to my home in the US and I will show you parts of California you have never seen."' Don thought nothing of the invitation until a follow-up letter arrived from Fess. A year later when the Beards were in Canada at a surgical conference Don took up his invitation. 'I forgot you had to have a visa to go from Canada to the States so it was a mad dash on a hired aircraft from Vancouver Island to the US Embassy and we managed to catch a plane to be met by Fess in Hollywood.

'We stayed at his home in Palm Strings and one day he took Margaret and me to a sale in a menswear shop where he bought all sorts of wonderful

American linen and cotton for a 10th of the normal price. Another time Fess and I lounged in his swimming pool, looking up at a mountain and dodging the odd golf ball from a nearby course.'

Sir Edward 'Bill' Hughes made his mark at St Mark's Hospital, London, in 1949 where he was recognised for his work in colorectal surgery. He was assistant surgeon at Royal Melbourne Hospital and was about to start private practice when he met the DGMS General Kingsley Norris at the races and was told he was needed in Japan. A few days later he found himself 'volunteering' for service in the Royal Australian Army Medical Corps. The Korean War had started and he was posted to Kure Hospital in Japan, where his organisation and documentation of Australian casualties made a long-term impact.

Don regarded him highly: 'He was probably the best surgeon in Australia and wrote hundreds of papers and lectured throughout the world on a variety of surgical topics. Sadly, he died in his 60s from Parkinson's disease. His research was meticulous. He taught me a tremendous amount and at one stage invited me to stay at his home for two weeks to accompany his day and night consulting and operating.'

In Adelaide after his study tour of England, a few years beyond the ceasefire in the Korean War, Don Beard met one of the soldiers he cared for during the conflict. 'Despite not having much use for authority and always being in strife with his superiors, Sergeant Frank Browne was a good soldier,' he recalled. 'We were walking in Adelaide and stopped together at traffic lights in King William Street. Sgt Browne had been shot in the chest in Korea and I looked after him. Although I didn't regard the wound as serious, Frank always insisted that I saved his life.

'"What are you doing now?" he asked.

'"Well, I haven't started work since my return from the UK, so I have a bit of free time."

'"Good," he said, "why don't we go to see that new film, *The Bridge on the River Kwai?*"

'The film, starring Alec Guinness, William Holden and Jack Hawkins, all masters of their craft, was getting rave reviews, so I readily agreed to accompany Frank.'

Within a few weeks he again met up with Frank in the city. Dr Beard was looking longingly at a leather-covered chair. 'Frank said to me, "Do you like that chair, Doc?" I nodded and mentioned something along the lines that I might one day afford such a chair.'

The men went their separate ways. Then, two days later, the very chair he had spotted in the shop window mysteriously appeared at Dr Beard's home.

'Frank explained to me, "You saved my life, Doc, surely you deserve a comfortable chair!"'

Don told Frank that he had done enough for him and not to lavish him with gifts. Two weeks later a brand-new television arrived, but there was a twist: this time it was a gift for Don's mother.

'Well, Doc, you can't refuse this gift, because it's for your mother – the television is not for you!'

The age of television had just begun in Australia, so usually all you saw on the screen was the test pattern, yet people, including Mrs Beard, would sit in their lounge room and watch the test pattern as intently as one might today take in the nightly newscast. At the time Frank Browne was on the board of DAVCO, which was involved in the development of a new-fangled sandwich machine and the 'somewhat shonky' management of a gold mine in Queensland.

'One day Frank asked me, "What are you up to Doc?"

'I told him I was heading to Sydney for a medical conference and he said, "You must see Al Shackman (Frank's American boss). He'll look after you." I instinctively knew that it might be imprudent to say no to Frank Browne. When I arrived in Sydney, Al Shackman took me to a number of clubs. There he got the best seats in the house and soon after we arrived a couple of girls appeared.'

Al suggested they go sailing the following day and Don sensed that Al Shackman was, like Frank Browne, a man whose invitation you would not dare refuse. They sailed on Sydney Harbour in a Chinese junk, resplendent with red sails and highly polished timber. Don suspected there could have been a few deals done by Frank and Al, but he would never delve into their business dealings and took them at face value. At one stage the Adelaide police attempted to extradite Al Shackman from Sydney to Adelaide to face a number of charges. Shackman pleaded not guilty in a Sydney court on the grounds that he that he had sustained a 'severe illness that causes giddiness and falling attacks'. While in court pleading his case, Al suddenly fell forward and struck his forehead a fearful blow on the thick, polished wood at the top of the dock. The judge immediately declared that Al Shackman was unfit to stand and next day the American wheeler-dealer flew back to the US and disappeared.

'We became good friends,' Don said. 'I found these fellows were kind and in Frank Browne's case he was a good army mate, the sort of fellow you'd want to be with you in the trenches.'

Don said the men who fought and worked in Korea during the conflict were from an amazing array of backgrounds. 'There were veterans from WWII, youngsters looking for excitement, men wanting to erase their past, especially fellas who needed to get away from their wives or lovers; yet when the going got tough on the battlefield these soldiers fought magnificently. They proved to be tough, loyal, combative and especially protective and caring for their fellow soldiers.'

One man, Private Leigh Turton-Sainsbury, amazed everyone in Korea when he turned up one day in clean uniform, sporting the Royal Air Force's coveted Distinguished Flying Cross (DFC) and the British Army's Military Medal (MM).

'He said he had been court-martialled from the RAF and that he then joined the army and was posted to the Khyber Pass where he claimed to have won the Military Medal, then migrated to Australia and volunteered for Korea. After Turton-Sainsbury returned to Australia from Korea, the army had suspicions about his story.'

Private Turton-Sainsbury later caught up with Don in Adelaide at the Britannia Hotel, whereupon he immediately spun a yarn about having some bills to pay to Encyclopaedia Britannica. He asked Don to lend him £10. Don readily agreed to lend him the money, but the days passed and repayment was not forthcoming. Turton-Sainsbury had disappeared.

A few years later, Don Beard walked into the Fox & Hounds Hotel in Melbourne, run by Major Wes Lloyd, registrar at 3 General Hospital in Kure. There he set eyes on one Leigh Turton-Salisbury holding court among a group of men enjoying a drink together. Don gave the former private some credit, for Turton-Sainsbury was quick off the mark.

'Gidday, Doc. Oh, I owe you £10 and I lost your address. I'll just duck outside to get the money from my jacket in the hall.'

'While he was away I paid for a round of drinks Turton-Sainsbury had ordered before he left. The time passed and no sign of him. He'd done me. Not only did I not get the tenner he owed me, but I was left to pay for the drinks. Such is the power of a good con-man.'

Whether they be gems or rough diamonds, Don mixes well with them all. He always sees the positive in situations and the good in his fellow man. Queen Elizabeth II is, of course, a world treasure and a sparkling gem. In the 1980s, the Federal Government appointed Doctor Beard to be the official surgeon to the Queen whenever she visited Australia.

'She never got sick,' he said. 'But she did say to me, "I assure you, doctor, that I do not need your surgical services, however, come down and have tea with us on the Royal Yacht *Britannia*."

'It was very exciting being driven down Port Road in dress uniform and sword, with people lining the route and the crowd became bigger as Margaret and I approached the Royal Yacht. We went up the gangplank to be received by the Duty Officer and taken to Her Majesty. Prince Philip and I discussed the Lord's Taverners Cricket Society, of which he is the "Twelfth Man", and Her Majesty spoke to us about the advances in surgery. Indeed a memorable day.'

Thirteen

Power of the Human Spirit

I deal with a lot of patients, and I find that, with those who are believers – I do not mind whether they believe in Christ, Mohammed, Buddha or whoever – as long as they believe that there is a God or someone greater than them then they can face up to death better.

Donald Beard

Donald Beard knows all about the power of the human spirit. Countless times in war and peace he has witnessed great bravery and an unquenchable will to live by the wounded, the sick and the dying. During his long medical career there have been seen some amazing advances in medicine and patient care. Dr Beard well remembers penicillin becoming available from 1945 and the first batch of the wonder drug arriving at Royal Adelaide Hospital. South Australian-born and educated Howard Florey was one of three men credited with discovering the practical use of penicillin. In the 1930s Florey got a team together at Oxford University and set about finding a way make penicillin work for the good of mankind. The urgency to find a practical use for what was to become a 'miracle' antibiotic became all the more acute with the onset of a world war. Florey's team undertook an experiment with eight mice, which turned out to be one of the most important medical experiments in history. On 25 May 1940 Florey's team injected the eight mice with a lethal dose of streptococci bacteria. Four of the mice were treated with penicillin, the remaining four were not. The treated ones fully recovered, all four of the untreated rodents died.

With the early dark days of the war upon the world and the Battle of Britain about to begin, the lives of eight mice must have been seen as insignificant, but Florey's team had made an extraordinary breakthrough for medical science. Tests were carried out by Florey and Major Hugh Cairns, a neurosurgeon in North Africa. They were classmates in physics at Adelaide University along with Mark Oliphant, one of a team of scientists who created the atom bomb.

By D-Day in June 1944, wounded Allied soldiers were being treated and saved in the their thousands by penicillin. Don Beard was working at the

RAH at the very cutting edge of the new and exciting technology which saw penicillin save so many lives throughout the world.

That very year streptomycin was introduced as the first drug for the treatment of tuberculosis, which had been up until that time a dreaded and often fatal disease. Tuberculosis was highly contagious and many medical students contracted the disease. Late in his career as a surgeon, medical science hit upon antibiotics for peptic ulcers. Up until that momentous discovery, the usual procedure was for a patient to have about two-thirds of his stomach removed. Nowadays an antibiotic treats the condition, so that any drastic surgery is rare.

However, before the new technology, Dr Beard performed about 40 gastrectomies. Advances in heart surgery – bypass and open-heart procedures – and joint replacement surgery – especially knee and hips – have relieved much distress and disability for thousands of people worldwide. From the outset Dr Beard has been at the coalface of this technology. Heart, hip and knee operations seem like shelling peas to the clever and talented surgeons, however, he knows all too well how careful medical practitioners and nurses have to be in a hospital environment to ward off the constant threat of infection.

In 1946, the young and enthusiastic medical student Donald Beard diagnosed a three-year-old neighbour with a patent ductus arteriosus, a congenital disorder of the heart. This condition arises when the newborn child's normal foetal blood vessel to the lung fails to close after birth. Because the vessel does not close and is 'patent' the result is irregular transmission of blood between two of the most important arteries close to the heart, the aortas and the pulmonary artery.

Early symptoms are uncommon, but as the child grows shortness of breath increases along with poor weight gain. Left untreated the toddler will develop congestive heart failure. His diagnosis saved the little girl a debilitating disease and an uncertain future.

Donald Beard devoted his life to the care of the sick, the wounded and the dying, but he vehemently opposes euthanasia, regarding the practice to be 'morally and ethically wrong'.

'Doctors should not be forced to play a part in it. Not only do I not believe in euthanasia, I am in total opposition to it and have been all my medical life. I have written many letters and appeared before a parliamentary inquiry to put my case in total opposition to euthanasia. It's too complicated and dangerous to leave in the hands of politicians and lawyers. I believe in doing what you do best and they (politicians and lawyers) don't handle the dying patient very well.'

There is, according to Dr Beard, no argument to justify euthanasia, which is fiercely opposed by the Australian Medical Association the British Medical Association, the American Medical Association and the World Health Organisation.

'The Law Lords in London have considered this matter fairly recently. Whatever you think about the rather peculiar system of justice in the United Kingdom, the Law Lords represent the pinnacle of legal knowledge and debate in the UK. When such an august body can be so certain in their opinion against euthanasia (five to none), then it can't be easily ignored. They heard a case in 2001, the sort of case that is used by euthanasia proponents to support their calls for euthanasia. In this case, a 42-year-old woman with motor neurone disease asked the court to lay aside the criminality of her husband assisting her suicide.

'She brought the case as a denial of her rights under the European Convention of Human Rights, and her right to privacy. Another woman, a Briton with spina bifida, went through years of wishing to end her existence. She ended with the words, "If you are surrounded by people who make you feel as if your life has the same unfathomable value as theirs, then you are able to cope with tomorrow."'

Australian-based doctor and a leading proponent of voluntary euthanasia Dr Phillip Nitschke is pushing for governments to make it legal for dying patients to take their own lives. 'There are of course a few most strange doctors like Dr Nitschke,' Dr Beard said firmly. 'And I don't know who pays for him to carry on this program. The trouble is it gets out of hand. It is supposed to be on the patient's request. In 60 years of medicine I've never been asked by a patient to terminate his or her life. The trouble is some patients are dying slowly and the friends and relatives can't themselves stand to see the person suffering. A lot of the pro-euthanasia letters are written by people for their own sake not for the sake of the patient.

'Certainly the patient doesn't want to suffer but palliative care today is very good. We can relieve a lot of the pain of a dying patient, symptoms such as nausea, dizziness and loss of appetite. We can't relieve them completely. I maintain it should be left to the patient's doctor. I've had a number of patients in my time who've said to me, "I don't mind dying, but I don't know whether I can handle all the pain." I will sit with them, hold their hands and look at them and say, "Do not worry about the pain or other symptoms. I will look after it." They know what I mean and we sit quietly hand in hand.'

Dr Beard gave evidence to the South Australian Parliament's Social Development Committee at the Voluntary Euthanasia Inquiry at Old Parliament House, Adelaide, on 5 March 1999. He told that inquiry: 'I have looked after a great number of patients with cancer – most of whom, I am pleased to say, have recovered – despite the dreadful publicity that cancer gets in the media. In fact, a great percentage of patients with cancer anywhere – breast, bowel, but not so much brain and lung – survive and do very well. But you do not hear about that. I spoke at a euthanasia meeting six years ago (Medical and Legal Aspects of Death and Dying: Seminar Topic: 'Early death is better than life', Victor Harbor, 26–27 March 1993), three weeks after I had come out of hospital after a bowel cancer operation. So I know what it is all about.'

On 16 September 1996, a letter from Dr Beard on the subject of euthanasia was published in *Australian Medicine*. He wrote (in part): 'Proper terminal care is not euthanasia. We treat the terminally ill by palliation of their symptoms. We do not need the intrusion of third parties, lawyers, agents, politicians etc. Euthanasia is morally and ethically wrong. Doctors should not be forced to play a part in it.'

However, the pro-euthanasia lobby would argue that not all medical practitioners have the same depth of care and moral fibre of Dr Donald Beard.

'Death is inevitable. It is a part of birth, life and death and, to me, being a Christian I am not frightened of death, because I believe that it is not the end. I deal with a lot of patients, and I find that, with those who are believers – I do not mind whether they believe in Christ, Mohammed, Buddha or whoever – as long as they believe that there is a God or someone greater than them then they can face up to death better. A majority of non-believers – the atheists etc – are scared of death and have great trouble in dealing with it. So, religion does help.

'Do we need euthanasia? I do not believe so. I have to admit that not all my patients survive, some of them die. One of the things that the pro-euthanasia lobby says is that we (doctors) practise euthanasia. We do not. What we do is attempt, to the very best of our ability, to modify the dreadful symptoms that some patients have such as pain, vomiting, abdominal distension – all sorts of distressing complaints for which we can help. The euthanasia lobby claim we kill them, that we practise euthanasia. That is not true; what we are doing is easing suffering.

'There are other things we can do. When a patient gets to the point of not being able to eat or drink and I know that they will not survive, I do not believe that I should pump fluids into them which I know will help them survive maybe a few more days. Then comes the difficult situation of removing the drip.

'Again, the pro-euthanasia lobby may say, "Oh, you go up and take the drip out of the patient. This is a terribly traumatic experience," but I do not and we do not do it that way.

'When the drip slows down, and at times it stops and has to be replaced, I will say to the patient, "Look, this drip has stopped. Your veins are not very good, so we will give them a rest until tomorrow and think about putting the drip back." I do not actively remove a running drip, but I will explain to the patient, "We will give the veins a rest." Sometimes, just rarely, the patient may understand what I am saying and sometimes they may say, "Look, could I have the drip back?" "Of course, I will rest the vein and replace it tomorrow," I tell them, and tomorrow never comes. But it is important to keep the patient's mouth moist and clean and also his skin.

'Now, it does pose difficulties. I had a patient who had come to this situation. He was riddled with cancer and his distress was only just being held by the various drugs that I was giving him, so I did not replace the drip. That night I had a telephone call at home from a man in Mount Gambier who abused me and said, "I hear you've taken the drip out. You'll kill my father!"

'"Look," I said in reply, "I haven't taken it out, it's blocked."

'"Well, you'll have to put it back in again."

'"The family doesn't want the drip put back again."

'He said: "Well, I do."

'"But, you haven't seen your father in hospital while he's been sick. You've never come up here from Mount Gambier."'

Next day the irate man arrived at the hospital and got stuck into Dr Beard, who remained calm and told the man he must discuss his concerns with the rest of the family who had agreed with the course of action he had decided to take.

'"Oh," he said, "I don't talk to them!"

'The patient died a few hours later. We kept him comfortable, ensured he didn't have any pressure sores, his mouth moist.'

'Some members of the family want them to die because they don't want to see their loved one in pain. Unfortunately, there are others who want them to die because they can't stand going into the hospital every day and it's a very unpleasant thing to go in at a bedside while someone's dying. Sadly, some in another category want to get their hands on the estate. On rare occasions, some people stand to gain if the person lives. Maybe they are a carer or something. They are being paid to look after them.'

In 1984 Julie Richards lost her battle with cancer after a 12-year fight under Dr Beard's care. Near the end of her life, Julie wrote to her doctor:

> Dear Mr Beard,
>
> I would like to take this opportunity to thank you for all your care and concern not only over the past three months, but going back over 12 years.
>
> There should be a medal for doctors who go 'beyond the call of duty'. I feel at times you must become tired of the same old face popping up like a bad penny every few weeks. However, you always have a kind word and hopeful outlook, which I think is the only thing that has kept me sane through all this.
>
> To you and your dear wife (in my opinion the definition of 'a lady' is Mrs Beard) I, along with Doug and Peta, wish you the very best for Christmas and the New Year.
>
> Love
> Julie

Just before she died, Julie penned a last letter to him. Dated 4 April 1984, it reads (in part):

> What seemed important before now takes a back seat to being grateful for good health and a better understanding of their partner's worth to them. Doug and I became so close. I felt sorry that it had to take something as serious as this for us to realise how much each meant to the other. We had what others would say to be an average marriage; a few tiffs along the way. We didn't work at making each other happy all the time, which I now know should be the ultimate goal of everyone. Wealth, possessions, etc, are of no use if you're ill and can't be cured; it can happen to the lowliest beggar to kings and queens.
>
> Thank you for your untiring efforts on my behalf. I know you really battled and did everything possible. You already know I …

Julie didn't have the strength to finish the letter or to sign her name. Her writing just trailed away. 'You know,' Dr Beard said, his eyes misting over, 'I couldn't save her, but I'll never forget the night I went to see her in hospital. I wore my evening army dress uniform and the instant Julie saw me her face lit up and she reached up and embraced me.'

In November 2011, 27 years after Julie Richards passed away, her sister Sandy Scott wrote to Dr Beard, part of which follows:

> Just had to let you know that on Friday 11 November, when Julie would have turned 62, you happened to be on Channel 7 news. Now how incredible is that, almost like a sign. Doug and Peta taped it because they were out that night, but I saw it. Just to see you again (and you have barely changed) and hear that wonderful voice of yours, brought it all back. The eulogy you did for Julie was incredible and I still listen to the tape yearly, so I would recognise your voice anywhere. You are looking so well and still stand ever so straight. I think of Julie every day and speak of her often to my partner, Bob, who never met her, but says he feels like he knows her from all my stories about her. You made such a difference in her life, that special bond you shared was evident. So thank you so very much for helping her through the darkest time of her life.
>
> With gratitude always,
> Sandy Scott

In 1987 ex-SA and Australian batsman Les Favell developed cancer of the kidney, which was removed by Don Beard's close friend, Dr Peter Harbison, a former Australian pole vault champion. Sadly the operation came too late for Les, the cancer had spread. Because of Les's fabulous contribution to sport, the South Australian Cricket Association and Lord's Taverners decided to give him a farewell match on the Adelaide Oval. The non-playing captains were Les Favell and Sir Donald Bradman.

'What a wonderful match it was, the appreciative crowd revelling in the dancing feet of Neil Harvey, the glorious driving and explosive power of Graeme Pollock. When the captains went out onto the oval to toss, Les turned to me and said, "Doc, would you come with me. I can get out there to toss, but I doubt if I can get back."

'After the match, as black clouds skirted the southern end of the ground, Les went home for a rest, but returned for a memorable dinner when Sir Donald spoke so beautifully about Les as a cricketer and a man. Within a month Les was confined to bed and nursed by his beloved wife, Berry. I sat at his bedside a few days before he died, holding his hand while he said, "Doc, I am not afraid to die, but I don't want to leave Berry – I love her so much."'

One of the more remarkable personalities in Dr Beard's life was journalist and author Elizabeth Auld. She inherited a unique sense of adventure from her grandfather, William Patrick Auld, who went with John McDonnell Stuart on an exploratory expedition from Adelaide to Darwin in 1862.

In the early summer of 1932, Elizabeth was among a throng of journalists and photographers who flocked to the wharves at Port Phillip Bay to interview members of Douglas Jardine's touring England cricket team. All Australian newspaper editors were jostling to get a new angle on the stories emanating from England about Jardine, the Scottish-born, lean and mean captain. When the press arrived *en masse* they found to their anger that the gangway to the tourists' ship was blocked. As they argued with the ship's crew, Elizabeth slipped away from the mob and walked to the stern of the ship where she searched for another way to board the vessel. There she spotted a tall, slim man in a suit and grey hat leaning against the rail of the ship smoking a cigarette. He asked Elizabeth what she was doing and the young journalist introduced herself, explaining how she was a journalist for the *Herald Sun* in Melbourne and her assignment was to interview the England captain. The tall man smiled, held out his hand and helped Elizabeth aboard.

'How might I find Mr Jardine?' she asked.

'You are speaking to him,' he grinned. 'Come with me and I'll tell you all you wish to know.'

Much to the annoyance of her male colleagues within the newspaper industry, Elizabeth Auld got the scoop of that Ashes summer, which became known as the Bodyline series. For all her more than 50 years as a journalist, Elizabeth worked for the Murdoch News Ltd publishing empire. She wrote for the *Herald Sun* and, from its launch in 1964, the *Australian*. Elizabeth lived next door to Don and Margaret Beard when they lived in Marryatville. They became great friends. At the age of 90 Elizabeth's journalistic career had long ended, but it was then that she sat down to write a book, the story of *The Kidnapped Kitten* (Peacock Publications). The foreword was penned by Barry Humphries, who regarded Elizabeth as 'the most charming person I've met', and her book was launched by Lachlan Murdoch, who flew from Sydney.

Barry Humphries wrote: 'I first met Elizabeth Auld in the early 1960s when she was a devastatingly attractive Murdoch journalist at an age when most of her colleagues had retired. She now lives in a charming house full of flowers in Adelaide. When you leave – usually because you can't stand the pace of morning tea with Elizabeth Auld – she comes to the gate in traditional fashion to wave you off. A nice old custom rarely seen these days.'

Dr Beard fondly recalls Barry Humphries' frequent visits to the Auld household. Clutching a bunch of gladiolas, the international celebrity would waltz down her driveway, making straight to her front door. As Elizabeth neared her century in years her health began to deteriorate. One night when Dr Beard visited the ailing Elizabeth at home, she said to her friend, 'Ninety-seven, ready for Heaven. I think I'll pop off now.'

'And she did exactly that,' the doctor said. 'Elizabeth rolled onto her side and took her last breath.'

About three years ago when Barry Humphries was in Adelaide delivering his immensely popular one-man show, Dr Beard received a late evening phone call from the veteran showman.

'I'm pretty unwell,' Humphries told him as the doctor's grandfather clock in the background gently struck eleven o'clock. 'I need you to take a look at me.'

Throughout his working life the doctor was used to calls on his services and he quickly dressed and drove to the Grosvenor Hotel in North Terrace. When he got to see Humphries in his hotel room he found the showman lying in bed in a lather of sweat. 'He was running a high temperature and shaking involuntarily. Barry looked terrible,' Dr Beard recalled. 'I thought he was getting pneumonia and while I was writing a script for a course of antibiotics, I told my friend that he was so sick he should slow down and take things easy. He should stop touring and retire from show business.'

The antibiotics must have done the trick, but Dr Beard's advice about retirement fell on deaf ears for the very next night Barry Humphries was back on stage, seemingly as bright as a button and as sharp and as clever as ever.

On 1 June 2005, Dr Don Beard delivered, arguably, his *pièce de resistance* of medical papers, *Music and Warfare*, to a 500-strong audience at The Quincentenary Conference, Royal College of Surgeons in Edinburgh. He was invited to provide this presentation in the wake of delivering it to the annual conference of the Royal Australasian College of Surgeons. His talk covered all the major wars from the ancient to the most recent and how attitudes to war had drastically changed. While no one wanted war, he argued, they will always happen because of the 'fight for power, disputed lands, religion or simply the love of a woman such as Anthony for Cleopatra'. Speaking about the changing attitude of those composing music for warfare, Dr Beard succinctly described how at first battles and war were glorified with stirring battle hymns, but now the music of war reflects the reflective mood of nations: the music of war is now a lament. The victory of the Russians was commemorated by Tchaikovsky's *1812 Overture* and more than a century later, at the height of the unpopular Vietnam War, came Pete Seeger's 'Where have all the flowers gone?' His audience could never have envisioned the time he took to gather material for this speech. Over a period of two years, Don grabbed any spare time he could to go to the State Library, The War Memorial, Art Gallery, Museum and Elder Conservatorium for Music to fossick among the archives for the information he needed. There was no Google then, no immediacy for a researcher as there is today.

In his speech first given to the Royal Australasian College of Surgeons in 2002, he said:

Two hundred years ago the French military surgeon, Larrey, said, 'Casualties must be removed promptly and properly from the battlefield to the best possible care.'

In the Franco-Prussian War, German surgeon, Bernhardt Langenbeck, said, 'No art, no science is too great when caring for the flower of the nation's youth bleeding on the battlefield.'

Management of battle injuries deteriorated through the Dark Ages, but improved in medieval Spain when Queen Isabella insisted that all armies be accompanied by surgeons. She was criticised for visiting battlefields, but said: 'Let me alone, the only consolation our soldiers have is the presence of their sovereign. It may at least inspire them with the courage to bear their painful wounds with dignity.' She was the mother of Henry VIII's wife, Catherine of Aragon.

Military surgery is a saga of forgotten lessons. In the 1st Century AD, the Roman, Celsus, recommended ligature of a bleeding vessel. This was forgotten and replaced by the red-hot cautery. In the Russo–Japanese War in 1900, the Russian surgeon, Princess Vera Ignatieva Gedroitz, advocated pushing her ambulance train close to the front line to facilitate early surgery, particularly on abdominal wounds. This too was forgotten, even in WWI.

In the 15th Century, surgeons were attached to individual generals and gave only what time they could spare to the soldier. In Spain Ambrose Pare was the surgeon to the Commander of the French Army but still made fundamental observations on the management of injuries. He made the famous statement, 'I dress the wounds and God heals it.'

John Hunter, the father of British surgery, considered it important to devote time to the soldier and he served at Belle Isle. Charles Bell attended the wounded at Waterloo and as part of his records he made paintings of the wounds. The Napoleonic Wars produced two outstanding French surgeons, Pierre Francois Percy, who introduced trained stretcher-bearers, and Dominique Jean Larrey, who designed the light flying ambulance. The technology of war and surgical techniques has improved with every battle.

All of this was accompanied in the lecture room by music of the battle; The Gordon Highlanders' stirring rendition of *When the Battle was Over*. Don posed the question: What of the role of music in warfare?

> It does much more than express emotions. The regulation of daily camp life was played out by the 'Reveille'; the trooping of the colours on parade; the retreat; and, finally, the Tattoo. Orders were passed with musical instruments on the battlefield until the noise became too great. Even at the Battle of Kapyong in Korea in April 1951, an overwhelming force of Chinese advanced upon the Australian battalion with a frightening scream of whistles and trumpets, which I will never forget.
>
> Finally is the music that is dedicated to the soldiers to express their suffering and protests. In Ancient Egypt they used trumpets and horns and the Greek soldier used a pottery salpinx. The Romans used various curved instruments made of ox horn. Bands, such as the Black Watch, lead the soldiers into battle in Iraq, but often members of the band were assigned other duties, such as stretcher-bearers in the Australian Army and they gave magnificent service.

On a lecture tour of India and Pakistan in 1996, Dr Beard spoke in Lahore on 'The Surgery of the Injured Soldier'. He outlined war music over the ages, including *Spartacus* by Khachaturian, in the opera *Sampson and Delilah*, and the stirring battle song, *Chanson La Guerre*, where, at the Battle of Marignano in 1515, two armies clashed with the sounds of weapons, then music of trumpet, fife and drum, the shouting of the soldiers and finally the cries of help from the defeated army.

Dr Beard noted that in 1796, while on Belle Island fighting against Napoleon, John Hunter, the father of British surgery, made significant observations on vascular injuries and surgical management. While Hunter was in the army, Handel composed *The Messiah* in London, and 'Hunter's wife, Anne, wrote a libretto, which was eventually discovered in the vaults of the Royal College of Surgeons of England'.

'Ludwig van Beethoven penned some stirring war music, including the *Wellington Victory Sympathy*, *Rule Britannia*, and *God Save the King* for the British, and for Napoleon, whom he admired, the composer composed the *Emperor Concerto* while he hid in a cellar from the bombardment of the outskirts of Vienna.

'Beethoven also composed the *Eroica*,' Dr Beard continued, 'but when Napoleon declared himself Emperor, the composer considered it was against all his republican ideals and he tore up the title page. Napoleon's advance across Europe stopped dead in its tracks due to the merciless weather, which ended in the dreadful retreat in 1812; source of Tchaikovsky's celebrated *1812 Overture*, commemorating the victory of the Russians.'

During the tour in the Subcontinent Don Beard had the opportunity to travel up the Khyber Pass to the border with Afghanistan. He had to keep strictly to the Pass, but in the distance he could see a cloud of dust. When he reached it he found it was due to a cricket match being played by the Arab tribesmen. He was able to meet with Major Khan to whom he had written from Australia and invited to lunch with Margaret at the Officers Mess of the Khyber Rifles. They turned off the Pass up a dusty track and came upon an oasis of headquarters, at which a Pakistani pipe band was playing stirring military music on the parade ground. The reception had somehow been organised and their welcome was followed by a 'delightful lunch'. On their return journey they went down the Khyber Pass to Peshawer, capital of Khyber-Pakhtunkhwa and the economic hub for the federally administered tribal areas of Pakistan. Steeped in history and something of a mysterious place for Westerners, Peshawar is situated in a large valley near the eastern end of the Khyber Pass. As they walked through the alleyways and bazaars the Beards happened across a man in tattered clothing but of great presence. Don and Margaret had inadvertently happened upon Peshawar's famed Qissa Khawani Bazaar ('The Storytellers Market'). The storyteller, an Indian signaller, Kahn Singh, sitting blind and cross-legged at the bazaar would talk to anyone about 'Murphy Sahib', the famous Simpson and his donkey.

'There was no Victoria Cross and no medal, but Simpson was mentioned in dispatches for his gallant and distinguished service. Captain Ken Fry, 3rd Field Ambulance, and later an Adelaide physician, wrote to Simpson's sister: "Your mother can take comfort that he gave his life in a performance of gallant and dutiful service but has been excelled by no one."'

The legend of Simpson and his donkey has long captured the hearts of the Royal Australian Army Medical Corps. Simpson's legend grew in just a few short weeks on the bloodstained beaches and gullies of Gallipoli. His disregard for his own personal safety and care for the soldier was such an inspiration to all Australians that it transcends our greatest expectations of loyalty and commitment under fire. Simpson's enduring example of bravery immortalises the men and women of the medical corps who put their lives on the line at the battlefront to care for the wounded. Amid myriad stories of gallantry at Gallipoli, the story of Simpson and his donkey is perhaps the greatest tale of them all.

Don Beard believes the legend of Simpson and his donkey is the 'shining light' for the Royal Australian Army Medical Corps. 'Simpson's inspirational courage in caring for the wounded soldiers while walking his donkey through a hail of bullets is the greatest example for the men and women of our medical corps who put themselves in harm's way on the battlefield.'

John Simpson Kirkpatrick, deserter from the British Merchant Navy at Fremantle in 1910 and on the Gallipoli peninsula for less than four weeks, became a national hero. He enlisted in the AIF hoping that his service would get him back to England. The 22-year-old adventurer avoided any prospect of being arrested as a deserter from the British Navy by enlisting in the AIF under the name of Simpson. While he might not have been a good peacetime soldier, Simpson was fearless on the battlefield. His job was to recover and help the wounded in the hellish war that was Gallipoli. Famously, with bullets whizzing and mortars exploding all around him, he used a donkey to carry men down from the front line. The bravery of this 'man with the donkey' who carried no arms soon became the most prominent symbol of Australian courage and tenacity on Gallipoli.

In a fitting tribute, Dr Beard gave an address to the Lions Club of Adelaide on 21 June 1990 entitled 'A Service to society with special reference to John Simpson Kirkpatrick'. He said (in part):

> On the night of 24 April 1915, General Birdwood gave his message: 'Tomorrow at dawn we will make a landing at the Dardanelles. I am sure you will do your best for Australia and the Empire.' E.C. Buley wrote of the stretcher-bearers: 'They carried their wounded with a rain of bullets around them, their only concern not being to stumble with the tortured man they were carrying. One victim later said that when they heard a shell coming, they lay down the stretcher and draped their bodies across him.' The Australian plans had been excellent with field ambulances and the stationary hospital with Major Henry Newland in charge. The same could not be said of British medical arrangements. There were insufficient hospital ships and doctors. Conditions were dreadful. Seriously wounded lay on the decks or dirty unventilated spaces below. These inadequacies were recompensed by Private John Simpson and other men on the beach.
>
> On the first day of the landing he carried men down the dreaded Shrapnel

Gully. On the second day he went missing and it was then that he found the frightened donkey. The two became an independent unit. By day and night he scurried up Shrapnel Gully to the heavily shelled area around Monash Gully and Quinn's Post. He carried or dragged casualties to his donkey dubbed a variety of names including Abdul, Duffy and Murphy. Before he lifted his wounded comrade onto the donkey, he tended to him with what was said to be 'quick, gentle skilled hands'. And off they went with Simpson supporting the man with one arm and guiding the donkey with the other. An officer had wanted to give him a sovereign but Simpson replied: 'Keep your blinking quid, I am not dong this for money.' They referred to him using the Hindi word for hero, 'Bahadur – the bravest of the brave'. He had no time for letters from Gallipoli, but on 9 May sent a card to his mother saying, 'I am well. Received your letter, will write. Jack Simpson, 3rd Field Ambulance.'

For almost 20 hours on 11 May 1915 he struggled down with his casualties and lost none of them. On 15 May, General Bridges set out with Lieutenant R.G. Casey on his daily visit. At Monash Valley he stopped to talk to Captain Thompson at his aid post, but when he stepped onwards, he was hit. Simpson arrived and wanted to take him down with his donkey but General Bridges said he did not want to endanger any of the stretcher-bearers and died soon afterwards bleeding from a penetrating wound of the femoral artery.

On 19 May, the Turkish assault was at its height. When Simpson went up the valley he normally stopped at the water point to have breakfast, but it was not ready and he said, 'Never mind, get me a good dinner when I come back.' On the way down he was shot through the heart by a machinegun bullet at the same spot where General Bridges had been killed. He fell beside his donkey. Captain Davidson, 3rd Field Ambulance said: 'We covered his body and put it in a dugout by the side of the track and carried on with our job and went back for him at 1830 and buried him at Hell Spit with a simple wooden cross.' The word quickly spread through the trenches and there was great sadness.

During his service in Korea Dr Beard knew a man after Simpson's heart: stretcher-bearer and drum major, Sergeant Tom Murray, a man who displayed courage above and beyond the call of duty. Murray was awarded the George Medal for heroism under fire, which included saving a man who had fallen into the icy depths of the Taeryong River. When the 3rd RAR B Company reached the town of Kujin on the Taeryong River, only three kilometres from their destination, the town of Pakchon, they found one span of the

300-metre bridge across the Taeryong River had been destroyed. Amid fierce fighting with the North Koreans, our men could cross the 'broken bridge' but tanks and other vehicles could not. Fighting to retain possession of the bridge continued throughout the night and the Australians were up against Russian-made T-34 tanks and superior numbers of North Korean infantry.

In the early hours of the morning the North Koreans unknowingly moved onto the road where A Company was dug in. When the Australians and the enemy were only metres away from each other, A Company opened fire with small-arms fire, mortars and grenades and the enemy forces, including a T-34 tank, fled the scene. However, clearing the bridge brought a heavy cost to the regiment. The Australians lost eight soldiers plus another 22 injured. Sergeant Tom Murray spent hours evacuating the wounded across the broken bridge and at one point risked his life by stripping off and jumping into the freezing water to save a man who had fallen from the bridge. Murray's George Medal was only the second awarded to anyone attached to the 3rd RAR in Korea. Private Horace Madden was awarded a George Medal posthumously for his selflessness and bravery as a prisoner.

About 10 years ago a small group of South Australians got together to form the Simpson Foundation, with a view to raising awareness about the Simpson and his donkey legend and to raise funds to commission a bronze statue to be erected in a prominent place in Adelaide. Dr Donald Beard became the Simpson Foundation patron and Brigadier Rob Atkinson, who worked as an intern under the tutelage of Dr Beard and served in Vietnam, was the driving force behind the project.

'The idea of a Simpson statue went back to the 100 years celebrations of the Australian Army,' Brigadier Atkinson said. 'Ideas were being tossed about and we went to the Adelaide Lord Mayor (then Michael Harbison) and told him that the city had strong links with the Simpson and the Donkey legend and that we should so something. He was immediately enthusiastic about the idea of a statue and suggested we get Robert Hannford to do it.'

Local artist Robert Hannaford, who was commissioned to fashion the famous Don Bradman statue that stands in the Park Lands outside Adelaide Oval, readily agreed to do the job. After six years only about $80,000 had been raised and the project had lost momentum. The Simpson Foundation then appointed Colonel Viki Andersons, who as Colonel in the Royal Australian Army Medical Corps saw service in Timor, as chair.

Within a few years the Foundation had raised $450,000 (which included two separate donations of $50,000) and the 2.4-metre-tall bronze statue was unveiled where it now proudly stands on the corner of King William Road and War Memorial Drive. Simpson's unit, the Royal Australian 3rd Field Ambulance, had its headquarters in Adelaide from the start of WWI until 1995. In February 2012, SA Governor, Rear Admiral Kevin Scarce, unveiled the work, describing it as a 'wonderful tribute'.

Dr Beard believes the Simpson statue is a mute reminder to us all of the magnificent service provided by myriad defence force medical corps.

Fourteen

Hawkeye's Guardian Angel and Other Miracles

Neil's wife, Beverley, displayed the most wonderful courage and commitment I have ever seen in my medical life. She is an angel.

Donald Beard

Neil Hawke was a champion athlete, a Test cricketer and league footballer with the physique of an Amazon. Tall, broad-shouldered and toned of muscle, Hawke was poetry in motion when playing football across the forward line for Port Adelaide or South Australia, but as a clever fast medium swing bowler he had the action of a crab's sideways waltz about the flames of a fisherman's fire.

Just as Max Walker's tangle-footed method proved a plus for Victoria and Australia, Hawke's unique method worked wonderfully well for him. He could swing the ball both ways and on flat, unresponsive wickets he changed his pace cleverly and got the ball to move off the seam. His fingers had a tensile quality to them for they seemed to stretch and mould to the shape of the cricket ball. Neil would pick up the ball and the object seemed to fit his hand as if it was the most natural thing in the world. He taught me a lot about the need to change pace on the Adelaide Oval wicket, 'a key factor for success, whether you bowl fast or slow, is to break the rhythm of the batsman by subtle change of pace'.

Hawke played district cricket against Don Beard and me and I was lucky enough to join him in the SA team in 1967/68 and to tour England with the Australian team in 1968. I have this enduring image of Hawkeye – as he became affectionately known – in a slow waltz-cum-stroll with the Queen Mother at Clarence House. They shared a love of horses and there they were skipping along the corridor taking in the gilt-framed watercolours of dozens of famous horses and giggling like excited schoolkids.

In a long and distinguished career as player and commentator, former Test all-rounder Richie Benaud said Hawke was one of the best medium pacers he had seen. High praise given that Benaud batted against some great fast-medium bowlers, including England's Peter Loader, Trevor Bailey and the legendary Alec Bedser; South Africa's Trevor Goddard; Pakistan's Fazal Mahmood and the West Indies' Frank Worrell, plus Garfield Sobers, whose fast-medium stuff sometimes, when the mood struck him, turned to pace like fire. In 27 Tests Hawke took 91 wickets at 29.41, including a Test bowling best of 7/105.

He also excelled as an Australian Rules footballer and set the football world abuzz with his adopted new-style kick, the drop-punt. As a forward with East Perth in Western Australia Hawke used the drop-punt, which spun in the manner of a drop kick and travelled reasonably long distances. He always said that he found the drop-punt more reliable than the long-favoured drop kick or screw-punt. A few years later Subiaco and South Melbourne full-forward Austin Robertson added to the fame of 'the Neil Hawke special', booting hundreds of goals and always kicking a drop-punt. At East Perth, playing alongside Graham 'Polly' Farmer, arguably the greatest Australian Rules player in history, Hawke kicked 50 goals in his first year, 1958. The following season Hawke booted 114 goals helping the East Perth Royals to their second successive flag and was selected in the WA side. As the team's full-forward, he stood his old Port Adelaide teammate, the tough, unforgiving full-back John Abley. But Hawke kicked four goals to help WA to a comfortable win.

After a few years in WA where he excelled for North Perth in grade cricket, hitting 189 and figuring in a record 282-run fifth wicket partnership with Peter Wishart (122*) in the 1958/59 grand final, plus starring for East Perth and playing for WA in both football and cricket, he returned to Adelaide in time for the 1961/62 Sheffield Shield season. Back with Port Adelaide Cricket Club, he scored 137 and took 12/49 in what statistically was the finest all-round performance in district cricket – and a launching pad for what would become a brilliant career for SA and Australia. Hawke played football for Port Adelaide, East Perth, West Torrens, WA and SA and he was a member of the SA team which famously beat the mighty Victorian 18 at the MCG in 1963. He played with and against some physically tough characters: among them Neil Kerley, Ron Barassi, Kevin Murray, Jack Sheedy, Darryl Baldock, Sergio Silvagni, Brian Dixon, Ken Eustice, Geof Motley and John Cahill. Late in the last quarter of the 1958 East Perth–East Fremantle grand final, East Fremantle's giant ruckman Jack Clarke had the ball and was moving across the goal front when Hawke met him front on with a hip and shoulder. Off balance, Clarke careered headlong into the point post, snapping it off at ground level. There was no time to get a replacement so a tall, slim policeman stood like a Grenadier Guardsman as the point post and the game continued, with East Perth winning an epic clash by two points. A few East Perth supporters got hold of the post and nailed it to the back wall of the bar at Perth Oval. Under the post that Hawke broke is the caption: 'We hit them with everything including ...'

Hawke enjoyed a wonderful sporting career, but in his time top sportsmen often struggled to eke out a living away from the game. Soon after his sporting career ended in Australia, Neil went to live in England. He played cricket for the Nelson Club in Lancashire League and was involved in the Nelson Golf Club. A keen and good golfer (Neil once played off a two handicap), he was enjoying life in the UK and managed to make ends meet with a number of enterprises, including a few speaking gigs with the great England fast bowler Freddie Trueman. Then one day he got the biggest wake-up call in his life.

> In 1976 I had undergone emergency surgery for an intestinal blockage, caused by adhesions from an appendix operation many years earlier. It had been serious, but I soon got over it and resumed normal life. I thought of a hospital then as a garage. You had a problem, so you took your car in, got it fixed and all was well again. Later I was to learn how very wrong I was.
>
> Neil Hawke in *Neil Hawke – Bowled Over*, 1982

In 1979 Hawke sold his business interests in the UK. There was every chance that he would be taking up a business deal in South Africa, marketing pool tables in the republic. However, before travelling to South Africa, Hawke wanted to visit Adelaide, catch up with old friends and play a bit of golf. He had two marriages, and a daughter, Janet, from his first marriage, whom he hoped to see in Adelaide. In the summer of 1980, he met and fell in love with Beverley Meyers, an attractive single mother of two daughters, Natalie and Debra. They met at a Cheltenham race meeting. It was a classic case of love at first glance. Neil and Beverley had a whirlwind romance. Neil was in his element, perhaps truly in love for the first time in his life.

'It was like I was born again,' he said at the time. 'Beverley is such a wonderful, vivacious, passionate girl. I am so much in love.' The months passed and their love grew stronger. Marriage was in the air when Neil fell desperately ill.

Neil and Beverley had stayed up late to watch the 1980 ladies' Wimbledon final between the Australian favorite, Evonne Goolagong Cawley, and US champion, Chris Evert-Lloyd. Neil ate peanuts and drank a beer as Goolagong Cawley won 6–1, 7–6, her second Wimbledon crown. By the time the game had finished he was in excruciating pain.

When Neil was operated on for a bowel obstruction more than five years before, the condition was thought to have been caused by his eating peanuts but, for some reason, doctors there did not insist he never again eat peanuts. Beverley took Neil to see her own doctor and then to nearby Modbury Hospital.

Dr Beard soon heard of Neil Hawke's arrival. 'The registrar didn't know of Neil Hawke the great all-round sportsman, but he rang me and said he had admitted a chap with a small bowel obstruction. I told him – Dr Siew-Kiong Tham – to operate, normally a small bowel obstruction is a pretty straightforward operation, and that I would come up and give him a hand. I had every confidence in Dr Tham. He was a pretty good, qualified surgeon.'

Unbeknown to either doctor, Hawke's bowel was something of a time bomb. In wake of his abdominal operation in the UK he had developed adhesions of the small bowel, which was partially blocked. He had a virtual cesspool of muck and rubbish that had not built up sufficiently to completely close off the bowel. However, for five years food waste had dribbled past the partial obstruction of the small bowel into the lower bowel and the peanuts proved the last straw. Peanuts are notoriously difficult to digest and when eaten in quantity they form a mass. The small bowel was completely blocked. Dr Beard believes that the complete closure was inevitable, although peanuts probably brought on the condition sooner. By the time Don Beard got to the operating theatre, Dr Tham had begun to operate.

'In the operation carried out on Neil in the UK five years before, a hernia of the abdominal wall had to be repaired. The operation left a gaping wound, too big for the surgeon to be able to bring the two ends together and stitch them … so metallic mesh was stapled to the abdominal wall. Now Dr Tham was faced with cutting free the metallic mesh. This required very steady hands and a lot of patience. It was a very delicate procedure and Dr Tham was being extremely careful.'

Dr Beard was instructing Dr Tham in his work to separate the bowel from the abdominal wall, essential to enable the surgeon to see the extent of the problem and deal with the rest of the adhesions.

'It was an extremely delicate procedure, like separating the skin from a fish without damaging the flesh. But as Dr Tham was carefully cutting away the bowel from the abdominal wall, a tiny little nick gave off a little puff of gas. Nothing seemed wrong.'

Dr Beard told Dr Tham to sew up the little hole, which he did. What the doctors could not have known was that that little puff of gas was the most toxic gas imaginable. The scalpel had just touched the outer wall of the small bowel containing a build up of toxic gunk. Neil's small bowel was a potentially fatal toxic mass that proved to be the catalyst of the nightmare that followed.

Neil was pleased to see the familiar face of Dr Beard walk into the recovery room. He had known him for years, having played for Port Adelaide against Don when he was opening the attack for Sturt and, of course, throughout his time as the SACA doctor. But, within a few hours of the operation, Neil's condition had deteriorated dramatically.

'His body simply shut down and he had turned yellow. Neil had suffered total organ failure. That small nick on the wall of the bowel had a catastrophic effect, releasing a flood of infection which had laid dormant all those years. It spread rapidly throughout Neil's body. He suffered renal failure, gas gangrene and septicaemia. At Modbury Hospital we did not have the facilities to cope with such an emergency, so I transferred Neil to Royal Adelaide Hospital.'

When Beverley Meyers arrived at the RAH, Neil was on oxygen and a drip and medical staff indicated to her that he was not expected to last the night. But Neil did survive, although that was the start of a nightmare of hallucinations and the unreal and often frightening world that sometimes confronts an intensive care patient.

'From that first traumatic evening, Beverley sat beside Neil. She held his hand and wouldn't let him die. That extraordinary dedication and love, allied to Neil's courage and determination not to let go were, no doubt, crucial to his survival. Beverley displayed the most wonderful courage and commitment I have ever seen from a carer. She is an angel. For months Neil hovered between life and death. Because of the gas gangrene, his bowel was exposed for much of the time. Every time dead skin from the exposed bowel area was removed, skin-graft specialist Dr Don Robinson came in to do the repair work. Over the months Neil had undergone more than 50 operations, survived numerous cardiac arrests and had been administered more than 1000 pints of blood.'

From the outset, Neil's fiancée Beverley Meyers was totally committed to helping him get through his nightmare. It was for Don Beard the most loving, compassionate and caring act he had seen in all his medical life. Beverley was more than Neil's nurse: she was his guardian angel. Dr Beard had observed similar devotion on the battlefield.

'Beverley just sat at his bedside and held his hand and would not let him die. He didn't want to die because he loved her, she didn't want him to die because she didn't want to lose him and so she stimulated him and nursed him day and night, until she was able to do more than any of the nurses in the way of dressings, drips, putting in transfusions, giving him blood and other fluid and antibiotics. Neil had a number of cardiac arrests. She pumped him and got him going before the nurses arrived. That's a remarkable story of courage and devotion. Eventually after all the surgery, the countless skin grafts, the blood transfusions and recurrent cardiac arrests, the RAH administration said to Beverley: "We are sorry, but we can do no more."

'Beverley replied: "Well, I'm taking him home." Medical staff asked her how she would manage all the necessary procedures, such as clearing his airways, putting in the drips and changing his dressings. She reminded them she had been providing this care for the months Neil had been in hospital, fighting for his life.'

Beverley had set up a room in her house especially to care for Neil. There was a State-wide fundraiser to help buy the expensive equipment, although a lot of the money she raised by herself. Neil was just 41 years old, yet he had aged like a man who had endured years on a starvation diet and maltreatment in a POW camp. But he did survive and became well enough to lead a productive life, working as a cricket and football writer at the *News*, doing commentary work with Channel Nine and public speaking of his ordeal. His survival was considered a medical marvel by doctors and he was the subject of study by researchers on how long a patient could be drip fed.

In 1990, Neil Hawke suffered heart failure and then blood poisoning, central nervous system damage, cirrhosis of the liver and later contracted hepatitis B and C before a brain dysfunction in 1996 severely impaired his speech, leading to severe bouts of depression. Through all of this medical expenses mounted and he sought to sell some of his cricket memorabilia in England. Unfortunately, the man to whom he entrusted the memorabilia, a fellow cricket writer, was later found to have allegedly pocketed the profits of the sale after telling Hawke the items had been damaged in transit. In his last few years on earth, Neil Hawke became a born-again Christian and joined the evangelical Assemblies of God Church. He died in Adelaide on Christmas Day, 2000, aged 61. Survived by his third wife, Beverley, and his daughter Janet, tributes poured in from throughout the world and on Day Two of the Boxing Day Test match in Melbourne the Test players wore black armbands as a mark of respect. Don Beard has seen the good and the great on the battlefield and in peacetime he has seen his fellow men and women display courage in a variety of circumstances, but no devotion to duty, compassion and love of a fellow human being ever eclipsed Beverley Hawke's love for her husband, Neil; one of South Australia's most loved sporting sons.

Don Beard was greatly saddened by Neil's death. He had made time to look in on his old cricketing mate almost every day at the RAH when Neil was fighting for survival. Old mates such as Ian Chappell, Bob Simpson and the doyen of ABC radio, Alan McGilvray, used to visit Neil occasionally, but it was Beverley who did the hard yards. Dr Beard considers Neil's recovery from the trauma of his body completely shutting down from the toxic shock of gas gangrene to be one of the most remarkable in his medical experience. And the doctor received a lot of very unfair criticism from those who didn't know the circumstances of Neil's illness, how the toxic time bomb had lain dormant in his upper bowel all those years before the July 1980 emergency. A Sydney commercial radio man blamed Dr Beard, saying he was at fault for 'a simple operation gone wrong'. It is extraordinary how such ignorant voices find their way to the airwaves or into the press in a modern Australia of so-called tolerance, equality and fair play. But Don Beard knows that all that could have been done for Hawkeye was done. 'Neil Hawke's courage and recovery was the most amazing I've seen in peacetime medical practice, but there were one or two horrifically injured soldiers who virtually came back from the grave in Vietnam.'

Don Beard has seen first-hand some other amazing feats of courage. There was, of course, Julie Richards, for whom Dr Beard was her 'shining light'. He has never been anything but the most compassionate, caring medical practitioner; the complete professional who always followed up on his patients. Here are some of their stories.

In 1987 Dr Beard was on call at Modbury Hospital when a 17-year-old soccer player who had recently represented South Australia at the national level was brought in with a severe injury to his right leg. Neil Fuller had been involved in a heavy tackle and had both of his bones broken in his right shin, but the critical concern was that the accident had also resulted in his artery being severed. He spent three weeks in Modbury Hospital and because of the severed artery and complications arising from it, Don knew that in order to save the young man's life it had to be amputated, just below the knee. He knew that when the young man recovered from the surgery he would be greatly distressed because the injury meant the end of a promising soccer career. Dr Beard did for Neil Fuller what he has done for countless people – in the trenches of Korea and the field hospital in Vietnam, for patients suffering a variety of illnesses and injuries – he talked to him and he confided in him.

'After his recovery from having his right leg amputated, I sat by Neil Fuller's bedside. I held his hand and told him the best story I know of a man who had lost not one but both legs and yet he recovered to make a most wonderful contribution to public and family life. I told him the story of Digger James, the Australian soldier who lost his legs when he was blown up in Korea. Digger, as we've seen, wanted to stay in the army and I advised him to study medicine and become a doctor. Of course, Digger did so and gave great service to the Australian Army in Vietnam and beyond. The young man listened intently and while he didn't say a lot to me at that time, he certainly took the advice on board and really made a wonderful comeback.'

Neil Fuller spent three weeks in hospital. Sadly he would never play soccer again and have the chance to realise his dream, to play for the Socceroos. But he set new targets. Neil was determined to represent his country and through his grit and determination he became one of the world's best amputee athletes. Neil won 34 medals representing Australia – 16 gold, 10 silver and eight bronze. Since 1995 he dominated the 400-metre event for below-knee amputees, slashing the world record. He broke the record of 56.26 seconds by nearly five seconds, a sensational time of 51.89 seconds, just two seconds slower than the time set by the world's best 400-metre female runner, Cathy Freeman. He represented Australia at four Paralympics from 1992 – Barcelona, Atlanta, Sydney and Athens – winning a total of six gold, six silver and three bronze medals. He also introduced the spring-loaded splint and was awarded an OAM for his achievements.

Motorbike enthusiast and racing rider Paul Keily was badly injured in a motorcycle accident. The doctor repaired his punctured lung, fractured left femur and ruptured liver. Keily recovered fully, but the surgical team, which had toiled so well to save Paul's life, missed something. They forgot to check Keily's right big toe. It had been broken in the accident and was left unattended. Paul Keily made a complete recovery – except for his big toe. It still throbs with pain on occasion. That the surgical team overlooked ensuring that all was well with Paul was a good lesson to them.

Another interesting case was that of Ralph Turner, a lacrosse player. He was training at Woodville Oval when he copped a stray elbow under the rib cage. He was in pain, but it didn't deter him riding his bicycle the 20 kilometres from Woodville to his home at Tea Tree Gully, whereupon he collapsed and was taken by ambulance to Modbury Hospital. There Dr Beard removed

Turner's spleen, bringing back memories of a similar operation he performed on an army batsman he struck with the new ball in a cricket match at Kure in Japan. At that time Don Beard left the field with the injured batsman, operated to remove the spleen of the man he struck, and returned to the bowling crease to finish off the opposition batting.

And, of course, there was the market gardener, Paul Camilleri, who fell off the back of his truck and landed on an upturned pitchfork, the prongs penetrating his rectum, the very day Test opening bowler Jeff Thomson suffered a dreadful fracture dislocation of the shoulder when he collided with Allan Turner at the Adelaide Oval. Don could not leave the Modbury Hospital operating theatre where was in the middle of repairing Mr Camilleri's rectum and giving him a colostomy. (He survived and three months later the colostomy was closed.) Don sent a message to the Adelaide Oval to contact an orthopaedic surgeon to operate on Thommo. He performed a delicate and complicated operation but then had to go overseas to a conference, and Don took over the rehabilitation. They became great friends.

In the late 1980s eccentric England spinner Phil Tufnell, who could bowl but couldn't catch a cold, fell foul of the early stages of pneumonia and Dr Beard had him rushed to the RAH. With a temperature of 103 degrees, Tufnell spent hours on an intravenous drip and a course of antibiotics. Without warning, he disappeared from his hospital bed and first thing next day, much to Don Beard's amazement and concern, Tufnell opened the England bowling. There was the time Rod Marsh was hit on the head in an attempted hook off one of the rampant West Indies fast men. The doctor quickly assessed Marsh's condition and when he found that the Australian wicketkeeper was shaken, but not stirred sufficiently to prevent him playing on, he was immediately on the phone to Rod's wife, Ros. 'Given Ros was in WA and probably heard about the incident over the radio or saw it on TV, I thought I would allay her fears.'

On another occasion Dr Beard rushed to the aid of Doug Walters, who, in the attempt to hook a ball from South Australian speedster Wayne Prior, got his boot sprigs stuck in the turf and with the momentum of his body something had to give. It did. Doug sustained a dislocation of the patella (kneecap), an injury which ruled the NSW batsman out of contention for any Test matches in the 1975/76 season. Another time, another tough guy, David Boon, broke a bone in his little finger of his right hand and, sensibly, Boonie came off for treatment.

All the patients mentioned revealed courage in their own different ways, but perhaps the most remarkable of Dr Beard's experiences with courage from a top-level sportsman was the time in the early 1960s when world cycling great Nino Solari was badly injured while racing. Having survived war-torn Italy, the country of his birth, 18-year-old Nino Solari came to Adelaide in 1955. He quickly developed a love of sport and excelled in cycling. Adelaide's local morning newspaper, the *Advertiser*, reported on 7 December 1963: 'Pocket-sized Italian cyclist Nino Solari resumed cycling in the Six Day Race at the Norwood Velodrome with a broken collarbone. In obvious pain and riding one-handed, Solari stayed on the track to keep his team in the race … a true hero.' Don Beard knew the whole story.

'On 6 December 1963, I was on surgical call at the RAH when Nino Solari was admitted with a fractured clavicle and a very nasty lacerated leg he sustained in a fall at the Norwood Velodrome (now the site of a tenpin bowling alley in Osmond Terrace). His partner was the great cyclist, Sid Patterson. The race required two riders working as a team to ride non-stop for six days. In Solari's absence, Patterson continued to ride, hoping for his partner to return. Solari had a general anesthetic to repair the damage and he was returned to the ward where I expected him to stay for a couple of days. I was unaware of the drama at the racetrack later in the day. I called into the ward to check his recovery. Nino was not there! He had signed a risk form and discharged himself, whereupon he returned to the Velodrome in time to take over from Patterson, who had been riding for about 10 hours. The pair went on to win the race.' Apart from his success in the sport, Nino's son David became a world champion cyclist, and followed his dream to represent Italy. He won the Italian national junior titles and was a member of the Italian cycling team at the Seoul Olympics.

Fifteen

'My fortunate life'

Don Beard draws a crowd as well as standing above it; veterans ebb and flow about him for a word or two; punctuated with many handshakes and laughs. The easy comradeship has a special touch: Don Beard is 3RAR's family doctor.

Alan Millett in *Their War for Korea*

Don Beard smiles the smile of a man who has tasted life to the full; all its joys and tragedies: 'If ever a man enjoyed a fortunate life, it was me.' He lived through the darkest days of the Great Depression and the Beards struggled, as did many thousands of Australian families, but his childhood was a happy one. Don didn't inherit a silver spoon. Two key elements were at play: Don's insatiable thirst for knowledge and Harold Beard's determination to do all in his power to provide a good educational pathway for his son.

Away from war, one of Dr Beard's greatest battles was to campaign towards greater road safety in Australia, specifically in the State of South Australia. In the 1960s Australian television featured a US police show, *Highway Patrol*, hosted by veteran actor Broderick Crawford, who signed off each episode with these sobering words: 'Leave your blood at the Red Cross, not on the highway.' Surgeons know all too well how devastating road accidents can be: for the victim and the family.

Don Beard's interest in road trauma began when he was a medical student working in casualty at Royal Adelaide Hospital. 'Later Sir Edward Hughes (who was associated with me in caring for casualties of war in Korea) and I recommended to the Royal Australian College of Surgeons a number of factors which would reduce the road roll. I was always concerned as to why so many accidents occurred and was very upset with the number of road crashes, which seemed to steadily increase each year. In fact, much road trauma results from irresponsible driving by a driver affected by consuming too much alcohol and by driving too fast in the wrong place.' Don says there is a tendency for drivers involved in road crashes to try to divert the blame.

'They talk about poor roads, bad signals or hazardous traffic rules. But in the end the only way people can avoid crashing is to drive at a speed suitable for the particular road, intersection or weather conditions.'

Dr Beard helped the SA Road Safety Council and the Australian Medical Association (AMA) in 1970 to lobby government to legislate for compulsory blood alcohol testing for all victims of road crashes. He believes such testing should include all passengers, cyclists and pedestrians over the age of 14.

'Some in authority say you can't test people as young as 14, however, a lot of 14-year-olds are drinking out there.' He said that a 'bad feature' of the present licensing system was the test might prove the ability of the driver to handle a vehicle, but it cannot test the motorist's behaviour. 'When we introduced blood-alcohol testing, the number of deaths per year was 373. Two years later it was 273 – reduced by 100.

'Similarly the compulsory wearing of seatbelts has reduced the death rate considerably. In fact, statistics reveal a 20 per cent reduction of serious injury or death by drivers and passengers involved in car crashes compared with those who did not wear a seatbelt.'

The great trauma and tragedy visited upon hundreds of people in the wake of a vehicle accident was never more evident than in Dr Beard's sad story.

'One Christmas Eve I had a ring from the Modbury Hospital. A 16-year-old girl had been brought in. She had just finished her matriculation studies and was looking forward to attending university. She'd been to town to celebrate with friends. She arrived home, got off the bus, walked round the back of the vehicle and was hit by a car, which had failed to stop. I raced to the hospital and we went straight into theatre.

'We worked five or six hours trying to save her; she was losing a lot of blood. The more I worked, the more blood Bob Edwards administered, but we were getting nowhere. Eventually, sometime after midnight, she died. I see her now lying on the table and I could imagine what her parents would be thinking.

'Next morning I felt that I would like to speak to the parents so I drove up to their home, knocked on the door and went into the hallway where there was a large Christmas tree surrounded by presents; presents that were not going to be opened. The family didn't want to play a part of Christmas Day. They sat around, they talked of her and I'll never forget two things – in the operating theatre when I lost her and going into that house and seeing the Christmas tree and all the decorations.' On many occasions a surgeon has the unpleasant task of telling loved ones at the hospital that the patient did not survive. Don said this task was never easy.

In 1969 the Australasian College of Surgeons held a conference in Melbourne to discuss the number and cause of road crashes throughout Australia. Twelve surgeons present were given a project to research. Dr Beard was nominated as the South Australian-based surgeon to investigate two areas – the merit or otherwise of drivers wearing seatbelts and the effect of alcohol and drugs on drivers. Over a period of 12 months he looked at more than 10,000 road crashes and their records and found other important factors in the cause of road trauma. For instance, his research found that 40 per cent of victim drivers who died in road accidents were aged 16 to 25.

'These drivers love the thrill of speed and are sometimes at the wheel of a faulty vehicle, often without thought of the consequences, and they sometimes drive recklessly on dangerous back roads away from police surveillance. Unfortunately whenever there is a crash involving alcohol or speed or whatever, people tend to say that is the cause and immediately recommend the lowering of speed or alcohol. The politicians think they have fixed the problem and want to be seen to be doing something. Things are not so simple. There is no single cause of a crash and no single method for reducing the toll. Crashes all have other causes – large and small. They all need to be examined.

'Some 30–40 per cent of all deaths on the roads were related to the drivers being under the influence of alcohol. Despite there being a far greater volume of vehicles in the city and suburbs, about 40 per cent of all fatal crashes occurred in country areas. Again, there are many factors.

'People say to me, "I was only doing 100 kilometres an hour." But if the driver is doing 100 kilometres an hour on a dirt road with soft shoulders and is faced with a bend in the road there is precious little time to correct. And this ends in an inevitable crash.'

The SA State Government, active in seeking ways to reduce the road toll, came up with a scheme that over the following 20 years helped reduce fatalities by a huge margin. Gil Langley, Don's old wicketkeeper at Sturt, recommended him to become part of the Road Safety Council in South Australia. Langley was then the ALP Member for Unley and later Speaker for the SA House of Assembly. He knew only too well about Don's concern for road safety and finding a way to drastically cut the road toll. A brilliant all-round sportsman, Langley played football and cricket for Sturt and South Australia, and four VFL games for Essendon, including the 1943 Grand Final, which Richmond won by five points. He also played 26 Tests, catching 83 batsmen and stumping 15.

In 1974 Dr Beard was appointed chairman of the SA Road Safety Advisory Council. At that time he listed the five main factors that contribute to road crashes. He calls them the 'Five Fingers of Death':

- Speed
- Alcohol
- Reckless driving
- Country roads
- Youth and inexperience

'Each of these Five Fingers of Death contributes to 40 per cent of road crashes. When speed is combined with drinking too much in an un-road-worthy car on a dirt road in the country a bad road crash is almost certain to occur.'

What of drugs? Dr Beard said in the early days of investigating the causes of road crashes, drugs were not perceived to be a major problem. However, an enormous variety of drugs became easily accessible and there was a general awareness of the detrimental rffects these drugs can have on the nervous system. 'Depressants like alcohol either excite or modify the reaction of the brain and as such reduce the ability to adjust quickly to an emergency situation. Years ago we knew little of how various drugs affected people. They were difficult to detect. Now we know a great deal more and we realise how important they are in the crash scene.'

There are other less frequent causes of road crashes. 'They are countless and include the medical – heart attacks, strokes, epileptic fits – fatigue, suicide, un-roadworthy vehicles, roads, single occupancy, stress.

'There are many more factors that combine with the "five fingers" to produce the crash situation. Driving a vehicle on our roads is a privilege, not a right and every driver should consider the other drivers.'

For years, using his position as chairman of the Road Safety Council, Don lobbied government for changes to legislation so there was mandatory blood testing of all drivers and passengers over the age of 14 involved in a motor accident; random breath testing; and the compulsory wearing of crash helmets for motorbike riders and cyclists, and seatbelts for driver and passengers.

Dr Beard also wrote dozens of letters to the editor of the morning newspaper, the *Advertiser*, warning of the dangers on our roads. In 1985 there was a huge media campaign in Adelaide which carried the catchcry, 'Arrive Alive in 85'. The campaign was designed to help keep the SA road toll below 270. By 2005 the toll was 147 and in 2011 it was just over 100. Despite a far greater number of cars on the road, high-powered vehicles with the capacity to reach ludicrous speeds, the road toll has gone down significantly in the past 25 years.

In May 1973 Dr Beard was quoted in one of Singapore's leading newspapers, *New Nation*, saying 'it is safer to be injured in the Vietnam War than be severely hurt in a road accident in Australia. Furthermore, it is safer for a young soldier driving in Vietnam than it is driving a high-speed car in Australia'.

'A crash victim in Australia had less chance of survival than in war-torn Vietnam because of the speedy military style of rescue operations and emergency services.' He said at the time that there was a plan underway in Australia to implement the military-style operations to rescue road accident victims by means of helicopters. 'One of the biggest lessons we learnt in Vietnam was that no matter how serious the wounds were, the victims could still be saved.'

About 10 per cent of accident victims were maimed, deformed or permanently disabled.

'Death is the ultimate injury,' he says. 'Drivers really do not think it is going to happen to them, their friends or relatives. They do not see the brain injuries, deformities and disabilities of limbs and the abdomen, the ruptured bowels and bladders and the crushed chests and damaged lungs. Surgeons see first-hand these terrible injuries caused by road crashes. Every day, especially at the weekends and during the holiday periods, they witness the trauma. They fight for the victim's life and in many cases where the patient survives they are then confronted with the reality of a list of serious disabilities. But the trauma to the victims, their friends and relatives is virtually incalculable in the wake of a bad road crash.'

The road toll has almost halved since Dr Beard became chairman of the SA Road Safety Council, and all the stakeholders in helping to reduce the carnage on our roads – his team, police, ambulance and the media – should take a bow. 'Yet the road toll is still far too high,' he maintains. 'The fight must continue until there are zero deaths on our roads.'

Peter Goers, actor, director, reviewer, columnist and radio host, has the highest regard for Doctor Donald Beard; indeed deep respect for all Vietnam veterans. 'I've met Dr Donald Beard many times and do you know every time we speak he focuses totally on you and makes you feel the most special person in the room. And every time you are left feeling so much better about yourself. He is a remarkable man with a range of talents, including having acted in number of plays and operas.' Peter recalled one Anzac Day march when the doctor arrived from the 3rd RAR Kapyong Parade interstate too late to join the Korean contingent or his Vietnam colleagues, so he 'straightened up and marched proudly down King William Street alone'. 'There was a time when I was experiencing excruciating stomach pains. My self-diagnosis was that I had pulled a muscle in my stomach. But I thought I'd better seek help from Dr Beard. I rang and he told me to come immediately to his home and there – after complaining about the annual fee of $1000 to maintain his medical licence to practise – he spent more than two hours giving me the most extensive and thorough medical examination I've ever experienced. He scolded me for being too fat and told me in no uncertain terms that I needed to shed weight, then said that I was right after all, I had sustained a pulled stomach muscle.'

By the time Dr Beard had met Peter Goers, his distinguished career was very much behind him. But as far back as Korea in 1951, the young Capt Don Beard was making a huge impact with the officers and men of the 3rd RAR as a 26-year-old Regimental Aid Post (RAP) commander. He also came under the keen eye of US war correspondent Alan Millett, who years later wrote a book about the Korean conflict entitled *Their War for Korea*, which included a chapter, 'A Doctor in Korea', about Capt. Don Beard. Years later he caught up with Colonel Beard at the Chief of Army's annual history conference in Canberra and in July 2000 penned these words:

> At seventy-five Don Beard appears to have held on to every inch of his 6'4" (193 cm) of height without weighting his bayonet-straight body with extra 'stones'. In appearance – dapper, clipped moustache – Don Beard could be a retired general. Indeed, he clearly chats easily with General Sir Thomas J. Daly, KBE, CB, DSO, one of the former commanders of 3 Battalion, Royal Australian Regiment (3RAR), which provides the largest and most vocal group of 'mates' at the conference. Don Beard draws a crowd as well as standing above it; the veterans ebb and flow about him for a word or two; punctuated with many handshakes and laughs. The easy comradeship has a special touch: Don Beard is 3RAR's Diggers' doctor.'

Having rubbed shoulders with Don Bradman, Harold Larwood, Viv Richards, Dennis Lillee and others of the 'Walking Wisden', Don is convinced that the very best cricket of all is club cricket, State and county competitions and, of course, Test cricket. He played club cricket for more than 50 years throughout the world – South Australia, Victoria, New Zealand, Papua New

Guinea, Sri Lanka, India, Gibraltar, England, Nova Scotia and Jamaica. 'I have enjoyed every game and have never met an unpleasant opponent. I have made many friends, some of whom have endured to this day.'

He particularly enjoyed seeing his father come to grade matches at Unley Oval to watch him play. Armed with a thermos of tea and a bag of sandwiches he'd sit quietly in the stand taking it all in. He has seen it all: from Bodyline to T20. Donald Beard was with his father at the Bodyline Test match in Adelaide in the summer of 1932–33.

'We were on the southern mound. The atmosphere was electric, especially when (Bill) Woodfull and (Bert) Oldfield were hit – but weren't struck by short balls. In retrospect I believe the reaction was somewhat excessive and threatened not only cricket but diplomatic relations. It was sad to see Larwood take the brunt of the criticism and virtually hounded out of the game – but then he migrated to Australia and was welcomed by open arms – wonderful Australian sportsmanship.'

Jane Inverarity, wife of ex SA, WA and Test batsman and current Australian selector John Inverarity, recalls the time when John was playing for SA at the time he was vice-principal at Pembroke School. 'Inver' lived in Holden Street, Kensington Park, two doors from Sir Donald Bradman's home. One day, on a run around the block, he stopped to speak to his near neighbour who was in his front garden pruning the roses.

'Hi, Sir Donald.'

'Hello, John, what are you doing?'

'Getting myself fit for the coming summer of cricket. What did you do to prepare for the new season?'

'Not a lot, John. Early on as a young man I played squash. I played a bit of golf, but rarely did I go off running down the street. I just ensured that on the first grade match of the season I scored 200 and ran a lot of ones, twos and threes.'

Soon after the Inverarity family got to Adelaide, John's wife Jane took their two young girls, Alison and Kate, to Adelaide Oval to watch a Shield match. The girls had taken off their sandals and were playing in the old members' grandstand. 'Kate, who was then about six, let out a scream after getting a horrible, crumbling big splinter in her foot,' Jane recalled. 'I took one look at it and realised it would require considerable digging to get all the pieces of wood out. One of the officials came down with Doc Beard to see what had happened. The doctor generously took Kate and me back to his surgery to "operate". He put Kate up on the table and told her he had treated the Queen on this very table and how brave she had been. He then went on to tell Kate that he thought she was coping very well. His calm, gentle and reassuring manner put Kate completely at ease. Dr Beard would not hear of sending us an account.'

Former Defence Minister in the Howard Government, SA cricketer and ex-President of the South Australian Cricket Association, Ian McLachlan has long been a close friend of Doctor Beard. 'I think I met him when I first played for Sturt,' McLachlan recalls. 'My impression was he always turned up late for a grade game. And there were two reasons. One he hadn't finished operating on some poor chap and secondly he had a condition called colitis so if he was at the ground he was on the loo and if he wasn't there he was operating. Usually John Lill was at first slip, and either Peter Lovett or Gil Langley kept wicket.

'The Doc bowled serious outswingers and he got most of his wickets caught at slip or behind. Gil Langley said it was all you needed to get the rabbits out. Cricket was a great outlet for his work as a surgeon. I got to know him well and was in his wedding party as the groomsman. My wife Jane and I attended a number of the Test match dinners he and Margaret hosted at their home, always memorable occasions.'

McLachlan said Don Beard was a good speechmaker and was so because he prepared for every one. 'A good speech takes seven weeks of preparation and a bad one takes three minutes. He is such a cricket tragic; a cricket nut and he gets quite horrified by people like me who don't read cricket books all the time. Once he told me to "avoid the knife" at all costs.

'"But doctor, you've made your whole life with the knife."

'"I just tell you. Keep away from the knife; don't be operated upon unless it is absolutely impossible to avoid it."'

Just before he left Australia to take the 1972 Australian team to England for an Ashes series, Dr Beard was alerted to a wound on Test captain Ian Chappell's chest by none other than Australia's 'man of the century' Barry 'Nugget' Rees. Chappell's skin was discoloured in exactly the same spot that he had been burnt by a cigarette after a great Test win at Old Trafford in 1968.

Chappell explains: 'We were having a beer under the shower and I asked "Cho" (John Gleeson) to put out his cigarette. I threw water over it and he immediately lit up another one. I warned him that I would throw water at him again, so he hurriedly squeezed the lighted end between forefinger and thumb, then stubbed me in the chest with it. Trouble was the thing was still alight. Three years later the Doc took one look at it and said he had to operate straight away. It had turned malignant.'

Chappelli had the cancer cut out under a local anaesthetic. He was scheduled to appear at a SACA function that evening. As the doctor inserted nine stitches to close the wound, he said, 'Well, Ian, you'll experience a little pain tonight … but a few beers should fix it.'

John Lill, former Sturt and SA batsman and secretary of the Melbourne Cricket Club, always calls Don Beard 'the long doctor'. John has known Don for a long time, ever since they were Sturt Cricket Club teammates; John catching at first slip many outside edges created by Beard's sharp pace and late outswing. But there was always a suspicion among teammates and opponents that Beard sometimes bent his elbow in delivering the ball.

'Later in his career, one Saturday afternoon, during a lower-grade game played on a concrete pitch near the Victoria Park Racecourse, Beard was bowling and a man, who had just left the races, wandered across the oval and sidled up to the square leg umpire.

'After two deliveries he said to the umpire, "That bowler is chucking them, why don't you call him?"

'"I know," the umpire said sadly, "but the bowler is my surgeon and he is due to operate on me on Monday!"'

In the late 1980s, when the producers of Richard Strauss's *Elektra* were searching for a 'tall wraith-like man' to play the role of a ghost, Dr Donald Beard, who stands 193 centimetres tall, was a leading contender. He was consulting when Opera SA rang to inform him that the director was seeking someone of his description and asked to see him. Opera SA's headquarters were near Don's rooms and he told the next patient he had a call and would be away for a short time. He shot off, walked into the office of the director, Bruce Beresford, and was thought suitable for the part. Upon returning to his rooms his patient asked whether he had dealt satisfactorily with the emergency.

Don played the part of Agamemnon, looking decidedly ghost-like and, true to the part, he didn't have to utter a word at the $600,000 State Opera production featuring a 94-piece orchestra and a 60-member cast in its long performance. Greek mythology tells us that Agamemnon was the King of Mycenae, a kingdom of legendary Greece.

'Don had a great presence on stage,' Margaret said proudly. 'He was never nervous although I sometimes wonder how he didn't fall off the stage as he walked across having to negotiate all manner of furniture on the set. I think Don has always loved dressing up, whether it was for cricket, the army or fancy-dress parties. Although sometimes, when you see him getting about the garden in old clothes and going to the local shops, you wouldn't think he likes dressing up.'

His operatic career continued with parts in *Samson and Delila* and as King Duncan in *Macbeth*. During an interval in *Samson and Delila*, director Lindy Hume summoned the men's chorus into the rehearsal room and hauled Don and others over the coals. The instant the last member of the cast entered the room Lindy leapt on a table and gave them a verbal dressing down. 'You've all behaved far too realistically in the orgy scene,' she complained.

Don Beard, eminent surgeon, and A grade cricketer used to dishing out a barrage of bumpers at breakneck pace, was in this opera, playing a tall walk-on Philistine. 'I quaked a little at Lindy's fury,' he said, 'but I thought it unfair that she did not provide us with any detail about the complaint, nor would she reveal who made the complaint.' Playing Agamemnon in *Elektra* and King Duncan in *Macbeth* thrilled him.

Margaret derived a love of the theatre from her father's fascination with the arts. 'Our father always took us to the theatre. We went to the opera at Her Majesty's and attended all the big shows at the Theatre Royal. I remember seeing shows such as *Annie Get Your Gun* and many others.

While Don was still hard at work as a house surgeon at the Royal Adelaide Hospital, Cecelia Obst was dancing her way across Europe, collecting various charm bracelets and jewellery from admirers in a number of countries, including gifts from members of the Luftwaffe and the German Army. Coincidentally, Cecelia's mother had migrated to Australian before her as a migrant and lived as a housekeeper in the very house that years later became Don and Margaret Beard's family home. Cecelia's mother worked for the previous owners, the Menz family, who lived there from about 1890 to 1950.

'I got to know Cecelia as a patient. One day she said to me her mother worked in Adelaide for Mr Menz and they lived at Norwood but she didn't know the name of the street. She came here and went to the very room that had been described by her mother. I was her doctor right up to the end. Finally someone from the Queen Elizabeth Hospital rang me and asked me when I was going to come and make the arrangements. I asked what they meant.

'They explained that Cecelia had placed a letter in the hands of the trustees and she had left everything – house, furniture, clothing, jewellery – to me. I told them that I could not accept this because to do so would be unethical.

'Margaret and I went to her flat. First we discovered that she did not own her home, the flat was rented from the SA Housing Trust. Cecelia also did not own any of the white goods in the flat, or the furniture. There were a lot of furs that she used as a dancer and 200 pairs of dancing shoes. She asked in the letter if I could take anything I didn't want to the Guide Dogs Association. Margaret had little use for those tiny dancing shoes. We opened a drawer and there we discovered the reason for her rather pecuniary state, the drawer was full of betting tickets – useless betting tickets. It seemed Cecelia spent most of her money on the horses. We gave most to the Guide Dogs and there were a few odd things like a jewellery box, most of which we've given to our granddaughters. It was all a wonderful gesture. However, I couldn't get out of organising the funeral. She had also asked me to deliver the eulogy.' As usual Don Beard did his homework, gathering information from Cecelia's relatives and friends living in Germany.

Another of Dr Beard's patients, a woman who hailed from Wales, also wished to leave her entire estate to him, but he politely declined.

'No, doctor, I want to leave you everything because you have been so kind to me,' she said. Don stood firm and refused to accept her offer. But she used a subtle tactic, not unlike Frank Browne, who gave his mother a television set in 1957. She left in her will $200 each to Don and Margaret's two sons, Matthew and Alastair.

Cricket was always Don's much loved sporting activity. In A grade cricket Don Beard took a total of 333 wickets at an average of 17.55. From the summer of 1943/44 until 1947/48 he took 91 wickets for University at an average of 19.57. From 1952/53 until 1961/62, Beard took 242 wickets for Sturt at an average of 16.80. His batting didn't quite match his fast swing bowling. In all matches for the two clubs, the Doc played 89 innings, scoring 207 runs (a highest score of 19) at an average of only 4.22.

Don played alongside Ian McLachlan, his son Matthew and State players Ashley Woodcock and Peter Herbert for the Don Beard XI against former England captain Mike Denness's XI at St Peter's College in December 1982. As England arrived in Australia for the second round of the Ashes contest of 2013/14, Don Beard presented the University CC with his 1946 club blazer.

Don's career as a surgeon and his involvement in cricket were inextricably bound. 'Sir Vivian Richards – Viv Richards – was, of course, a wonderful batsman, possessing an array of glorious strokes that I still recall, but people thought he was a bit stand-offish and didn't mix freely. I got to know him. He had an injury one day during a match at the Adelaide Oval and I drove him to the hospital for X-rays. We talked a bit about his cricketing life. It came out how much he loved cricket and how much he loved boys who played cricket and what he did for them. He did a tremendous amount coaching young boys both in West Indies and in England. He talked about this in a most sincere manner. He opened up and I was fortunate to have had the chance to talk to him in this way. I saw the other side of Richards, the humble, caring side. In his photograph he looks supercilious, looking slightly upwards as if the rest of the world didn't matter. I think that was, partly, shyness. There was a long-held perception that Viv was arrogant. He was much like Bradman – many people thought he was a bit arrogant. There is no way Richards was arrogant. He loved cricket and he loved people.'

Don got to know Wes Hall, a West Indian fast bowler with a 'magnificent action', whom Margaret reckoned to be a fabulous conversationalist and Don highly regarded. The doctor looked up from his study chair and indicated that I cast my eye on a photograph hanging on the opposite wall. There was the image of three great West Indian cricketers – Wes Hall, Viv Richards and Clive Lloyd. Wes Hall wrote a few words in ink at the bottom of the photograph.

'I've always treasured this photo,' he said, reading the notation aloud: *To Doc Beard, a true friend of all West Indian people. An ardent fan of the noble game. A great doctor and one of the nicest men I've ever met, sincerely Wes Hall.*

'I saw Keith Miller play for a short while in postwar years. He batted, bowled and fielded the same way – with great flair. I first met him as a friend. He had set up residence in a caravan at the back of the western stand at the Adelaide Oval. There he was, the great Keith Miller, sitting next to John Selth's catering hut. He set himself up there at most Test matches and he'd virtually interview the droves of people who'd turn up to his caravan to say hello. He spent far more time there than he did watching the cricket or in the committee room. This happened a good deal in the 1980s. He didn't talk about the war, although his flying record was very good in England and, indeed, he was a hero to the English people. (Eventually his health started to deteriorate early in 2000.) I took the opportunity to see him whenever I could. Finally I was in Melbourne at a surgical conference and I took the day off, caught the train down to Mornington, then a bus and then I had to get a taxi from the bus stop to Keith's home. When I got to his home the taxi driver said to me, "Why have you come down here?" and I said, "I've come to see my friend Keith Miller."

'"Oh," he said, "Keith Miller? Does he live here?"

'I then asked how much the fare was and he replied, "I could not charge a fare to someone who was coming to see Keith Miller."'

Dr Beard also admired Dennis Lillee. 'Dennis used to tell me how to bowl,' he said. 'He invited my son down to the nets and I'll never forget how he used to encourage Matthew to "reach for the sky" with his non-bowling arm. He always told his charges to "bowl as fast as you can, forget about control and reach as high as you can with your left arm. Keep your left arm high so you can look over your left shoulder and you can bowl forever."

'Dennis used to come to our house for dinner. He was ever popular. I know Don Bradman loved to be in Lillee's company. Sir Donald thought Dennis a great fella. They talked cricket and tactics. Bradman would extol the virtue of getting inside the line of flight to hook and pull the short ball, or, as an alternative, make room to cut it behind point. I admired him for the way he dealt with his own injuries – he had an injured groin, knee and, of course, his dreadful back injury.'

Dennis says of Dr Beard: 'As old friends we still catch up for the occasional lunch. I like that the Doc feels comfortable in ringing me to ask if I could look at how his grandson, Julian Beard, a good young cricketer, is progressing with the ball. The Doc is a great friend of cricket.'

Dr Beard had heard of Geoff Boycott, the bespectacled Yorkshire opening batsman, as early as 1964 when he debuted against Bob Simpson's touring Test side in England, but he had never met him and did not then know of Boycott's eccentricities. The 1965/66 England Team left Heathrow Airport in October 1965. They stopped in Colombo en route to Singapore, when their young opening bat, Geoff Boycott, complained of headaches. When the team landed at Singapore, MCC manager Billy Griffiths had Boycott seek medical help. Boycott was examined by Dr L.R. Taylor at St Mark's Hospital and Maternity Home in Joo Chiat Place, Singapore, on 21 October 1965. There the youngster was found to have 'colicky abdominal pain, followed by severe watery diarrhoea'. The batsman's vital signs were found to be okay, but he was running a temperature (100.8° F) and his pulse rate was in the 90s. His medical history revealed that Boycott had, at the tender age of nine, survived a splenectomy for a ruptured spleen. Dr Taylor ordered Boycott to bed for four days. He was placed on a diet of liquids and was to be given an injection of Largactil, to help prevent vomiting. By 27 October, Boycott was deemed fit enough to fly out of the country and rejoin the MCC team in Perth. The doctor gave the injection and as the needle entered his body close to the sciatic nerve, Boycott reeled at the excruciating pain. He later told Dr Beard that 'the further the needle went in, the more pain I felt'. In the wake of the injection, Boycott experienced numbness down his leg. By the time the side arrived in Adelaide, he was in real trouble. Don was called to his side and admitted him to the Queen Elizabeth Hospital.

'I suggested to the MCC manager that when Boycott left hospital in a few days, he could come and stay at my home at Marryatville for a week. At the end of the week I would let him know whether Boycott was okay to continue the tour or be flown back to England.'

Dr Beard placed Boycott on an exercise program of walking and running, which Boycott religiously adhered to in his usual determined Yorkshire manner. 'My two boys – Matthew was then about three – were intrigued with our visitor from England. Matthew and Alastair used to peep round the door of Geoff's bedroom and look at him.'

After a few days of intensive training, Margaret's good cooking and the general well-being associated with being in the Beard family environment, Don announced one morning, 'Righto, Geoffrey, let's go and have a net; I'll find somewhere we will not be observed by the media.'

They set off together for a net at Marryatville High School. Beard marked out his full run and charged in to bowl, just as he had umpteen times to Don Bradman or Gil Langley at the State squad training all those years ago. He might have lost a yard in pace, but he was still lively and could get the ball to rise awkwardly off a good length.

'Boycott used his feet and really got stuck into me. He belted me all over the park and I said confidently, "Well, Geoff, you can go to Brisbane." He wasn't going to open, but one of the openers was sick, and Boycott did open the batting.'

In fact, Boycott played in all five Tests of the 1965/66 series. He scored 45 and 63 not out in Brisbane (the match Doug Walters hit a debut 155); 51 and 5 not out in the MCG Second Test; 84 at the SCG; then a double failure (22 and 12) in Adelaide, and 17 and 1 in the final Test at Melbourne: a total of 300 runs at an average of 42.8 in a series which was drawn 1-all.

'From that time we became friends. A little doubting of my action, he used to let it be known to friends. Geoffrey Boycott was determined, certainly not to my mind selfish, as some claimed. There are English, Scots, Welsh ...

and Yorkshiremen. He was single-minded and determined to become the best opener in the world. When he got out he often went and had a long net session, however many runs he scored. He didn't care what people thought of him. I liked Geoff, I still do. Throughout life if you keep an open mind you simply find good people come into your life.

'There has been a wealth of great all-rounders in cricket – Ian Botham, Richard Hadlee, Imran Khan, Keith Miller, Alan Davidson. However, one man – Sir Garfield Sobers – stood above all the rest. Sobers may well have been the greatest cricketer who ever lived. My first memory of Sobers was when I was playing for Sturt against Prospect at the Adelaide Oval. Out came the great Sobers and I charged in to bowl. I had decided to bowl like fury that day, centre stage at Adelaide Oval before an unusually large district match crowd of more than 2000 people. I got one past his bat with a beauty and I raised the heavens with my raucous appeal. The umpire disallowed my appeal and as I walked back I said, "Pretty close, Colin?"

'Umpire Colin Egar replied, "Do you think that all this crowd have come to see a district cricket match to watch you bowl out Sobers? Not out, Don!"'

Dr Beard also admired Kim Hughes for his courage in batting on against the West Indies attack with a broken toe. '"Doc, don't send for an X-ray. We know it's got a crack in it, but I don't want those West Indian fast bowlers to know it's broken, because they'll aim at it."'

In Justin Langer's first Test match he was hit on the head by a rising ball from Courtney Walsh, the West Indian fast bowler. He collapsed on the pitch, but by the time Dr Beard had reached the middle of Adelaide Oval, Langer had struggled groggily to his feet. His helmet was off and he was shaking his head. The doctor looked at Langer.

'Justin didn't have a fractured skull, but his helmet was broken. I said, "Justin, you'd better come off the ground."

'"Doc, if I come off, I'll never get back again. Can you leave me out here?"

'"Okay," I said, "but I'll be sitting at the pickets and if I see one sign of your being groggy you'll be off the ground."'

As a young man retirement never entered Donald Beard's head. But he later realised that everyone has to retire or at least slow down. 'Retirement doesn't worry me as much as I thought it might. One day I went to work and the next day I didn't. But I certainly miss my patients. I miss the atmosphere of working in a hospital.' Don attends increasingly more funerals and the older he becomes the more frequent those occasions will occur, for he is now in his late 80s and funerals go with the territory of old age. In recent times he has lost many old mates and friends. 'I feel great sadness when friends die, but strangely enough I don't feel, "Well they've gone, so I'll be next." Life is still marvellous and I'm enjoying it, and I have no thoughts of it ending. I went to a funeral recently and the undertaker came up and I said to him, "You keep away from me, you're not getting me yet!" Life's taken on many other features. I'm really not a great gardener but I do the clearing work and making compost, which goes back into the garden. Eventually I had to stop cricket. And so I took up lawn bowls, which I've enjoyed just as much. And so bowling has become a joy. The Adelaide Oval is a great club, and I have a lot of wonderful friends; we play pennant bowls in the summer and we play throughout the winter. I read every night on a variety of subjects. My goals are to remain fit as I can in order to look after my family – my wife and my two boys and my grandchildren – for as long as I can. I think it's the family that is of the greatest concern. I wake up at night thinking about them, and wonder if there is something more that I could or should be doing. Joy is just about everything in this beautiful world of ours. I love it. There's a joy in gardens, there's a joy in the sun, in the sunlight and in the blue sky. I get up each morning looking forward to what the day will hold. And at the end of it, I look back and find that there were a lot of very enjoyable hours.'

From the time he was a boy Don Beard learnt to give. 'Giving was something my mother handed down to Beryl and me. You know as humans we must learn to give and to forgive. This was a wonderful trait of "Weary" Dunlop, the doctor who saved hundreds of ill and injured servicemen on the infamous Burma Railway.'

While serving on the battlefield Donald Beard resisted the very concept of carrying a weapon, although other medical men did so. Even when under fire he continued to work, as ever caring for his patients as he did during the height of the Battle of Kapyong. In 2001 he returned to Korea for a reunion of those who served at the time of the Battle of Kapyong. The frenetic morning rush hour at Seoul's main railway station held the incongruous sight of young white-collar workers frantically getting their takeaway coffees before running to their designated platforms, while a group of war veterans, resplendent in regimental blazers, military berets and clusters of well-polished medals, began to muster on the highly polished concourse.

'We were recognised as veterans of the allies in the Korean War and station workers bowed as we passed; staff in kiosks and the small shops which lined the concourse stopped selling their coffee and pastries and broke into spontaneous applause. Australia lost 339 men in the conflict in what was a war that was virtually forgotten at home. My return to Korea to walk the battlefields of Kapyong was a nostalgic and poignant time.'

Don Beard has hundreds of files loaded with transcripts of the hundreds of his speeches. He has kept letters from an amazing variety of people – from former patients to residents of Buckingham Palace; so much has he packed into his time on earth.

'I come to the most important part of my life – my family and it is here that I realised that I have failed. I thought I was doing the "right thing" for them. I have been selfish and inconsiderate, but worse still I have not realised what I was doing to them in my aim to help. I love them all so much and I would do anything for them. My thoughts have always been with them. But I have been too dominant and domineering. Margaret would want to do things and to go places to get ideas to improve her life and her house and her beloved garden and her children. But time and again I resisted. I was worried about finances and the need to ensure there would be sufficient money to provide an adequate future. This was upset by my accountant and the Government superannuation that further eroded the financial situation making it more important to be careful. With regard to my sons, Matthew and Alastair, I wanted very much for them to have a future and I felt a good education and good results were important. And so I drove them too hard. I did not realise what I was doing to them by interfering with what they wanted to do.

'But succeed they did and I am very proud of all their achievements at school and university and in their subsequent lives. I now see what a rough time I gave them and I don't deserve the wonderful things they have done for me. I love them all and would do anything for them in my remaining years.

'When I first went to the Royal Adelaide Hospital treatment was simple. There were no antibiotics, no joint replacements, no laparoscopes, no specific psychotic drugs, no specialised nurses and few specialised medical officers. There was no plastic surgeon, no vascular surgeon, no cardiologist. They all came later. At times we feel we have reached the top, but there are still mountains to climb. Bacteria and viruses are just waiting to invade the body.

'In my younger days we just drained the infection when suppuration occurred and laudable pus was produced. Now we use antibiotics and no sooner do they become effective that they become resistant and a new generation of antibiotics must be created. It will be infection that will kill the world, not a combination of illnesses such as cancer and deaths on the roads.

'My fortunate life'

We must resist at all times the temptation to use antibiotics just because they may be effective at this moment.

'As to my service with the Australian Army: in my youth weapons, tanks, artillery and communications were all very simple. Now the tanks are almost impenetrable, weapons fire long-distance high-velocity missiles that cause dreadful destructive injuries. But even so, anti-personnel mines are simple and easily made by the enemy and cause just as severe injuries as our high-velocity bullets. It needs a dedicated service of military surgeons and their assistants to deal with them – not only the physical injuries but the psychological effects. During my long service in war and peace I have been impressed by the Australian officers and soldiers in their dedication to the fighting role for which they have been trained and for their care of their fellow soldiers in spite of the inherent dangers. I feel humble in their presence and would do anything for them. I salute them.'

One thing is certain. The man who has dedicated his life to the giving of his time and skill to others will live forever in the hearts of those who have known him. In a long, distinguished and well-lived life, metaphorically and literally Donald Douglas Beard has created a mighty large footprint.

'I look back with great joy on my life. It has been a fortunate one,' concludes Dr Beard, 'but I should have and could have done much better.'

Bibliography

Green, B. *The Battle of Kapyong*, Headquarters Training Command, The Australian Army, 1992, p. 57

Grey, J. *The Commonwealth Armies and the Korean War: An Alliance Study*, Manchester University Press, 1998

Hawke, N. *Neil Hawke: Bowled Over*, Rigby Publishers, Adelaide, 1982, p. 158

Millett, A.R. *The War For Korea, 1950–1951: They Came from the North*, Potomac Books, US, 2002

O'Dowd, B. *In Valiant Company*, University of Queensland Press, 2000, p. 90

Robertson-Glasgow, R.C. *Wisden Cricketers' Almanack*, Sporting Handbooks for proprietors, John Wisden and Co. Ltd, London, 1949

Swanton, E.W. (ed.) and Woodcock, J. (assoc. ed.) *Barclays World of Cricket: The Great Game from A to Z*, Collins in association with Barclays Bank International, 1980

Acknowledgements

My thanks to Dr Donald Beard for his amazing breadth of knowledge and depth of memory in the journey of his biography. We had many talks, face-to-face chats, whereby we got to know one another better, which enabled the writer to weave his craft in a more informed and succinct way.

Don Beard has walked this earth for 89 years, but mere age is of no moment to this man in terms of getting things done: he's a highly respected surgeon in the medical profession, a legend in the Australian Army and a cricket enthusiast whose interest exceeds almost anyone I've ever known.

The Beard family have all been extremely supportive of the project and I thank Donald's wife, Margaret, for her input, although at one stage she reckoned the author was trying on a Barbara Cartland script for their lives together. That said, Margaret took the blue pencil to Chapter Eight, but, dear readers, I think some good stuff passed muster.

Donald and Margaret's two sons, Alastair and Matthew provided great insights to their growing up in the Beard household. I thank them and their wives, Jennifer and Marie. I must also thank Donald's sister, Beryl, for her articulate and detailed description of her years growing up with brother Donald in Ashford, Moonta, and in various parts around Adelaide.

My heartfelt thanks to Major General W.B. 'Digger' James who wrote the Foreword; also I appreciate the help of Donald's good mate and fellow surgeon Colonel Peter Byrne, who tells of Donald the man and the doctor and of Vietnam, and General Peter Cosgrove, who has agreed to launch *The Diggers' Doctor*, 'whenever or wherever'.

I've interviewed many people who have helped in the crafting of this work. Thanks to Janet and Ian McLachlan, Rosemary and John Lill, John and Jane Inverarity, Barry Jarman, Dennis Lillee, Ian Chappell, Barry 'Nugget' Rees,

Colonel Viki Andersons, Dianne Gall for her splendid painting of the Doc and many more. Ex-television executive Patsy Gardner helped in providing feedback after reading the manuscript. Whereas a writer tries to paint a word picture, TV people have a particular image in mind. Their concepts are enlightening to a wordsmith. Journalist-author Trevor Gill did me proud with his sound literary advice and encouragement.

I am delighted that Wakefield Press has taken on this project, for I know Michael Bollen and his team always produce the goods in terms of a book of substance and in its presentation. Thanks to Julia Beaven for her editing and Michael Deves for his final sort of the wheat from the chaff.

This book probably should have been out sooner but for a slight hiccup with the author. As I lay in my hospital bed in the wake of a heart ailment, my physiotherapist said, 'Well now, who do we have to write the final few chapters?'

Matthew Beard is not only a good man to repair the physical mishaps in the human body. He also knows a thing or too about psychology.

'I'll write them, Matthew; me, yours truly.'

And so it came to pass.

Ashley Mallett, Adelaide 2014

Index

A

A Ton of Spirit, Penny Smith 86
Abley, John 173
Aboriginal Men of High Degree, A.P. Elkin 145
Adams, Flt Lt Bay 10
Addis Ababa Fistula Hospital 40
Adelaide Club 29, 132
Adelaide Oval 68, 91, 123, 131, 135, 136, 138, 142, 162, 172, 180, 188, 193, 196
Adelaide Technical High School 27, 30, 31, 35, 107
Adelaide Turf cricket 60
Adelaide University Baseball Team 44
Adelaide University Boat Club 93
Advertiser, the 34, 46, 49, 92, 132, 135, 181, 185
Afghanistan 18, 22, 167
Agamemnon 190
Althorp, John 64–65
American M16 112
Andersons, Col. Viki 170, 202
Anzac Day 1, 17, 92, 97, 113, 130, 187
Argent, Hazel 149
Archer, Ken 44
Archer, Ron 44
Argyll and Sutherland Highlanders, 1st 4, 8
Atkinson, Brig. Rob 170
Auld, Elizabeth 162–164
Australian Army 24, 53, 55, 61, 71, 99, 144
Australian Army units –
  1st Australian Field Hospital (Vung Tau, Vietnam) vii, 19, 104, 108, 115, 118
  3rd Royal Australian Regiment (3rd RAR) vi, 1–7, 8, 10–22, 53, 58, 59, 93, 105, 113, 115, 145, 167, 169, 171, 187
  8th Field Ambulance (Vung Tau, Vietnam) 102–103, 118
  Royal Australian 3rd Field Ambulance 167, 169, 171
  1st Royal Australian Regiment (1st RAR) vii, 19, 104, 108, 111, 115, 118
  2nd RAR 5 Platoon B Company 111
  212th Company, 1st Mobile Strike Force (Vietnam) 117
  Australian Army C Company 7, 109

Australian Army Training Team (Vietnam) 115
Australian Military Forces 114
Army Medical Service viii, 51
Australian Cricket Team, 1953 68
Australian Cricket Board of Control for International Cricket 55, 132
Australian Logistic Support Group (ALSG) Vietnam 103
Australian Medical Association (AMA) 161, 187
Australian War Memorial 22, 165
Australian War Memorial Battlefield Tour Group 89

B

Badcock, Jack 127–131
Badcoe, Major Peter (VC) 105,117
Baldock, Darryl 173
Barassi, Ron 173
Barr, Major Marshall 103–104
'Barbasol' Beard 14
Barbour, Dr Russell 61, 73, 98
Bardsley, Mick 140–141
Bardsley, Warren 141
Battle of Britain 62, 156
Battle of Kapyong vi, 1–23, 55, 59, 98, 166, 197
Battle of Kapyong 2, 200
Beard, Alison (née Wright) 24–25, 156
Beard, Alastair 85–86, 87, 89–94, 97, 100, 101, 137–138, 192, 195, 198
Beard, Beryl 24, 29, 33, 34, 44, 201
Beard, Harold 24–27, 34–36, 37, 40, 182
Beard, James 85, 94–95
Beard, Jennifer 85–86, 93, 94, 201
Beard, Julian 85–86, 94, 194
Beard, Margaret vi, viii, 41, 82, 84–89, 93, 95–96, 97–101, 108, 114, 116, 134, 137, 139, 143, 151, 155, 163, 167, 189, 190, 191, 192, 193, 195, 198, 201
Beard, Marie 85, 88, 94–96, 201
Beard, Matthew viii, 85, 87–91, 92–96, 97, 100–101, 137–139, 192, 194, 195, 198, 201, 202
Beard, Myrtle 24
Beard, Phoebe 85, 86, 94
Beard, Dr Roland 32
Beard, Sophie 25, 85, 88, 95
Beare, Col. Tom 99, 103, 116, 124
Bedi, Bishan 137, 139

Bedser, (Sir) Alec 173
Bell, Charles 165
Bennett, Chester 33
Benaud, Richie 172
Beresford, Bruce 190
Birch, Dr Hugh 47
Birdwood, General 168
Bleechmore, Lt Col. John 54
Blinman, Roy 127
Blumfield, Lt Col. Lou 111
Bodyline Test, Adelaide Oval 188
Bonnin, Jim 51
Bonnin, Dr Lance 51
Bonnin, Dr Mark 51
Bonnin, Dr Noel 51
Bonython, Kym 146–148
Boon, David 180
Boone, Daniel 91, 151
Botham, (Sir) Ian 196
Bowley, Bruce 72, 81
Boycott, Geoff viii, 194–195
Boyle, Major Mick 103
Bradman Albums 135–136
Bradman, Sir Donald vii, viii, 43, 45, 91, 126–143,144, 162, 170, 187, 188, 194
Bradman, Lady Jessie 130–131, 135, 137, 141
Bradman, John 141
Bridges, General 169
British Army 62
British Commonwealth Brigade 2, 5
British Commonwealth General Hospital, Kure 8
British Commonwealth Occupational Force 6, 8, 9, 15, 19, 52 54–55, 104, 126, 152, 154, 180
British General Hospital, The 29th 53
British Gloucester Battalion 4
Brittain, Major RSM 62–65, 69
Broadstock, Jack 30
Brokensha, Peter 44
Brown, Dean 28
Brown, Gordon 28
Browne, Sgt, Frank 152–154
Buckingham Palace 64–65, 66–68, 72
Bullwinkle, Nurse Vivian 71
Burdett, Les 138
Burdon, Dr Ken 39
Burdon, Dr Roy 39
Burgess, Jack 34
Burma Railway 197
Butler, Keith 49

Byrne, (Dr Maj., Col.) Peter 116–118

C
Cahill, John 173
Cahill, Lik Lak 30
Cairns, Maj. Hugh 156
Camp Hospital, EBISU, Tokyo 56
Cape Canaveral, Florida 41
Carmody, Keith 76
Casey, Lt. R.G. 169
Cattle, Mr A.C. 30, 31
Chappell brothers 30
Chappell, Greg 91
Chappell, Ian viii, 178, 189–190, 201
Cheshire, Group Capt. (VC) Lionel 76
Christofani, Bob 76
Cilento, Rafeel 48
Cilento, Diane 48
Citizen Military Forces (CMF) 7, 51–52, 88, 99, 116
Claxton, Norrie 52
Claxton Shield 52
Clarke, Jack 173
Club Cricket Conference 77
Coco 95
Colebatch, Mr 30, 38
Colquhoun, Des 135–136
Commander of St John's, Jerusalem 85
Commonwealth contingent 65, 67–68
Cooper, Dave 148
Coral Sea Memorial 151
Cornish, Dr Brian 7, 52, 55, 103
Cornwall, Dr John 39
Coronation Day 61, 63–68
Coronation Fleet 69
Coronation Tour, 1953 62–72, 73
Cosgrove, General Peter 55, 201
Coumbe, Lt Col. 100
Craig, Ian 68
Craker, David 35
Credlin, Sgt 111
Crile, George 150
Crippled Children's Association (South Australia) 135
Crosier, Mr 24
Cunningham, Ken 136
Cush, Frank 140
Cush, Mrs 140

D
D-Day 156
Da Nang, Vietnam 115–119
Daily Express 68
Daily Mail 68
Daly, Gen. Sir Thomas 187
Dardanelles 168
Darling, Len 60
DAVCO 153

Davison, Brian 123–124
Davidson, Alan 196
Davidson, Capt. 169
Dennis, C.J. 34
Depression, The Great 26, 28, 36, 128, 132, 182
Deputy Director Medical Services (DDMS) 99, 116
Dixon, Brian 173
Dickson Wright, Arthur 75, 148–149
Dickson Wright, Clara 75
Distinguished Flying Cross (DFC) 154
Don Bradman & Co 133
Douglas, Sgt 110
Douglas, Hugh 7, 52, 55
Dowling, Jack 41–42
Downer, Alexander 29
Duke of Edinburgh 66, 67
Dunkirk 37
Dunlop, 'Weary' 61, 197
Dunn, Alexander 84, 89–90, 100
Dunn, Margaret 82, 84
Dunque, Pte 'Nugget' 5
Dunstan, Dr Dick 99
Dunstan, Sir Donald 146
Dwyer, Dr J.M. 'Barb' 51–52
Dyson, John 91

E
Earl Spencer, the 8th 65
Earl's Court, London 65–66, 68–69
East Molesey 76
East Molesey Cricket Club 76
East Perth Royals 173
Edmonds, Frances 139–140
Edmonds, Phillipe 139
Egar, Colin 196
Eisenhower, US President Dwight 58
England Eleven 126
Ern, Uncle 29
Eustice, Ken 173

F
FA Cup final 149
Fadden, PM Arthur 8
Fairfax, Sister 81
Fairley, Sir Neil Hamilton 75
Fairweather, Pvt. 112
Farmer, Graham 'Polly' 173
Farrar–Hockley, Maj. 4
Favell, Les 162
Favell, Berry 162
Ferguson, Lt Col. Bruce 2–4, 12, 59
Fermoy, Frances 65
Field Marshall Viscount Montgomery 67
Fisher, Guy 132
'Five Fingers of Death' 185
Florey, Howard 156
Forbes, Pvt 110

Fraser, Malcolm 105
Fry, Capt. Ken 167
Fuller, George 39
Fuller, Neil 178–179
Fulton, Pvt. 112

G
Gallipoli 17, 32, 167–169
Gandevia, Capt. Bryan 10, 53
Gavaskar, Sunil 91, 137
George Gosse Ward 71
George Medal 20, 21, 169–170
Giap, Gen. Vo Nguyen 102, 104
Gleeson, John 'Cho' 189
Glenelg 24, 43, 81
Goers, Peter 186–187
Gordon-Taylor, Sir Gordon 75–77, 83, 149
Gosse, George 29, 30, 70–71
Gosse, Sir James 29
Government House (Adelaide) 59, 65, 85
Gowrie, Lord 133
Grace, Dr W.G. 32
Grant, Col. Ray 99
Grey, Jeffrey 7
Griffiths, Corp. 112
Grimmett, C.V. 'Clarrie' 33, 35, 127–128, 141
Gunn, Sir James 83
Gurner, Maj. Gen. Colin 99
Guttmann, Ludwig 61

H
Hadlee, (Sir) Richard 196
Haenga, Pvt. Roger 106
Haldane, Capt. Douglas 4
Hall, Wes viii, 91, 193
Hamlin, Catherine 40
Hamlin, Dr Reg 39–40
Hammond, Wally 46
Hands, Pvt. 112
Hannaford, Robert 170
Harbison, Michael 170
Harbison, Dr Peter 32, 74, 162
Harris, Jim 74, 75
Harvey, Neil 162
Haskard, Mr 34
Hassett, Lindsay 68, 76
Hawke, Beverley 172, 174–178
Hawke, Neil 172, 172–178, 200
Hell Spit (Gallipoli) 169
Henry Simpson Newland J. Estcourt Hughes 149
Herbert, Peter 192
Heydon, Harold 128
Hillary, (Sir) Edmund 66, 72
Hindmarsh Volunteer Fire and Ambulance Brigade 49
Hiroshima 44
Hobley, Pvt. 112
Hone, Dr 'Papa' 129
Hughes, Lt Col. E.S.R. 14, 53

Index

Hughes, Sir Edward 'Bill' 152, 182
Hughes, J. Escourt 149
Hughes, Kim 196
Humphries, Barry 163–164
Hundt, Gunner 110–111
Hungry Horse Art Gallery 147
Hunter, John 165–166
H.V. Millard Trophy 60
H.W. Hodgetts & Company 128, 131, 133
Hodgetts, Harry 126–129, 131–133
Hyde, Jim 77

I

Imperial Japanese Army 37
Inchon 9, 58
Indian 60th Parachute Field Ambulance 2, 4, 16–17, 19–20, 22, 122
In Valiant Company 6, 200
Inverarity, Alison 188
Inverarity, Jane 188
Inverarity, John 188
Inverarity, Kate 188–189
Invincibles, The 135
Iroquois UH-1D helicopter 98
Israeli Philharmonic Orchestra 95
Italian Cycling Team 181
Iwakuni 11, 52

J

James, Maj. Gen. 'Digger' vi, 112–113, 179, 201
Japan 7–8, 9–11, 14, 15, 19, 20–21, 44, 51, 52–55, 56, 104, 152, 180
Jarman, Barry 82, 84, 201
Jardine, Douglas 163
Jones, Alan 136
Jones, Geoff 135
Jose, Dr (Sir) Ivan 48, 78–79, 133

K

Kalashnikov AK-47 rifle 112
Kapyong Bridge 22
Kapyong Day 95, 191
Kapyong Valley 1–7, 17, 22, 98, 120–122
Keily, Paul 179
Kerr, Capt. 68
Kerr Grant, Prof. 38–39
Keswick Army Barracks 24, 25, 61, 105, 116
Khan, Imran 196
Khe Sanh 102
Khyber-Pakhtunkhwa 167
Khyber Pass 154, 167
Kierse, Jack 142
Kim Il Sung 57
Kingsford-Smith, (Sir) Charles 131
King George VI 64

Kippax, Alan 129
Kirkpatrick, John Simpson (Simpson and his donkey) 168–169
Knott, Alan 139
Kooyonga Golf Course (Adelaide) 137
Korean War vi, vii, 1–7, 8–23, 52–54, 55, 56–59, 97, 112–113, 120–122, 124–125, 144–145, 146, 152, 169–170, 179, 182, 187, 197–198
Kure (Japan) 6, 8, 17, 19, 52–55, 152, 154, 180

L

Lane, Penny 84, 86–87, 95, 118–119
Lancaster Bomber 41, 90
Langer, Justin 196
Land Rights 145–146
Langenbeck, Bernhardt 165
Langley, Gil 49, 60, 80–81, 184, 189, 195
Langridge, John 46
Larrey, Dominique Jean 165, 166
Larwood, Harold 187–188
Lavarack Barrack (Townsville) 18
Lee, Bob 33
Lendon, Alan 77
Leslie, Col. Douglas 100
Lill, John 142, 189–190, 201
Lillee, Dennis vii, viii, 86, 91, 139, 187, 194, 201
Lindrum, Walter 137
Lions Club of Adelaide 168
Lippett, Dick 115
Lloyd, Clive 193
Lloyd, Lt Col. Russell 117
Lloyd, Maj. Wes 154
Loader, Peter 172
Lochiel Salt Lakes 42–43, 56
London vi, 61, 62, 65–69, 72, 74–75, 76, 77, 83, 130, 131, 137, 148–149, 150, 152, 158, 166
London Gazette 70
Long Binh Hills (Vietnam) 105
Long Hai Hills (Vietnam) 111, 118
Lord Ironside 67
Lord's Taverners Cricket Society 155, 162
Lord's Cricket Ground (London) 75, 83
Lovett, Peter 189
Luftwaffe 191

M

MacArthur, General Douglas 8, 9, 10, 11, 20, 54–55, 57–58, 145
MacBeth, Bill 78–79
Madden, Pvt. Horace 21, 170
Madigan, C.T. 38
Magarey, Dr Ivan 79
Maguire, Pvt. 109

Mahon, Capt. 68
Mahmood, Fazal 173
Mailey, Arthur 131
Malaya 57
Manhattan Project 39
Maryang San (Korea) 18, 145
Marsh, Rodney 91, 180
Marsh, Roslyn 180
Martin, Corp. 12
Martin, The Misses 27
Maud, Aunty 27, 29
Mawson, Sir Douglas 38
Marylebone Cricket Club (MCC) 32, 45, 77, 194–195
Maylands 27, 34
McCartney, L/Corp. 112
McGilvray, Alan 178
McGregor, Dr James 150
McKenna, Keith 77
McLachlan, Ian 84, 142, 189, 192, 201
McLean, Bob 82
Mead, Pvt. 112
Mehta, Zubin 95
Melbourne Cricket Club (MCC) 190
Menz family 191
Menzies, Sir Robert 8, 57
Meyers, Beverley 172, 174–178
Middle East 57, 102
Middlesex Battalion 2
Middleton, Roy 127
Mike Denness XI 192
Mike Force 111
Military Cross 89, 112
Mill, Jim 74, 149
Miller, Keith 76, 193–194, 196
Millett, Alan 182, 187, 200
Mills, Brenda 32
Modbury Hospital 116, 175–176, 178, 179, 180, 183
Monash, General Sir John 86
Monash Gully (Gallipoli) 169
Moonta 25–26, 27, 36, 201
Moore, Dick 34
Most Venerable Order of the Hospital of St John of Jerusalem 85
Mugabe, Robert 123
Murray, Sgt Tom 20, 169–170
Myren, Joe 49
Motley, Geof 173
Moyle, Sydney 34–35
Mt Erebus 30, 38
Mulligan, Gerry 148
Murdoch, Lachlan 163
Murray, Kevin 173
Murray, Tom 20, 169–170

N

Nantawarra 42
Napoleon 165–167
NASA 41, 42

National service (Australian Army) 19, 53, 57, 58, 107, 110, 112
Nelson, Willie 96
Nelson Golf Club (England) 174
Nestor, SS 73
New Nation (Singapore) 186
New Zealand 8, 10, 17, 29, 76, 105–106, 118, 187
New Zealand 16th Field Regiment 6–7, 10, 17
Newland, Maj. Henry 171
Newland, Sir Henry Simpson 149–150
Newland, Simpson 150
News Ltd (the *News*) 29, 135, 163
Nicholson, Dr Bernard 49, 80–81
Nitschke, Dr Phillip 158
Nkomo, Joshua 123
Noblet, Geff 46
Norrie, Sir Willoughby 64
Norris, Maj. Gen. Kingsley 53, 152
Norton, Charles 34
North Adelaide Cycling Club 52
North Korea 8–11, 18, 57–58
North Korean Army 55, 120, 121, 145, 170
North Vietnamese Army 101, 102, 117
Norwood Velodrome 181
Not Another Bloody Tour, Frances Edmonds 139
NSW Cricket Association 128
Nye, Col. C.W. (ADMS) 10–11

O
Obst, Cecelia 191–192
O'Dowd, Maj. Ben 4–5, 6, 14, 200
Officer Cadet Training Course 144
Oldfield, Bert 188
Old Trafford 189
Oliphant, (Sir) Mark 39, 156
Olive, Aunty 27
Opera SA 190
Opie's Bread 34
O'Reilly, Bill 131
Oxford University 32, 156

P
Paddington Station 65
Page, Maurice 42
Paget, Waterloo 151
Parker, Fess 91, 151
Parkside Mental Hospital 28, 47
Parkside Methodist Church 28
Parkside Methodist Church Eleven 28
Parkside School 27
Parliament versus Press cricket match 64
Pascoe, Len 91, 139
Patterson, Maj. Don 79
Patterson, Sid 181

Payne, Warrant Officer Keith (VC) 117–118
Pearl Harbour 39
People's Republic of Korea 57
People's Weekly, Moonta 36
Percy, Pierre Francois 166
Peter Badcoe Club 105
Peters, Dr Brian 84
Phillips, Father Joe 15–16
Phuoc Tuy Province 118
Pirbright 62–65, 69, 72
Pollock, Graeme 162
Ponsford, Bill 130
Pope, Dr Roly 129
Poplar Hospital for Accidents 150
Port Adelaide 56
Port Adelaide Cricket Club 173, 176
Port Adelaide Football Club 172, 173
Port Hughes 26
Portsmouth 69
Prest, Pvt. 112
Prince Alfred College 33
Prince Charles 65
Prince Philip 66–67, 155
Prince of Wales 133
Prince of Wales Hospital, London 148
Princess Diana 4, 65
Princess Elizabeth 62, 66
Princess Patricia's Canadian Light Infantry 5, 6, 7
Princess Vera Ignatieva Gedroitz 165
Pusan 22
Pyongyang 57

Q
Qantas 87, 101–102
Qissa Khawani Bazaar (Peshawar) 167
Queen Elizabeth II 30, 62, 66-67, 69, 144, 155
Queen Elizabeth Hospital 16, 99, 116, 191, 195
Queen Isabella 165
Queen Mother 172
Quinn's Post 169

R
Rabaul 41, 52
Radio 5DN 34
Radio 5KA 34
RAF 41, 42, 154
RAAF 8, 10–11, 19, 20, 41, 52, 78, 98, 115
RAAF, 77 Squadron, Korea 10–11
Rangaraj, Lt Col. A.G. 16
Rangaswami, Maj. 16–17
Rankin, Col. C.C. 61
Rann, Mike 22
Reagan, US President Ronald 91, 151

Red Cross 122
Rees, Barry 'Nugget' 189, 201
Regimental Aid Post (RAP) vii, 1, 2, 15, 19, 20, 53, 59, 108, 121, 122, 187
Regimental Medical Officer (RMO) vi, 1, 10, 53, 150
Renshaw's Ramblings 36
Republic of Korea (ROK) Division 1, 57
Rhodesian Bush War 123
Richards, Julie 161–162, 178
Richards, (Sir) Vivian viii, 91, 187, 193
Richardson, Arthur 45, 126, 132, 133
Richardson, John 107
Richardson, Vic 130
Richmond Air Base 115
Richmond Primary School 27
Ridgway, General 12
Ring, Doug 135–136
Robertson, Austin 173
Robertson-Glasgow, R.C. 126
Robinson, Dr Don 176
Royal Adelaide Hospital 31, 32, 41, 47, 51, 61, 77, 116, 127, 136, 150, 156, 176, 182, 191, 198
Royal Australian Army Medical Corps 103, 113, 152, 167, 168, 170
Royal Australasian College of Surgeons 76, 83, 164, 165
Royal College of Surgeons of England 53, 74, 76, 77, 149, 164, 166,
Royal Melbourne Hospital 53, 152
Royal Yacht *Britannia* 155
Ruhr Valley 42

S
Sacred Heart College 33
Saigon 101–102, 103, 116–117
St Andrew's Hospital (Adelaide) 96
St James' Palace 72
St John Ambulance 85, 147
St John Eye Hospital (Jerusalem) 85
St Mary's Hospital (London) 75, 148
St Matthew's Church (Kensington) 25
St Paul's Cathedral 65
St Peter's Cathedral (Adelaide) 97
St Peter's College (Adelaide) 149, 192
St Peter's Collegians Association 29, 46
St Francis Xavier Cathedral (Adelaide) 16
St Francis Xavier Cathedral (Port Pirie) 16
Salisbury, Police Commissioner Harold 105
Salvation Army 15, 20, 44

Index

Salvation Army Boys' Home (Adelaide) 41
Sampson and Delilah 166
Saunders, Harry 145
Saunders, Capt. Reginald 7, 144–146
Scales, Sheila 84
Scarce, SA Governor, Rear Admiral Kevin 171
School of Army Health (Healesville) 100
Schubert, Betty 143
Scrimgeour, Bernard 127
Scott, Sandy 162
Selth, John 82, 135–136, 193
SA Boy Scouts Association 29
SA Chamber of Commerce 29
SACA (South Australian Cricket Association) vii, 68, 98, 118, 127–128, 132, 135, 162, 176, 189, 190
SACA Ground and Finance Committee 127
SA Road Safety Council 183, 184, 186
SA Road Safety Advisory Council 136, 185
SA State Team 60
Shackman, Al 153
Sheedy, Jack 173
Sheffield Shield vii, 68, 127, 131, 173
Shepherd, Amy 34, 43
Shepherd, Lily 34, 43
Shields, Sir Douglas 130
Shrapnel Gully (Gallipoli) 169
Silvagni, Sergio 173
Simpson, Bob 178, 194
Simpson, Dr Donald 88
Simpson, Warrant Officer Ray (VC) 117
Simpson Foundation 170
Singapore Cricket Club 37
Singh, Kahn 167
Smith (nee Lane), Penny 84, 86–87, 95, 118–119
Sobers, Sir Garfield 'Garry' 173, 196
Solari, Nino 181
Solari, David 181
South Australian Hotel 85
South Australian Parliament's Social Development Committee 159
South Vietnamese Army 117–118
Spartacus 166
'Spike' Hill 70
Stansfield, Frank 74
Stoke Mandeville 61
Sturt Cricket Club 49, 60, 80, 84, 100, 136, 190, 192
Sunday Mail (Adelaide) 32, 80–81, 137
Sydney HMAS 58, 62, 66, 69–70

Sydney Harbour 100, 153
Sydney University 46
Syngman Rhee 57

T

Taeju 11
Taeryong River 169–170
Taipan SS 21, 56
Talbot, Don 137
Task Force HQ, Nui Dat 113
Taylor, Dr L.R. 194
Tampling, Sgt Noel 1, 12
Tanfield's Diary 68
Tet Offensive 102, 104, 108
Tham, Dr Siew-Kiong 175
The Bridge on the River Kwai 152
The Gordon Highlanders 166
The Kidnapped Kitten (Elizabeth Auld) 163
The Pathway of Honour, Government House (Adelaide) 59
The Quincentenary Conference, Royal College of Surgeons (Edinburgh) 164
Theatre Royal (Adelaide) 82, 191
Thomson, Cheryl 137
Thomson, Jeffrey viii, 137–139
Thompson, Warrant Officer Bob 113–114
Thousand Voices Choir 31
Toorak Services Club (Melbourne) 93
Toshack, Ernie 135
Tokyo 20–21, 56
Travers, Joe 127
Treves, Sir Arthur 150
Tropical Medicine Institute (Liverpool) 75
Truman, US President Harry 9, 58
Trueman, Fred 174
Tufnell, Phil 180
Turton-Sainsbury, Pvt. Leigh 154

U

Uijongbu Corridor 57
Ulysses SS 73
University of Adelaide 7, 32, 36, 37, 38–39, 41, 105, 132, 142, 149, 156
United Nations (UN) 9–11, 18
United States 5, 104
Unley Oval 59–60, 80, 188
US Mobile Army Service Hospital (MASH) vi, 16–17, 19–20, 53, 58, 99, 121
US 72nd Heavy Tank Battalion 3, 5, 7
US Presidential Distinguished Unit Citation 5

V

Verco & Gurner 84
Victor Harbor 27, 159
Victoria Cross 70, 117, 167

Victoria Park Racecourse 28, 190
Victory Tests, 1945 76
Viet Cong 102, 104, 108, 111–112, 117–119, 122
Vietnam War 97–99, 101, 111–112, 113–115, 116–119, 122, 123–125, 146, 151, 165, 170, 178, 179, 186, 187, 201
Viswanath, Gundappa 137
Voluntary Euthanasia Inquiry (1999) 159
Vung Tau (Vietnam) vii, 98, 102–105, 108–109, 113–115, 118, 122, 123–124

W

Wakefield Memorial Hospital 123
Walker, General 12
Walker, Max 172
Walsh, Courtney 196
Walters, Doug 180, 195
War Office 67
Ward, Frank 141
Watson-Hughes, Walter 37
Wau Valley 144
Webb, Ken 59
Wellington, Duke of 150–151
Wellington Road School 28
West Adelaide Football Club 30, 33
Westralia 52
Western Front vi, 89
Westminster Abbey 62, 67
Whiteley, Brett 147
Whiting, Bill 46, 136
Wigzell, Billy 148
Wilde, Oscar 26
Willhem Rhys 84
Wilson, Dr Graham 7, 52, 55
Wisden Cricketers' Almanack 126, 200
Wishart, Peter 173
Woking 62, 77
Woodcock, Ashley 192
Woodfull, Bill 128, 129, 188
Woodside Army Barracks 105
Workman, Jim 76
World Health Organisation 158
Worrell, Sir Frank 173
Wright, Alison 24–25
Wright, Charlotte 25
Wright, Henrietta 25
World War I 17, 32, 76, 86, 89, 144, 165, 171
World War II 7, 9, 10, 15, 32, 36, 37, 39, 41, 42, 57, 62, 75, 102, 112, 126, 144–145, 146, 154, 156, 193

Z

Zimbabwe Africa National Union 123
Zimbabwe Africa People's Union 123

Wakefield Press is an independent publishing and
distribution company based in Adelaide, South Australia.
We love good stories and publish beautiful books.
To see our full range of books, please visit our website at
www.wakefieldpress.com.au
where all titles are available for purchase.

Find us!

Twitter: www.twitter.com/wakefieldpress
Facebook: www.facebook.com/wakefield.press
Instagram: instagram.com/wakefieldpress

www.ingramcontent.com/pod-product-compliance
Ingram Content Group UK Ltd.
Pitfield, Milton Keynes, MK11 3LW, UK
UKHW021329180426
11947UKWH00017B/1526